Amarillo Junior League Cookbook

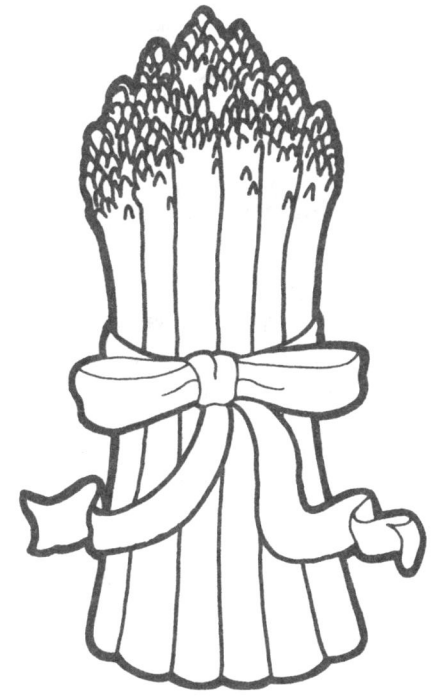

The Junior League of Amarillo, Inc.

Amarillo, Texas

The Junior League of Amarillo is a volunteer organization whose purpose is to train its members for service and leadership in the Amarillo community.

The proceeds from the sale of the *Amarillo Junior League Cookbook* will be returned to the community through the projects of the League. Since 1930 the League has devoted its energies and resources to various programs in the community, and it is to these seventy-two years of service that we dedicate this book.

For additional copies use the order blanks in the back of this book or write directly to:

The Junior League of Amarillo
1700 South Polk
Amarillo, Texas 79102-3151
806-374-0802
Fax: 806-374-8229

Library of Congress Catalog Number: 79-53706
ISBN: 0-9604102-0-1

Manufactured by
Favorite Recipes® Press
an imprint of

FRP

P.O. Box 305142
Nashville, Tennessee 37230
800-358-0560

Manufactured in the United States of America
First Printing: 1979 10,000 copies
Second Printing: 1980 12,000 copies
Third Printing: 2002 5,000 copies

Especially About Asparagus

A bunch of fresh, appetizing stalks of asparagus tied in pink ribbon! — Besides whetting your appetite, we hope the nosegay of asparagus on the cover of this volume will convey to you something special about the nature of the cookbook you hold in your hands.

Asparagus is an unusual vegetable. It requires extremely slow and careful cultivation with heavy labor requirements. No harvest is possible until the plants are several years old. Once established though, and with proper maintenance, asparagus plantations will produce a crop every year for a man's lifetime. Plantings are in existence which have produced profitable yields for more than 100 years.

This book is a product with many similar elements. It is the result of a carefully laid plan carried out with many laborious hours spread over several years' duration.

Fourteen hundred favorite recipes were submitted by Amarillo Junior League members. Each was tested at least twice and over 600 were approved for publication. Testing, tasting, and editorial production began almost three years prior to publication.

That perky, pink-tied cover symbol has meaning for us even beyond the publication of this volume. It also represents the role the Junior League has played in this community.

Published on the League's 50th anniversary year, the analogy of careful cultivation and continuing labor to establish a long-lasting, continually fruitful seedbed is still appropriate. With continuing effort and attention, the Junior League, expectantly planted in Amarillo some 50 years ago, continues to yield rich harvests of leadership, education, cultural enrichment, and maximized human resources for the benefit of the entire city.

Cookbook Committee

Co-Chairmen
Cordelia Man
Kay Brosier

Vice Chairman
Joann Thatcher

Testing Chairman
Sally Kritser

Editing and Indexing
Carolyn Conklin

Treasurer
Patty Buckley

Artist
Barry Fields

Creative Writer
Georgia Swift

Promotion and Publicity
Suzanne Curtis

Proofreader
Carol Cowan

Recipe Librarian
Rosemary Patterson

Typing Chairman
Julie Harris

We wish to thank the many members of the testing, editing, typing, proofing, and publicity committees who helped make this book possible. Our sincere appreciation to all who shared their favorite recipes with us.
4

Contents

The Junior Welfare League of Amarillo opened the Rose Bowl Tea Room in 1930. The profits realized from the Tea Room were used for the free clinic for underprivileged children.

This etching, done by Margaret Seewald Roberts in 1932, was used on the menu of the Rose Bowl Tea Room.

To Begin With . . .

A city of spectacular sunsets surrounded by panoramic prairie vistas sweeping as far as the eye can see, Amarillo is a new community, incorporated after the turn of the twentieth century. Result of a fortunate covergence of railroads, fertilized with oil, cattle, and grain, this city is the commercial hub of an area covering segments of five states.

Surrounded by vast ranches measured in sections rather than acres, Amarillo is inhabited by sons and daughters of the pioneers that claimed this Great American Desert. Fall still calls for the ritual dove and quail hunts. Lucky families still enjoy wild turkey for Thanksgiving dinner. Recipes reflective of this ranching heritage, game bird preparations, barbecue, beef varieties and cornbreads, are found throughout this volume.

Enthusiasm for the enticing foods of our Mexican neighbors are reflected in such treats as Taco Salad, Green Chili Souffle, Huevas Rancheros, Chili Rellenos, Turkey Stuffed with Tamales, and Hot Pepper Jelly.

Deep in the heart of the nation's breadbasket, the Texas Panhandle is the source of much of this country's corn and grain. Hence, we offer a reflection of our enthusiasm for breads. Soil here is very fertile, if only we can water it, and a large truck farming industry has evolved south of town. We make the most of Mother Nature's largesse and we share with you an abundance of vegetable dishes.

Special occasion fare we offer you too. Here is the Egg Nog served at Junior League Christmas parties, instructions on preparing beef as prepared at the Houghton Ranch Barbecue, and the formula for Steak on a Stick, our Funfest moneymaker.

A non-food recipe has come our way that we cannot resist sharing with you. Our dry winds and low humidity have kept ladies searching for moisturizers over the years. Here is an especially soothing concoction.

HAND OR FACE CREAM

6 ounces peanut oil
2 ounces pure olive oil
2 ounces rose water

2 heaping tablespoons
of pure lanolin

Mix all ingredients in blender. Place in bottle or jar. Use before bed. Never gets old.

Mrs. James H. Simms (Freeda Daugherty)

Not only do we offer local specialties for your table, we also offer a temptation of gourmet edibles. As interest in exotic cooking has prospered, Amarilloans have traveled near and far to perfect their culinary skills.

In preparation for the introduction of this cookbook, two master chefs were brought to Amarillo and each conducted a multi-session culinary academy. Each drew a capacity crowd.

Giuliano Bugialli, Italian gourmet, brought a demonstration of his expertise. Sharing our enthusiasm for the cookbook-to-be, he later sent us a recipe in honor of our asparagus logo. An ancient Italian recipe, medieval or older, Asparagi in Salsa was widely used at the beginning of this century in the area of Livorno, main port of Tuscany.

ASPARAGI IN SALSA
(Asparagus in
egg-lemon sauce)   Serves 4

2 pounds medium-sized asparagus	2 eggs
½ cup olive oil	1 teaspoon unbleached all-purpose flour
1 large clove garlic, peeled	Salt and freshly ground
2 lemons	black pepper to taste

Cut off the white part of the asparagus. Do not scrape the remaining green part of the asparagus. Place the asparagus in a large bowl of cold water for about 15 minutes. Cut the asparagus in 1½ inch pieces and let them soak for 5 minutes more. Heat the olive oil in a flameproof casserole, preferably terra-cotta. When the oil is warm add the peeled clove of garlic and saute for about 1 minute.

Drain the asparagus and add them to the pan. Sprinkle with salt and pepper, mix well and saute for about 2 minutes. Squeeze the lemons. Remove the clove of garlic, add the lemon juice, mix very well and cover the casserole with a lid.

Let the asparagus simmer for about 12-15 minutes.

Place eggs in a small bowl along with a pinch of salt. Beat well with a fork. Mix in the flour slowly, being careful to prevent lumps from forming. Transfer asparagus from pan to a serving dish. Add the beaten eggs with flour and salt to the casserole with the remaining juice from the asparagus, stirring slowly, until the sauce has half reduced (about 10 minutes). Pour the sauce over the asparagus and serve.

10

Ann Clark of Austin, founder of LaBonne Cuisine Cooking School specializes in Provencial cooking, an outgrowth of time spent in Aix-en-Provence where she researched and created many of her recipes. She is permitting us to share this one with you.

OMELETTE SOUFFLE' au Grand Marnier
(Sweet dessert omelet)   Serves 4-6

3 large eggs
3 tablespoons sugar

3 tablespoons liqueur
1 tablespoon sweet butter

Separate eggs, mix yolks, sugar and liqueur with beater. Beat whites until stiff. Fold into yolks. Use 10-12 inch pan. Heat butter as for an omelet. Pour in egg mixture, count to 60, shake. Fold and slide onto serving plate.

This volume is the third in a series of cookbooks published by the Amarillo Junior League. *"Junior Welfare League Recipes"* was printed in 1932 and revised as *"Rose Bowl Cookbook"* in 1957. Another cookbook, the *"Junior Welfare League Recipe Book"* was printed in 1942.

The following recipes are favorites from the earlier editions.

ROSE BOWL TEA ROOM ROLLS

2 cups sweet milk
1 heaping tablespoon shortening
1 yeast cake
1 egg

½ cup sugar
1 teaspoon salt
Flour to make stiff batter (not too stiff)

Heat, but do not boil milk. Add shortening and sugar. Dissolve yeast in lukewarm water. Sift flour and salt. Mix. Add egg and beat five minutes by hand. Let rise 1 hour or until double in bulk. Work down, let rise again. Knead on floured board until smooth and elastic. Make into rolls and set aside to rise in warm place. Bake in hot oven (425°) 15 minutes. When lightly browned brush with butter and finish baking.

LONAS'
SPANISH CUSTARD ("Fried Cream")

2 eggs
6 tablespoons flour
2 cups scalded milk
1 teaspoon butter
¾ cup fine dry bread crumbs

½ cup sugar
¼ teaspoon salt
2 tablespoons water
1 teaspoon vanilla
1 egg

Mix sugar, flour and salt; add eggs alternately with milk and beat until smooth. Cook in double boiler, stirring constantly until thick. Add butter and vanilla when partly cool. Pour into buttered pan to ¾ inch thickness. The next day cut into squares, roll each piece in crumbs, dip in the egg beaten with the water, roll again in crumbs. Fry in deep fat, drain on soft paper and roll in powdered sugar.

PARSLEY RING

½ cup thick mayonnaise
1 tablespoon gelatine

4 hard boiled eggs
½ cup chopped parsley

Mix mayonnaise, eggs, parsley and season with salt, pepper, paprika and lemon juice. Put gelatine in ¼ cup cold water and dissolve in ½ cup hot water. Mix, and put all in ring mold. When cold fill center with shrimp, crabmeat or tomatoes.

PROPORTIONS FOR BARBECUE FOR ONE HUNDRED PEOPLE.

Ninety pounds of meat
Fifteen pounds of pinto beans
Four pounds of coffee
Ten pounds of dried apricots
One gallon of pickles
Two hundred rolls
Six pounds of butter

Miles Bivins

BARBECUE SAUCE FOR THIRTY TO FORTY POUNDS OF MEAT.

1 quart of water
1½ quarts of tomato catsup
2 pounds of butter
¼ cup of sugar
3 tablespoons of salt
3 tablespoons of chili powder
½ teaspoon of cayene
2 tablespoons of Worcestershire sauce
1 cup of vinegar
2 teaspoons of tobasco sauce
3 tablespoons of black pepper
4 tablespoons of paprika
1 onion, chopped fine
1 clove of garlic, minced

Cook these ingredients together gently,
for thirty minutes before using.

Miles Bivins

Apple Pone

2 Cups Corn Meal
1 tsp. soda
3 tbsp. sugar
2 Cups sour Milk
1 egg
1 tbsp. baking powder
1 tbsp. Melted butter
2 Cups Chopped Apples

Combine as for corn bread. (Mix dry ingredients. Combine egg and milk, add to flour mixture. Stir in melted butter. Add apples last. Bake in hot oven 425° about 30 Minutes or until it draws away from side of pan.

Serve hot with butter or honey

Mrs. Aleck Anderson

Chef Tack's Dust Bowl Pudding

Use 1 pt of milk, ½ cup sugar, 1 tbsp. cornstarch and 2 whole eggs to make a custard cream in a double boiler. Stir this cream well until it becomes very smooth. Let set until it cools to 60°. Take ½ ounce of Knox gelatin and dissolve in 2 oz water. Heat a little to aid dissolving. Stir into custard until it begins to set. Beat ½ pint of whipping cream until firm. Sweeten to taste. Add a little vanilla. Chop 6 to 8 roasted almonds. Fold in whipping cream and almonds into custard. Fill 6 individual molds and let stand 4 to 5 hrs. Serve with tart fruit juice such as raspberry, strawberry or loganberry.

Serves 6

Caviar Dressing

For Aspic or Whole Tomato Salads.

To 1 pt or less of a
Lightly-seasoned Oil Mayonnaise
gently fold in 1 ounce tin Caviar. Add
finely chopped onion if desired.

Mrs. M. I. Johnson

Egg-Nog Ring

8 eggs beaten separately
1 cup granulated sugar
1 envelope gelatine
1/2 cup boiling water
3/4 cup whiskey
2 teaspoons vanilla
chopped almonds, whipped cream
8 macaroons

To the yolks add whiskey, to the whites
add a cup of sifted granulated sugar. Fold in
yolks. Dissolve gelatine in boiling water and pour
over the mixture.

Line ring or mold with lady fingers and
pour in the above mixture.

When ready to serve, turn onto a platter
and fill center with stiff whipped cream, in
which are mixed the almonds and macaroons,
rolled and sifted.

This delicious dish may be garnished,
if desired, by strawberries, cherries or raspberries.

Sophie G. Harrington.

16

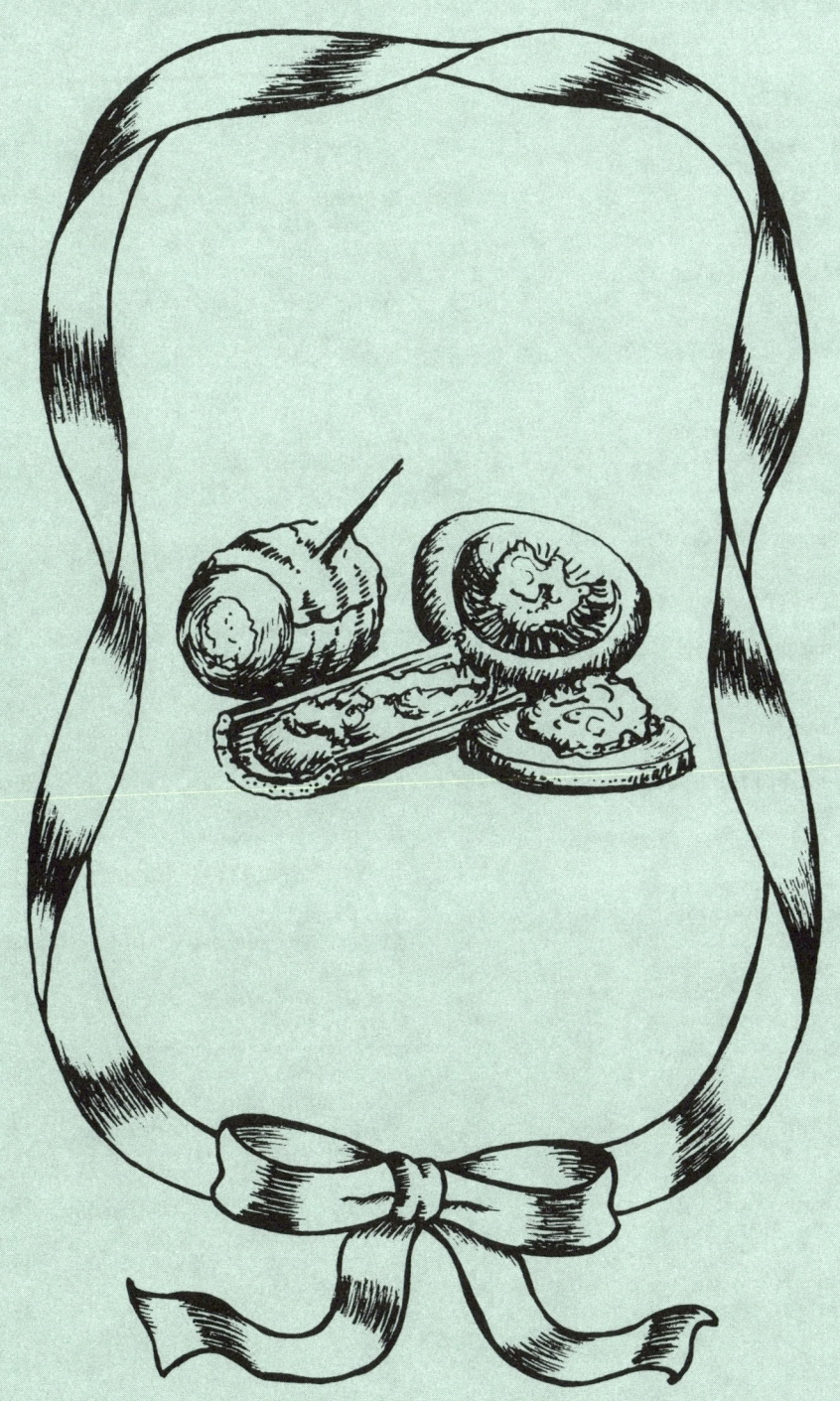

Appetizers and Beverages

Dips

Canapes and Hors d'oeuvres

Beverages

AVOCADO DIP

1 carton (8 ounces) sour cream
½ package of Good Seasons
   Italian Dressing Mix
2 tomatoes, diced

Dash of Tabasco
¼ cup mayonnaise
2 avocados, diced
Juice of ½ lemon

Mix together. Increase recipe by adding more sour cream or avocado.

Mrs. Don T. Curtis (Suzanne Stokes)

BAVARIAN DIP

1 pound Cheddar cheese,
   grated
⅛ pound blue or Roquefort
   cheese, crumbled
8 ounces cream cheese,
   softened
½ teaspoon salt

2 tablespoons grated onion
1 teaspoon
   Worcestershire sauce
⅛ teaspoon Tabasco
½ cup chopped pecans
1 bottle of beer

Combine all ingredients. Spread on Nabisco Sociable crackers.

Mrs. Joe B. Wells (Brenda Breece)

BEEF 'N PECAN DIP

1 package (8 ounces)
   cream cheese, softened
2 tablespoons milk
½ cup sour cream
¼ cup chopped green chilies
1 tablespoon instant
   minced onion

½ teaspoon garlic salt
1 jar (2 ounces) dried beef
2 tablespoons butter
½ teaspoon salt
½ cup chopped pecans

Blend softened cream cheese, milk and sour cream. Add green chilies, onion and salt. Rinse dried beef well, drain and chop. Add to cream cheese mixture. Spread in 8 inch baking dish and bake in 350° oven for 20 minutes. While spread is baking, melt butter in small skillet and add salt and pecans. Remove dip from oven and top with pecan mixture. Serve warm.

Mrs. Paul Cizon (Laurie Gray)

MOM'S CHILI CON QUESO

½ stick butter
1 large onion, finely chopped
2 cans chopped and peeled green chili peppers (Ortega)
1 can (1 pound) tomatoes, drained

2 pounds processed American or Old English cheese, grated
2 tablespoons Worcestershire sauce
Salt

Sauté butter and onions in large covered iron skillet. Do not brown. Add peppers and tomatoes to onions and cook 5 minutes. Add cheese, stirring constantly until melted. Add Worcestershire sauce and salt to taste. Stir constantly. Serve hot. May substitute 2 cans of Rotel for 1 can Ortega chilies and tomatoes.

Mrs. James E. Herring (Margaret Johnson)

MEXICAN KITCHEN DIP

1 tablespoon butter
3 tablespoons chopped green pepper
1 large onion, chopped
2 cloves garlic, chopped
2 tablespoons chili powder
½ teaspoon cumin seed

5 fresh tomatoes, chopped
¾ pound Cheddar cheese, grated
Salt to taste
½ teaspoon cayenne pepper
1 egg, well beaten with with a little milk

Melt butter in saucepan and cook green pepper, onion and garlic for about 3 minutes. Remove garlic. Add chili powder, cumin seed and tomatoes. Simmer for 20 minutes. Add cheese slowly. Stir in salt and cayenne pepper. When cheese has melted, stir in egg. Serve hot with tostados.

Mrs. David Kritser, III (Sally Simpson)

CLAM DIP

Serves 8-10

1 package (8 ounces) cream cheese
1 can (10½ ounces) minced clams
1 tablespoon mayonnaise
½ teaspoon grated onion

1 tablespoon lemon juice
½ teaspoon garlic salt
Worcestershire sauce
Tabasco sauce

Soften cream cheese and add remaining ingredients. Serve with chips.

Mrs. James E. Herring (Margaret Johnson)

EASY DELICIOUS CRAB DIP

2 packages (8 ounces each)
Philadelphia cream cheese,
softened
2 cartons (8 ounces each)
sour cream
1 onion, chopped

Seasonings or spices
to taste
Salt and pepper to taste
4–5 cans (6½ ounces each)
crabmeat, drained and
chopped
Capers

Mix together cream cheese and sour cream until smooth. Add next four ingredients. Add capers last. Serve with fresh raw vegetables: beets, celery, carrots, broccoli, cauliflower, turnips, etc.

You may also use blue cheese for crab and capers or substitute shrimp for crab.

Mrs. Stanley Marsh, 3 (Wendy O'Brien)

CRAB DIP

2 pounds cream cheese
1 package Lipton
onion soup mix
¼ cup water
1 pound lump crab
(fresh or frozen)
1 bunch green onion tops,
chopped

1 jar (7 ounces)
chopped pimientos
1 tablespoon chopped parsley
Paprika
Black pepper
to taste
Chicken-in-a-Biscuit
Crackers (optional)

Soften the cream cheese in a double boiler. Mix soup and water together. Strain the soup and add liquid to cream cheese. After the cheese is softened, add the remaining ingredients and heat. Serve hot in a chafing dish. This can be frozen.

Mrs. Robert Patterson (Rosemary Cherry)

KEMP'S
HOT CRABMEAT DIP   Serves 12

1 can or 1 pound crabmeat
4 hard cooked eggs
1 onion, juiced
½ teaspoon salt
¼ teaspoon cayenne pepper

3 tablespoons butter
1 heaping tablespoon flour
2 cups milk
1 pound Wisconsin
cheese, grated

Mix crabmeat, eggs, onion juice, salt and cayenne pepper. Melt butter and blend in flour until smooth. Add milk and cook until thick. Add cheese and crabmeat to mixture. Serve from chafing dish with melba toast. Also good with Triscuits and other crackers.

DILL DIP

Yields 2 Cups

1 cup sour cream
1 cup mayonnaise
1 teaspoon celery salt
1 teaspoon celery seed
1 tablespoon
  dehydrated onion flakes

1 tablespoon
  dried dill weed
1 tablespoon
  dried parsley flakes
1 tablespoon dried chives

Combine sour cream and mayonnaise, add remaining ingredients and mix well. Let marinate for 24 hours. Serve with fresh vegetables, such as carrots, celery, cauliflower, bell pepper, cherry tomatoes, cucumbers, etc.

Mrs. Royce Kelly (Charlotte Smith)

GINGER DIP

1 cup chilled mayonnaise
1 cup chilled sour cream
¼ cup finely chopped onion
¼ cup finely chopped parsley
¼ cup finely chopped
  water chestnuts

2 tablespoons
  finely chopped ginger
2 cloves garlic, minced
1 tablespoon soy sauce
  Dash of salt

Combine mayonnaise and sour cream. Add remaining ingredients in order. Mix and chill.

Serve dip with Wheat Thins, sesame crackers or fresh vegetables such as zucchini, jicama, turnips or carrot sticks.

Cannot be frozen.

Mrs. Sue Alice Stokes (Sue Alice Simpson)

LORRAINE'S SHRIMP DIP

Yields 2 Cups

1 can (5 ounces) shrimp,
  cut into small pieces
1 cup sour cream
¼ cup chili sauce
2 teaspoons lemon juice

½ teaspoon salt
⅛ teaspoon pepper
1 teaspoon horseradish
1 dash Tabasco

Combine all ingredients and chill well before serving.

Mrs. Stan Morris, Jr. (Kathleen Boyd)

BETTY McCUE'S SPINACH DIP

Yields 3 Cups

1 box (10 ounces) frozen
  chopped spinach, cooked,
  drained and squeezed dry
1 cup Hellmann's mayonnaise
1 cup sour cream
½ teaspoon salt
1 tablespoon dried parsley

½ cup chopped green onions
  and tops
½ teaspoon dill seed
1 teaspoon Beau Monde
  seasoning
1 teaspoon lemon juice

Combine all ingredients. Chill 2-3 hours. Serve with fresh vegetables — cucumber strips, turnips, cauliflower, carrots, celery, green pepper strips, broccoli florets, mushrooms, etc.

SPINACH DIP

1 package (10 ounces)
  frozen, chopped spinach,
  uncooked
1 cup sour cream
½ cup mayonnaise
½ cup minced parsley

½ cup minced onion
1 teaspoon salt
½ teaspoon celery salt
¼ teaspoon pepper
⅛ teaspoon nutmeg

Thaw spinach. Place in sieve and with the back of a spoon press out all water. Mix other ingredients together and fold in spinach. Let stand in the refrigerator for several hours.

Mrs. C.D. Hoover, Jr. (Jane Skillman)

HOT TOMATO DIP

Serves 10-12

1 can (16 ounces)
  tomatoes, mashed
1 can (6 ounces)
  tomato paste
2 pods garlic, crushed
5 green onions,
  finely chopped

3—5 small, fresh hot green
  peppers, finely chopped
1 teaspoon sugar
3 tablespoons salad oil
  Salt and pepper,
  if desired

Mix all ingredients. Bring to a boil. Refrigerate for several hours. Heat again before serving.

This is a low calorie dip that can be made the day before. Excellent served with Doritos. It is also good for seasoning Mexican dishes.

Mrs. Royce Kelly (Charlotte Smith)

VEGETABLE DIP

Yields 2 Cups

1 cup sour cream
½ cup Cheese Whiz
¼ cup chili sauce
2 tablespoons dry vegetable soup mix
½ teaspoon Worcestershire sauce

Combine all ingredients and refrigerate 2-3 hours. Use as a dip for celery, carrot sticks, bell pepper strips or chips.

Mrs. William Comerford (Pat Nunley)

CRABMEAT HORS D'OEUVRES

Serves 8-10

2 egg whites, beaten until stiff
1 cup mayonnaise
1 can (6½ ounces) crabmeat
Freshly ground pepper
Salt
Toasted bread slices

Mix first five ingredients together. Pile crab mixture on toasted bread slices and bake in 325° oven.

Mrs. T. Boone Pickens, Jr. (Bea Carr)

VELMA CRAIG'S MARINATED CRAB

Serves 4-6

1 can (10 ounces) Snappy Tom tomato juice
Dash of Tabasco, salt, and pepper
½ cup olive oil
½ cup cider vinegar
1 cup sliced water chestnuts
1 pound cooked crabmeat, drained
½ cup bean sprouts
4 green onions, chopped
2 medium tomatoes, diced
¼ bell pepper, sliced paper thin
1 celery heart, sliced paper thin

Combine Snappy Tom, tabasco, salt, pepper, olive oil and vinegar. Mix with remaining ingredients and marinate overnight.

24

CHEESE SPREAD

1 package (8 ounces)
  Philadelphia cream cheese
1 jar (2 ounces)
  red pimientos, chopped
1 tablespoon piccalili relish
1 tablespoon
  Worcestershire sauce
¼ cup grated onion
⅔ bottle (6 ounces)
  chili sauce
1 can (6½ ounces)
  crabmeat, drained
  and rinsed

Mix together cheese, pimientos, relish, Worcestershire and onion. Chill and shape. Glaze with chili sauce. Sprinkle with crabmeat.

Mrs. R.G. Morrision, Jr. (Esther Jones)

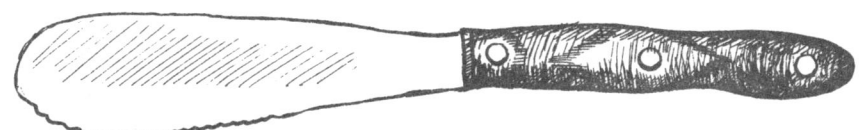

CHEESE BALLS

2 packages (8 ounces each)
  cream cheese
1 can (8 ounces) crushed
  pineapple, drained
¼ cup chopped bell pepper
2 tablespoons chopped onion
1½ teaspoons seasoned salt
2 cups chopped pecans

Combine first five ingredients and half of the pecans. Shape into a ball and roll in remaining pecans. Refrigerate for several hours. Best if made the day before serving.

Mrs. Michael Campbell (Maggie Larson)

CHEESE BALL

1 package (6 ounces)
  bacon and cheese roll,
  softened
1 package (6 ounces) jalapeno
  cheese roll, softened
1 package (6 ounces)
  garlic cheese roll,
  softened
1 large package (8 ounces)
  cream cheese, softened
1 jar (5 ounces) Old English
  cheese, softened
1 tablespoon chili powder
½ cup chopped parsley
¾ cup chopped walnuts or
  pecans, optional

Blend first six ingredients thoroughly. Roll into ball. May be covered with parsley or the parsley may be added to the cheese ball and the ball then rolled in nuts. Chill several hours or overnight. Keeps at least 2 weeks.

Mrs. J. Lee Johnson, III (Betty Knight)

CHEESE ROLL

Yields 2 balls

3 packages (8 ounces each)
Philadelphia cream cheese
3 tablespoons blue cheese
2 glasses (5 ounces each)
Sharp Old English cheese

1 tablespoon
Worcestershire sauce
1 tablespoon Accent
1 teaspoon onion powder
½ cup chopped nuts
¼ cup parsley flakes

Mix first six ingredients. Refrigerate until firm enough to handle. Shape into balls. Roll in combined nuts and parsley flakes. Refrigerate. Freezes well.

Mrs. Ken McCarty (Sue Sheriff)

HAM AND CHEESE BALL

1 package (8 ounces)
cream cheese, softened
1 tablespoon horseradish
1 tablespoon mustard

1 teaspoon grated onion
⅓ cup finely chopped nuts
1 cup finely chopped ham

Cream the cheese, horseradish, mustard and onion until smooth. Stir in ham. Chill for several hours. Shape into balls. Roll each ball in nuts. Wrap in foil and chill.

Mrs. William F. Countiss (Mary Dee Ledyard)

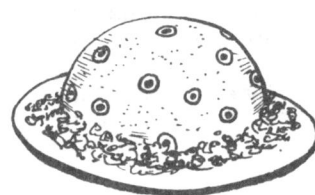

HAMBALL

1 pound cooked ground ham
½ cup white raisins
1 medium onion, grated
¾ cup mayonnaise
½ teaspoon curry powder
¼ teaspoon Tabasco

¼ teaspoon
Worcestershire sauce
2 packages (3 ounces each)
cream cheese
2 tablespoons milk
Fresh parsley
Stuffed green olives

Blend first seven ingredients thoroughly. Shape into one very large ball or two small ones. Chill on serving plate. Ice chilled ball with cream cheese which has been softened with milk. Decorate with parsley and olives. Chill several hours or overnight.

Mrs. Benny Lawrence (Ellen Yows)

SALMON BALL

Serves 16-18

1 can (1 pound)
  Red Sockeye Salmon
8 ounces cream cheese, soft
1 tablespoon lemon juice
2 teaspoons grated onion

1 teaspoon horseradish
¼ teaspoon salt
3 tablespoons snipped parsley
½ cup chopped pecans

Combine first six ingredients and chill. Shape into balls and roll in parsley and pecans. Serve with crackers (Stone Wheat Thins).

Mrs. James Herring (Margaret Johnson)

MINI-ASPARAGUS CRÊPES

Yields 20-24 Crêpes

1 recipe crepes
2 packages frozen asparagus
2 packages (8 ounces each)
  cream cheese

1 package Good Seasons
  dry Italian
  salad dressing

Cut each crêpe with a cookie cutter into three or four small crêpes. Cook asparagus by steaming slightly. Mix cream cheese and Italian dressing together. Spread some of the cheese mixture on each small crêpe. Place asparagus on each crêpe and roll the crepe. Cut off excess stalk end of the asparagus. May be heated or served at room temperature.

Canned asparagus works well also.

Mrs. Robert D. Forrester (Carol Tate)

27

CHEESE PUFFS

Makes 45 Tidbits

5 slices Texas toast
(bread about 1 inch thick)
1 package (3 ounces)
cream cheese

¼ pound sharp
Cheddar cheese
½ cup butter
2 egg whites

Trim crust from Texas toast. Slice each piece into 9 cubes. Melt cheddar cheese, cream cheese and butter over very low heat. Cool. Beat egg whites until stiff. Fold into cooled cheese mixture. Dip each bread cube in cheese-egg mixture. Place on cookie sheet and refrigerate for at least one hour or overnight. Bake in 400° oven for 12-15 minutes. Can be frozen indefinitely before cooking.

Mrs. Ed Harrell (Carol Flynn)

CHEESE PUFFS

Yields 4 Dozen

½ pound sharp cheese,
grated
½ cup margarine, softened
1 cup flour

½ teaspoon salt
1 teaspoon paprika
48 stuffed olives

Mix cheese, margarine, flour, salt and paprika. Wrap each olive with approximately one teaspoon of the mixture. Place the wrapped olives on a cookie sheet and freeze. Bake frozen in 400° oven for 10 or 15 minutes or until slightly browned on bottom. Serve while hot.

Mrs. John L. Milton (Sissy Thornhill)

CREAM CHEESE PUFFS

Yields 2 Dozen Puffs

4 ounces cream cheese
¾ teaspoon grated onion
¼ cup homemade mayonnaise
1 tablespoon chopped chives

⅛ teaspoon cayenne
⅛ cup Parmesan cheese
½ small loaf white bread

In a small bowl combine first six ingredients and mix well. Cut bread into circles (1½ inches round) and spread each with cheese mixture. Bake in 350° oven for 15 minutes; longer for crisper puff. The bread may be cut and spread with cheese mixture and then frozen. Bake when ready to use.

Mrs. Robert E. Aikman (Rachel Stockton)

HOT CHEESE SQUARES   Serves 20

¼ pound butter, softened
½ pound Old English cheese,
   grated
Dash each:
   Onion juice
   Cayenne pepper
   Tabasco
   Seasoned salt

Pinch dry mustard
2 egg whites,
   stiffly beaten
1 large loaf day old
   unsliced bread, cut
   into 1-inch cubes

Blend butter and cheese until smooth. Add seasonings. Fold in egg whites. Thinly ice sides and tops of bread cubes. Place on cookie sheets and refrigerate for several hours. Bake on ungreased cookie sheets in 350° oven for 10 minutes. Serve hot.

These may be frozen before baking for later use.

Mrs. Hollis B. DeGrassi, Jr. (Ann Moody)

CHILI BISCUITS   Yields 40

2 packages (40) Pepperidge
   Farm dinner rolls
1 can (15 ounces) Wolf Brand
   Chili without beans or
   2 cups homemade chili
   without beans

Green onions, chopped
1 package sharp
   Cheddar cheese

Using melon ball utensil, dig out a hole in each roll. Fill with chili, then onion and cheese. Bake in 375° oven until hot and cheese is melted.

Mrs. H. Fred Johnson (Olla Carter)

Homemade rolls or frozen rolls may also be used.

HOT EGGS   Serves 6

6 eggs, hard boiled
   and shelled

Jalapeno juice
Crackers

Place eggs in a 1 quart glass jar. Cover with jalapeno juice. Seal tightly and marinate in refrigerator at least 2 weeks. Remove eggs. Slice and serve with crackers. This is a tasty appetizer that men usually like. The eggs take on the hot taste of the jalapeno juice but do not change appearance.

Mrs. Hugh Gilmour (Michele Lamarca)

ENGLISH MUFFIN SNACKS

Serves 8-10

1 tablespoon minced onion
¾ cup mayonnaise
1½ cups grated, sharp
   Cheddar cheese
   Dash garlic salt

Dash Tabasco
2 tablespoons capers
6 English muffins,
   quartered

Mix first six ingredients and spread on English muffins. Broil until bubbly.

Mrs. Carter Kelly (Sue Whitney)

MUSHROOM CROUSTADES

Serves 8-12

24 slices white bread,
   very thinly sliced

Soft butter

Cut 24 croustades, using a 3-inch cookie cutter, fluted or plain. Coat each heavily with butter. Fit bread into tiny muffin tins. Bake in a 400° oven for 10 minutes. Do not over brown.

Filling: MUSHROOM DUXELLES

4 tablespoons butter
3 tablespoons finely chopped
   green onions
½ pound mushrooms, chopped
2 tablespoons flour
1 cup heavy cream

½ teaspoon salt
¼ teaspoon cayenne
1 tablespoon finely chopped
   chives
½ teaspoon lemon juice
2 tablespoons
   Parmesan cheese

Heat butter until foam subsides. Add onions and saute for 4 minutes. Stir in mushrooms. Sauté until moisture evaporates. Remove from heat. Sprinkle in flour. Stir. Add cream. Bring to a boil and simmer 1 minute. Add salt, cayenne, chives, and lemon juice. Refrigerate. Spoon into croustades. Sprinkle with cheese and dot with butter. Bake in a 350° oven for 10 minutes.

Freezes beautifully.

Mrs. E.T. Manning, Jr. (Sally Manning)

CHAMPIGNONS FARCIS
(Stuffed Mushrooms)

Yields 1 Dozen

12 large mushrooms
2–3 tablespoons melted butter
   Salt and pepper
2 tablespoons minced
   shallots or scallions
2 tablespoons butter

½ teaspoon flour
½ cup heavy cream
3 tablespoons fresh
   minced parsley
   Salt and pepper
¼ cup grated Swiss cheese
1–2 tablespoons melted butter

Remove mushroom stems and reserve. Wash and dry the caps and brush with melted butter. Arrange, hollow side up, in a baking dish. Season lightly with salt and pepper. Wash and dry stems and mince. Extract as much juice from stem as possible, by twisting in the corner of a towel. Sauté with the shallots or scallions in butter for 4-5 minutes until the pieces begin to separate. Lower heat. Add flour and stir 1 minute. Stir in cream and simmer 1-2 minutes until thickened. Stir in parsley and seasonings. Fill the mushroom caps with this mixture. Top each with 1 teaspoon cheese and a few drops of melted butter. Set aside until ready to finish cooking. 15 minutes before serving, bake in upper part of oven at 375°, until caps are tender and stuffing is lightly browned on top.

Mrs. John Mozola (Jo Rush)

PARMESAN TWISTS

Serves 12

1 cup grated
   Parmesan cheese
1 cup sifted flour
7 tablespoons sour cream

¼ cup butter
   Salt and paprika
   to taste

Work all ingredients together to a soft dough. Chill for 30 minutes. On a lightly floured board, roll out the dough about ¼ inch thick. Cut into strips ½ inch wide and about 9 inches long. Twist the strips into spirals. Put the twists on an ungreased baking sheet and bake in a 350° oven for 15 minutes, or until golden. Serve the twists warm. Dough may be frozen.

Mrs. John Baay (Nancy Middlebrook)

SOUFFLE SQUARES

Serves 12

½ cup butter, melted
½ cup flour
1 teaspoon baking powder
  Dash salt
10 eggs, beaten

1 pound cottage cheese
1 pound Monterey Jack
  cheese, grated
8 ounces chopped
  chili peppers

Combine butter, flour, baking powder and salt. In another bowl, combine the remaining ingredients. Combine the two mixtures and pour into a 10x13 inch baking dish. Bake in 400° oven for 15 minutes. Turn oven to 350° and continue cooking for 40-55 minutes. Cut into 1 inch squares and serve as hors d'oeuvres.

Mrs. Larry Paulk (Judy Feferman)

TYROPITES

Yields 3-3½ Dozen

1 egg
1 package (8 ounces)
  cream cheese
½ cup Feta cheese, crumbled
2 sticks butter

3 tablespoons
  chopped parsley
10 sheets filo pastry
⅔ cup grated Gruyere or
  Swiss cheese

Mix egg, cheese and parsley. Melt butter and set aside. Separate pastry sheets. Cut into 3 inch strips, lengthwise. Brush strips with butter. Put one heaping teaspoon of cheese mixture in one corner of pastry strip. Fold over in a triangle, as you would a flag. Place on buttered baking sheet. Repeat until each is folded. Brush each one with butter. Bake in 375° oven for 20 minutes. Best when warm.

Mrs. John Cottle (Sammye Kinkade)

ARTICHOKE HEARTS

Serves 6

1 small onion, chopped
1 clove garlic, minced
2 jars (6 ounces each)
  marinated artichoke
  hearts, chopped
5 eggs, slightly beaten
½ pound (2 cups)
  sharp cheddar cheese,
  shredded

¼ teaspoon salt
¼ teaspoon pepper
  Dash Tabasco
¼ teaspoon oregano leaves
1 cup (2 slices)
  bread crumbs
2 tablespoons
  chopped parsley

Combine onion, garlic and the liquid from one jar of artichokes in medium mixing bowl. (Discard liquid from second jar.) Microwave 4 minutes. Add remaining ingredients and mix well. Pour into 8 inch square baking dish. Microwave 10 minutes or until set. Cool slightly, cut into squares and serve. May be baked in a 350– oven for 35-40 minutes.

Mrs. William D. Campbell (Patsy Gannon)

CUCUMBERS HORS D'OEUVRES

Cucumbers
Lemon or lime juice,
to taste

Equal parts chili powder
and salt,
to taste

Peel and cut cucumbers into strips. Arrange on a platter and just before serving, sprinkle the chili-salt mixture over the strips and then the lemon or lime juice. Use enough of the dried ingredients to give the cucumbers a light orange coloring. Very tasty with drinks, especially beer.

Mrs. W.R. Klingensmith (Mary Wetzel)

MARINATED MUSHROOMS

Serves 6

⅓ cup red wine vinegar
⅓ cup Wesson oil
1 small onion, chopped
1 teaspoon salt
2 teaspoons dried parsley flakes or 3 tablespoons fresh

1 teaspoon Dijon mustard
1 tablespoon brown sugar
1 clove garlic, pierced
3 cans (4 ounces each) mushroom crowns, drained

Combine first eight ingredients in a small saucepan and bring to a boil. Add mushroom crowns. Simmer 5 minutes. Chill at least 24 hours. Drain just before serving.

Mrs. James Herring (Margaret Johnson)

STUFFED BAKED MUSHROOMS

Yields 24 Cups

24 whole fresh mushrooms
Salt
2 green onions, sliced thin
3 tablespoons butter
1 cup cooked crab, shrimp or combination
½ cup light cream

2 tablespoons bread crumbs
½ cup grated cheese, Cheddar or Swiss
Salt and pepper to taste
Dash garlic powder

Remove stems from mushrooms. Salt caps lightly. Chop stems fine and sauté with onion in butter several minutes over medium high heat. Add crab or shrimp, crumbs, cheese and seasonings. Mound mixture in mushrooms. Arrange in greased shallow baking pan. Pour cream around mushrooms. Bake in 350° oven for 20 minutes, basting several times. Serve hot. Can be prepared ahead and baked just before serving.

Mrs. James M. Goforth (Brenda Lee)

PEPPERS & ANCHOVIES
ITALIAN-STYLE

Serves 6-8

1 pound green or red
  bell peppers
3 tablespoons olive oil
1 can (2 ounces)
  anchovies, flat
2 tablespoons capers, drained
1 teaspoon dried oregano

Salt and freshly
  ground pepper
1 teaspoon finely chopped
  garlic
1 tablespoon red wine vinegar
1 tablespoon finely chopped
  parsley
Lemon wedges

Core and seed the peppers. Cut them into half inch lengthwise strips. There should be about 4 cups. Heat the oil in a heavy skillet and add peppers. Cook, stirring and shaking the skillet about two minutes. Drain and chop the anchovies and add to peppers. Add the capers, oregano, salt, pepper and garlic. Cook, stirring and shaking the skillet, about two minutes. Sprinkle with wine vinegar and remove from heat. Serve hot or cold. Sprinkle with parsley. Serve with lemon. Make ahead and let spices blend for a better flavor.

Mrs. W.R. Klingensmith (Mary Wetzel)

ZUCCHINI APPETIZERS

Yields 4 Dozen

3 cups (4 small) thinly
  sliced unpared zucchini
1 cup Bisquick
½ cup chopped onion
½ cup grated
  Parmesan cheese
2 tablespoons dried
  parsley, crushed

½ teaspoon seasoned salt
½ teaspoon dried marjoram
  or oregano
Dash of pepper
1 clove garlic, minced
½ cup vegetable oil
4 eggs, slightly beaten
½ teaspoon salt

Mix all ingredients and spread in a greased 13x9x2 inch pan. Bake in 350° oven, for 25-30 minutes, or until golden brown. Cut into pieces.

Mrs. Robert L. Bass (Allee Curtis)

HERRING
IN SOUR CREAM

Serves 6-10

1 large jar herring
  in wine sauce, drained
  and cut up
½ cup mayonnaise
½ pint sour cream

½ bunch green onions, diced
1 tablespoon lemon juice
1 tablespoon celery seed
1 tablespoon sugar
1 green pepper, diced

Combine all ingredients and mix well. Chill. Serve with crackers.

Mrs. David Waitt (Nancy Longtin)

BOURBON WIENERS

Serves 6-8

1 cup catsup
1 cup brown sugar

1 cup boubon
3 pounds wieners

Mix catsup, brown sugar and bourbon. Cut wieners into bite size pieces. Simmer in sauce over low heat for several hours. Serve hot. (Best when prepared 6 hours before serving.)

Mrs. Tom Cambridge (Norma Taggart)

TAMALE BALLS

Serves 20

1 pound ground beef
1 pound ground pork
1½ cups masa harina
1 teaspoon cumin
½ teaspoon rosemary
  leaves, crumbled
3 large cloves garlic,
  crushed

2 tablespoons chili powder
2 teaspoons salt
¾ cup juice from
  canned tomatoes
3 cans (28 ounces each)
  tomatoes
2 teaspoons salt
3–4 tablespoons chili powder

Combine first nine ingredients and form into 150 marble-size balls. Make sauce from tomatoes, salt and chili powder. Bring to a boil and drop balls into sauce and simmer for 2 hours. Stir carefully so meatballs will not fall apart. Correct seasonings and serve in chafing dish with toothpicks for spearing.

Sally Bivins

WAIKIKI MEATBALLS

**Serves 6 (Main Dish)
10-12 (Hors d'oeuvres)**

1½ pounds ground beef
⅔ cup cracker crumbs
⅓ cup minced onions
1 egg
1½ teaspoons salt
¼ teaspoon ginger
¼ cup milk
1 tablespoon shortening

2 tablespoons cornstarch
½ cup brown sugar
1 can (13½ ounces) pineapple
  tidbits, drain and
  reserve syrup
⅓ cup vinegar
1 tablespoon soy sauce
⅓ cup chopped green pepper

Mix thoroughly beef, crumbs, onion, egg, salt, ginger and milk. Shape mixture into ½ inch balls. Melt shortening in large skillet. Brown and cook meatballs, until done. Remove meatballs and keep warm. Pour fat from skillet. Mix cornstarch and sugar. Stir in reserved pineapple syrup, vinegar and soy sauce until smooth. Pour into skillet, cook over medium heat, stirring constantly, until mixture thickens and boils. Add meatballs, pineapple tidbits and green pepper. Heat thoroughly. Can be stored and/or frozen in plastic sealed bags.

Susan Roach

CHICKEN LIVER PÂTÉ

Serves 6-8

½ pound chicken livers
1 cup water
6 slices cooked bacon,
  crumbled

¼ cup mayonnaise
2 hard boiled eggs
2 tablespoons chopped onion

Cover livers, with water, in pan. Bring to a boil. Reduce heat and simmer 10-15 minutes. Drain. Combine with remaining ingredients in an electric blender. Shape and chill.

Easy in a food processor.

Mrs. John Mozola (Jo Rush)

DOROTHY DRAVIN'S CHICKEN PÂTÉ

Serves 20

1 pound chicken livers
1 hot yellow onion, chopped
2 hard boiled eggs
3 tablespoons butter or
  rendered chicken fat

Salt-pepper
Saltine crackers
Hard boiled egg slices
Yellow onions, sliced

Broil fresh chicken livers 5 minutes on each side. Do not overcook; these should still be a little bloody. Cool. Combine with next five ingredients and pass through a food mill or blend in a food processor. Serve with crackers and slices of hard boiled eggs and yellow onions. Men love this.

RENDERED CHICKEN FAT

Ask butcher to save chicken fat. Place fat in a pan with a small amount of water (enough to keep fat from sticking). Add 1 whole potato and 1 quartered onion. Bring to boil, then simmer for 3-4 hours. Cool. Strain and freeze. Will keep indefinitely in freezer and can be refrozen.

Mrs. Warren J. Freeman Jr. (Celine Seay)

MOCK PÂTÉ

Serves 20

½ pound liver sausage
1 package (8 ounces)
  cream cheese
2 teaspoons horseradish

½ cup mayonnaise
1 teaspoon prepared mustard
¼ teaspoon dill weed
1 cup toasted almonds

Let liver sausage and cream cheese reach room temperature. Mix with remaining ingredients and form into a ball. Wrap ball in plastic and refrigerate for 2 hours or more. Toast and chop almonds. To serve, roll ball in almonds and set on tray with crackers.

Can easily be mixed in food processor.

Mrs. James Upchurch (Nancy Brown)

PÂTÉ

2 envelopes Knox gelatin
2 cans Campbell's consomme
  Juice of 1 lemon
  Milk
2 rolls (8 ounces each)
  Oscar Meyer Brunswieger

9 ounces cream cheese,
  softened
1 envelope Lipton Onion Soup
  Garlic salt, to taste

Soften gelatin in one can cold consommé. Heat second can and combine with the first to dissolve gelatin. Add lemon juice. Divide mixture in half. Pour a thin layer into the bottom of bowl. Place in coldest part of the refrigerator for 10 minutes or until firm. Beat milk with cream cheese until it is the consistency of whipped cream. Mix brunswieger thoroughly with cream cheese mixture. Add dry soup and garlic salt. Beat thoroughly. Spread over gelatin in bowl. Cover pâte mixture with remaining gelatin. Chill. Can be made several days in advance. Makes two medium pates.

Mrs. T. Boone Pickens, Jr. (Bea Carr)

CHINESE BARBEQUE PORK (Char Siew)

Serves 6-8

1 cup soy sauce
1 cup sugar
1 teaspoon garlic powder
4 tablespoons catsup
1 teaspoon monosodium
  glutamate

½ teaspoon salt
3-4 pork tenderloins
  (1 pound each or less)
  Sesame seeds, toasted
  (optional)

Combine first six ingredients. Split tenderloins in half lengthwise. Pour marinade over strips and marinate at least 3 hours or overnight, turning occasionally. Drain pork and reserve the marinade. Broil on broiling pan, basting with marinade, and turn every 10 minutes, until thoroughly cooked (20 minutes). Lower the pan if meat has a tendency to burn. Slice into ¼ inch pieces and sprinkle with toasted sesame seeds. Serve hot with sauces of hot mustard and/or soy sauce.

Mrs. James D. Man (Cordelia Harris)

This was served at a league meeting (Pandora's Box Lunch) on a wooden skewer with pieces of Parmesan chicken, marinated mushrooms, fresh pineapple chunks and the pork. It was served at room temperature and cut into larger pieces (bite size).

SIMPSON'S SALAMI

2 tablespoons black
  peppercorn, divided
2 pounds lean ground beef
1 cup water

2 tablespoons Morton's
  Tender Quick Cure for Fresh
  and Frozen Meats
½ teaspoon garlic powder
1 tablespoon liquid smoke

Reserve one tablespoon of the peppercorns. Combine remaining ingredients. Mix well with hands. Divide into three equal parts. Shape each part into an eight inch log. Crush reserved peppercorns. Roll meat in pepper to coat. Wrap in foil. Seal well to avoid odor in refrigerator. Refrigerate for 24 to 48 hours. Place on a rack in an uncovered pan. Cook for 2 hours in a 300° oven. Freezes well.

SHRIMP-DILL
APPETIZER MOLD   Serves 8-10

2 envelopes unflavored gelatin
1½ cups tomato juice
2 tablespoons lemon juice
¼ cup chili sauce
1 tablespoon
  Worcestershire sauce
¼ teaspoon Tabasco

1 tablespoon dried dill weed
1 pint sour cream
¾ pound shrimp, cooked and
  finely chopped (2 cups)
  Whole shrimp
  Fresh dill sprigs

Sprinkle gelatin over tomato juice in a medium saucepan. Place over moderate heat and stir constantly, until gelatin is dissolved (about 3 minutes). Remove from heat and stir in lemon juice, chili sauce, Worcestershire, Tabasco and dill. When mixture is cool, stir in sour cream. Heat until smooth. Stir in shrimp. Turn into individual molds or a 5 cup mold. Chill until firm. Unmold and garnish with whole shrimp and sprigs of dill if desired. Serve with crisp crackers or rounds of bread.

Mrs. David Culver (Elaine Cash)

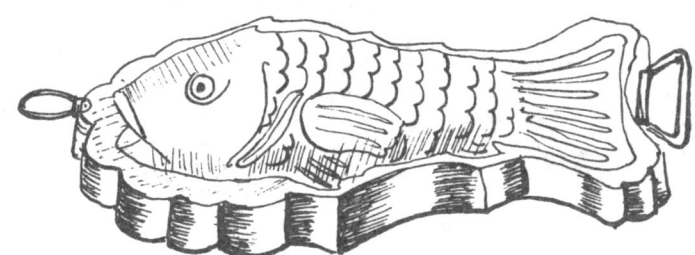

CAROLYN'S TIDBITS

Yields 48 Pieces

1 can (15 ounces)
  jumbo tamales

Bacon
Toothpicks

Slice each tamale into eight pieces. Wrap each piece with ⅓-½ slice bacon. Secure with toothpick. Line jelly roll pan with foil and bake tidbits in 300° oven until bacon is crisp. May be baked, refrigerated, and reheated.

MARINATED VEGETABLES

Marinade
1 cup red wine vinegar
⅔ cup olive oil
¼ cup minced dry onion
2 teaspoons Spice Islands
  Italian Seasoning

1 teaspoon seasoned salt
1 teaspoon garlic salt
1 teaspoon onion salt
  Sugar

1 can (4½ ounces) whole mushrooms, drained
1 can (8½ ounces) artichoke hearts, drained, cut in half
1 can (5¾ ounces) pitted ripe olives, drained
1 can (14 ounces) hearts of palm, drained, cut into bite sized pieces
Cherry tomatoes, cut in half (optional)

Combine all marinade ingredients and bring to boil. Pour the hot marinade over the vegetables, except the tomatoes. Refrigerate overnight. Stir occasionally. Tomatoes may be added for color 2-3 hours before serving. Serve with toothpicks.

Mrs. James D. Man (Cordelia Harris)

SUGARED PEANUTS

Yields 4 Cups

2 cups raw Spanish peanuts
  (10 ounce package)
  Salt

1 cup sugar
½ cup water

In heavy saucepan, combine peanuts, sugar and water. Place over medium heat. Cook and stir until mixture crystallizes and coats peanuts (about 10 minutes). Spread peanuts in a buttered 15x10x1 inch pan, sprinkle with salt. Bake at 300° for 15 minutes. Lift and turn peanuts with metal spatula. Continue to cook 15 minutes more. Cool and store in a covered container.

Mrs. Victor W. Shawgo (Mary Kaye Dolan)

SPICED PECANS

1 cup sugar	2 teaspoons cinnamon
1 teaspoon salt	½ teaspoon water
½ teaspoon nutmeg	½ pound pecans
½ teaspoon ground cloves	

Combine sugar, salt and spices with water. Cook to soft boil stage, stirring. Remove from heat. Add pecans. Stir until mixture, sugars and pecans are evenly coated. Pour out onto wax paper, cool and separate.

May be frozen.

Mrs. James H. Simms (Freeda Daugherty)

SPICED COFFEE MIX   Yields 20 Cups

1 jar (2 ounces) freeze dried decaffeinated coffee or instant coffee	1 cup granulated sugar
	1 tablespoon cinnamon
	2 teaspoons dried orange peel

Mix well; store in tightly covered jar.
To serve:
    1 Tablespoon mix to ¾ cup hot water.

About 30 calories per serving.

Mrs. Thomas A. Bunkley, Jr. (Myra Anne Stanley)

ALMOND TEA   Serves 20-30

1½ quarts water	Juice of 2 lemons
3 cups sugar	1½ teaspoons vanilla
3 lemons, juice and rind	1½ teaspoons almond extract
3 cups strong tea	

Combine first three ingredients. Boil for 5 minutes. Mix together with remaining ingredients and add enough water to make one gallon. Serve hot. Can be made several days in advance.

Mrs. James A. Hedgecoke, Jr. (Sallye Dees)

JEANNE WHITTENBURG'S
MINT TEA
Serves 8

4 cups boiling water
9 teabags, regular size
12 sprigs mint
Juice of 2 lemons

¾ cup sugar
2 cups boiling water
4 cups cold water

Pour 4 cups boiling water over teabags and mint. Let steep 10 minutes. Combine lemon juice and sugar. Pour 2 cups boiling water into the juice and sugar mixture stirring until sugar dissolves. Remove teabags and mint. Combine sugar mixture and tea. Pour into pitcher with 4 cups cold water. Serve over ice with a sprig of mint and a slice of lemon.

BETTY McCUE'S
SPICED TEA
Yields 16 Cups

4 quarts cold water
4 cinnamon sticks
1 teaspoon whole cloves
3-4 family size tea bags
   or 15 small bags

1¼ cups sugar
1 cup fresh orange juice
¾ cup fresh lemon juice
1 cup pineapple juice

Tie cinnamon sticks and whole cloves in separate bags of cheesecloth. Bring water, cinnamon, cloves and tea bags to a boil in an uncovered enameled pan. Let steep for 4-5 minutes. Remove tea bags and cloves, leave cinnamon. Add remaining ingredients. Serve piping hot.

STRAWBERRY TEA
Serves 75

4 cups sugar
2 cups water
2 cups strong tea
   (not instant) cooled
2 cups fresh lemon juice
2½ cups fresh orange juice

2 cans (46 ounces each)
   pineapple juice
2 packages (10 ounces each)
   frozen strawberries
   and juice
3 gallons water, chilled
2 quarts ginger ale, chilled

Bring sugar and 2 cups water to a boil and boil for about 10 minutes. Add tea, lemon, orange and pineapple juices. Chill several hours. Add remaining ingredients and serve over ice ring.

Ice Ring

Boil amout of water desired for mold (This is to keep it clean.) Chill water. Put small amount of water, mint leaves and whole strawberries in ring mold. Chill in freezer until slightly frozen. Add remaining water to fill mold. Freeze. Prepare at least 24 hours in advance.

Mrs. Don T. Curtis (Suzanne Stokes)

BANANA SLUSH

50 Cups

1 can (46 ounces)
   pineapple juice
   Juice of 5 oranges
   Juice of 2 lemons

5 bananas, mashed
2 quarts chilled ginger ale
1 recipe simple syrup*

Mix juices and banana pulp. Add cooled simple syrup. Freeze in a plastic container. Remove from freezer 1 hour before serving. Add ginger ale when ready to serve.

* SIMPLE SYRUP

4 cups sugar

6 cups water

Combine. Bring to a boil. Simmer for 5 minutes. Cool thoroughly.

Mrs. S.S. Stephens (Mikala Faville)

FRUIT SMOOTHIE BEVERAGE

Yields 1 Quart

1 apple
1 tablespoon lemon juice
2 cups orange juice
1 banana

1 fresh peach, seeded,
   peel if desired
4 ice cubes
1 tablespoon powdered
   protein, if desired

Core and chop apple. Place in blender with lemon juice. Blend until smooth. Add orange juice, banana and peach. Blend for 1 minute.

Mrs. Terry A. Curtis (Melonye Lowe)

LOW-CAL MINT LEMONADE

Serves 4

1 cup fresh lemon juice
5 tablespoons sugar
   substitute

2⅓ cups water
¼ cup mint leaves

Combine all ingredients in blender. Chill and serve over ice.

Mrs. Thomas A. Bunkley, Jr. (Myra Anne Stanley)

ORANGE-APRICOT-BANANA DRINK

Yields ¾ Gallon

1 banana
1 can (46 ounces)
  apricot nectar

1 can (12 ounces)
  concentrated orange juice
3 juice cans water

Blend banana with some juice in blender. Then pour all ingredients together and stir.

Mrs. A.W. SoRelle, III (Judy Jolley)

PERCULATOR PUNCH

Yields 10 Cups

1½ teaspoons whole cloves
1 stick cinnamon
⅛ teaspoon salt
3 cups unsweetened
  pineapple juice

3 cups cranberry juice
1½ cups water
⅓ cup brown sugar

Place cloves, cinnamon and salt in basket of percolator with liquids and sugar below. Perk full cycle and serve.

Mrs. Michael Musick (Sharon Prater)

CHILDREN'S ORANGE JUICE

Yields 3 Cups

⅓ cup frozen orange juice
  concentrate (half of
  6 ounce can
½ cup milk

½ cup water
¼ cup sugar
½ teaspoon vanilla
5 – 6 ice cubes

Combine all ingredients in blender, cover and blend until smooth, about 30 seconds. Serve immediately!

Mrs. James M. Goforth (Brenda Lee)

SPICED APPLE CIDER

Serves 20

1 cup brown sugar
1 teaspoon nutmeg
1 tablespoon cloves
1 tablespoon allspice
24 sticks cinnamon

1 gallon apple cider
1 can (6 ounces)
frozen lemonade
1 can (6 ounces)
frozen orange juice

Combine first five ingredients and tie in a spice bag. Combine cider, lemonade and orange juice in a large pot. Add spice bag and simmer for 20 minutes.

Spice bag may be omitted, if mixture is strained.

Mrs. H. Fred Johnson (Olla Carter)

HOT CHOCOLATE DRINK MIX

Approximately 80 Cups

8 quarts dry milk
1 pound Quick
chocolate mix

3 ounces powdered
Coffee Mate
1 pound powdered sugar

Mix ingredients together and store in airtight container. To make individual cups, add 3 heaping tablespoons to 1 cup of hot water.

Mrs. Dick Frazer (Sylvia Lindley)

TOMATO SIP YUMMY

Serves 6-8

2 tablespoons butter, melted
¼ cup diced onion
2½ cups V-8 juice
4 peppercorns
1 small bay leaf
3 whole cloves

¼ teaspoon tarragon
1 teaspoon salt
5 beef bouillon cubes
dissolved in
4 cups boiling water
2 drops Tabasco (optional)

Brown onion in melted butter. Add V-8 juice and spices. Simmer for 1 hour. Strain and add bouillon. Add Tabasco. Serve with a slice of lemon or dab of sour cream in mugs.

You can experiment with this. 1 tablespoon of parsley and ⅛ teaspoon thyme may be added, and 2 cans diluted consommé may be used in place of beef cubes.

Mrs. Hugh Umphres, Jr. (Carlie Barnes)

FUNFEST BOURBON SLUSH

Serves 2-4

- 2 tea bags
- 1 cup boiling water
- 1 can (6 ounces) frozen orange juice, thawed
- ½-1 can (6 ounces) frozen lemonade, thawed
- ½-1 cup sugar
- 3½ cups water
- ½-¾ cup bourbon

Steep tea in boiling water for 3-5 minutes. Mix with remaining ingredients and store in freezer. Serve with sprigs of mint and orange slices.

This refreshing beverage was served to our "Funfest '78" clean-up crew.

Mrs. E.T. Manning, Jr. (Sally Manning)

Mrs. Victor Shawgo (Mary Kaye Dolan)

BRANDY ICE

Serves 6

- 1 pint vanilla ice cream
- 4½ jiggers brandy
- 2¼ jiggers Drambuie

Put all ingredients in blender and blend well.

Mrs. William Comerford (Pat Nunley)

LOW-CAL IRISH COFFEE

Serves 1

- ½-¾ cup hot coffee
- 2 drops calorie free sweetener
- 1 jigger Irish whisky
- 1 tablespoon Cool Whip

In each cup put sweetener and whisky. Fill with hot coffee and top with Cool Whip.

Mrs. Thomas A. Bunkley, Jr. (Myra Anne Stanley)

ST. JOHN'S TIA MARIA

Yields 1 Cup

1 ounce Tia Maria Liqueur
6 ounces strong piping hot coffee

1 tablespoon whipped cream, sweetened

Pour Tia Maria in cup, add coffee. Top with whipped cream.

I love to serve this in living room after dinner with cookies. A good finish to a gourmet dinner. Equally as good aboard sail boat off isle of St. John.

Mrs. Ed Fancher (Shirley Feierabend)

FROZEN WHISKEY SOURS I

Serves 6

1 can (6 ounces) lemonade
1 can (6 ounces) lemon juice

1 can (6 ounces) bourbon
2 cans (6 ounces each) water

Mix well and freeze. Add Fresca if desired.

Mrs. Ken McCarty (Sue Sheriff)

FROZEN WHISKEY SOURS II

Serves 4-6

1 can (6 ounces) frozen lemonade concentrate, slightly thawed
½ can (6 ounces) frozen orange juice concentrate slightly thawed

1½ cups lemon-lime carbonated beverage
1¼ cups bourbon
¾ cup water

Combine all ingredients in a plastic container. Freeze until slushy.

This can be made in large quantities ahead of time. It is nice to have on hand for company.

Mrs. Stan Morris, Jr. (Kathleen Boyd)

46

DAIQUIRI-COLD DUCK PUNCH

Serves 20

2 cans (6 ounces each)
  frozen daiquiri mix

2 cups light rum
3 bottles Cold Duck

Combine all ingredients. Add ice or ice ring at the last minute. Lime slices and strawberries are a pretty garnish.

Mrs. Jairl P. Dowell (Lynn Ficke)

KAHLUA

Yields 2½ Quarts

3 cups sugar
3 cups water
2½ ounces instant coffee

1 pint brandy or bourbon
1 pint vodka or light rum
1 teaspoon vanilla

Boil sugar, water and coffee, until sugar dissolves. Add both pints of liquor. Serve when cool.

Mrs. Benny Lawrence (Ellen Yows)

HOT BUTTERED RUM

Serves 16

¼ pound butter, softened
1 pound dark brown sugar
¼ teaspoon cinnamon
¼ teaspoon nutmeg

¼ teaspoon ground cloves
Dark rum
Boiling water

Cream butter and sugar. Combine cinnamon, nutmeg and cloves. Sprinkle over creamed mixture and mix thoroughly. To store, refrigerate in covered container. To serve: into each mug place 1 heaping tablespoon of mixture and add 1½ ounces dark rum and finish filling with boiling water. Stir and serve hot. This mixture may be frozen indefinitely.

Mrs. William Comerford (Pat Nunley)

MAMA'S
EGG NOG

6 cups sugar
6 dozen eggs, separated
6 quarts whipping cream
   whipped

2 quarts straight bourbon
   whiskey (Old Grandad)
1 quart rum (light Bacardi)
1 cup brandy (optional)

Add 3 cups sugar to well beaten egg yolks and beat well together. Add 3 cups sugar to well beaten egg whites and beat well. Into beaten egg yolks and sugar mixture add whiskey drop by drop — then add Rum. Fold in the beaten egg whites and sugar mixture. Fold in the whipped cream. Mix well and enjoy!

Mrs. John Ballard (Sadie Claude Curtis)

Mrs. John K. Boyce (Margaret Curtis)

Served every year at Amarillo Junior League Christmas party.

My first taste of egg nog was made by my mother, Mrs. James O. Curtis, when we were growing up at 1620 Washington Street, the Curtis Home built for my Grandmother, Mrs. William Riley Curtis in 1910. She lived here for several years with my sister Carlie, until she decided she wanted to live in our home at 1705 Polk Street. She then decided she wanted to live with us after Sister Carlie was married. Grandmothers love to be with their grandchildren, and we loved it, too.

Mama always made us a glass of egg nog after an illness, to build us up, she said. We had egg nog at Christmas time and other festival occasions, but never when Mama entertained the Woman's Club. This club was organized in 1903 as the Social Dames. Incorporated in their by-laws was, ''No intoxicating drinks may be served at any meeting of the club.'' Later when Sister Margaret entertained the Woman's Club, she would invite the Junior Woman's Club, also. However, this by-law was not in the Junior Woman's Club year book; so Sister Margaret would put the egg nog in the dining room and punch in the library. It was interesting to note that many of the members of the Woman's Club casually came into the dining room!

Our father, Jim Curtis, always had his toddy in the late afternoon, the cocktail hour, as it is called today. He would stir and stir . . . a sign for us to come and get a taste, one spoon full, no more, no less. He believed if we grew up with a taste we would never crave it!

I hope everyone will enjoy Mama's Egg Nog, whether a glass full or in a punch bowl! It is very good to build one up after an illness, and it does give you courage.

Sadie Claude Curtis Ballard

MIKE CAMPBELL'S HOLIDAY EGG NOG

Yields 5½ Quarts

- 2 quarts commercial egg nog
- 2 quarts Golden Vanilla ice cream
- 1 quart whipping cream, whipped very stiff
- 3–4 tablespoons cinnamon
- 1 tablespoon nutmeg
- Bourbon*
- Brandy*

Pour egg nog in *very large* container. Add ice cream and mix well until ice cream is almost completely melted. Add whipped cream to mixture. Blend ingredients well, adding spices. Add liquor, heavy on *Bourbon and lots of *Brandy.

RED SPARKLE PUNCH

Serves 20

- 1 bottle (24 ounces) Red Burgandy
- 1 bottle (24 ounces) Sauterne
- 1 bottle (32 ounces) club soda
- 1 bottle (32 ounces) ginger ale

Chill bottles overnight and pour over ice ring to serve.

Cranberry juice frozen into ring mold is optional and very good.

Mrs. Gene Edwards (Elaine Johnson)

DIET WINE COOLER

Serves 1

- ½ glass Fresca
- ½ glass red wine

Combine ingredients and add ice.

Mrs. Thomas A. Bunkley, Jr. (Myra Anne Stanley)

49

AUNT EMMA'S BEER   5 Gallons

3 ounces hops
2½ pounds (1 pint)
    extract of malt

1½ pounds cane sugar
1 yeast cake

Boil 3 ounces of hops in 5 gallons of water for 1 hour. (Tie hops in cheesecloth bag.) Add 2½ pounds of extract of malt and 1½ pounds of cane sugar. Let boil 20 minutes. Remove from heat. Let stand until lukewarm. Then add one yeast cake dissolved in warm water. Let stand in vessel until finished fermenting (about 36-50 hours). Strain well and cork tight. Let stand 2 weeks.

Mrs. Glen Brosier (Kay Wagner)

O BE JOYFUL   Serves 50

1 fifth light Rum
1 pint Gin
½ pint Sloe Gin

½ bottle (32 ounce bottle)
    lemon juice
4 or 5 bottles (32 ounces each)
    Ginger Ale

Combine Rum, Gin, Sloe Gin, and lemon juice. Pour into punch bowl as needed, adding Ginger Ale at last minute. Use ice ring or crushed ice.

Warning — This is very tasty, but very strong. One could become too joyful.

Mrs. James Man (Cordelia Harris)

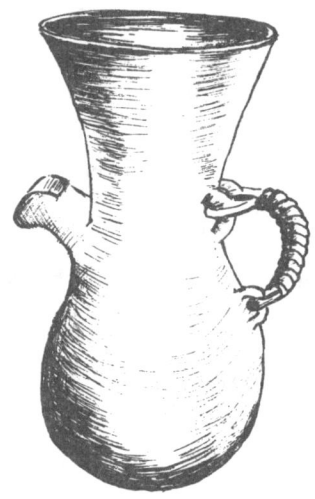

Soup

Sandwiches

ARTICHOKE SOUP

Serves 4

1 **can cream of celery soup**
1 **soup can of milk**
8 **ounces artichoke hearts**
   canned or frozen

3 **tablespoons sherry**
½ **cup grated sharp cheese**
   Dash Tabasco (optional)
   Grated onion to taste
   (optional)

Mix ingredients together. Heat in medium to large saucepan. Do not boil.

Mrs. Hollis Russell (Beth Knox)

AVOCADO SOUP

Serves 6-8

4 **fully ripe avocados**
2 **cups chicken broth**
2 **teaspoons lime juice**
½ **teaspoon salt**

⅛ **teaspoon garlic powder**
2 **cups heavy cream**
   Lemon slices

Peel and remove seeds from avocados. Slice and purée in electric blender with broth, lime juice, salt and garlic powder. Stir in cream and chill thoroughly. Garnish with lemon slices or with heavy cream whipped with a dash of garlic powder.

Mrs. Michael Campbell (Maggie Larson)

Half and half may be used instead of heavy cream.

BORSCHT

   Beef shank
1 **large onion, chopped**
   Salt
   Carrots (4 ounces), chopped
¼ **head cabbage, shredded**

1 **can (10 ounces) tomato juice**
1 **can (6 ounces) tomato puree**
1 **can (4½ ounces) diced beets**
1 **carton (8 ounces) sour cream**

Simmer beef shank until tender, the day before you want to serve the soup. Remove from broth, trim and chop, and return to the pan. Add onion, salt to taste, and carrots. Add cabbage and cook until the carrots are tender. Add tomato juice, purée, and beets. Simmer, then remove from heat. When soup is cool, add sour cream. Reheat, but do not boil. Serve with 1 tablespoon of sour cream on top of hot soup.

Mrs. Carter Kelly (Sue Whitney)

CREAM OF BROCCOLI SOUP

Serves 6-8

2 packages (10 ounces each) frozen broccoli
¼ cup chopped onion
3 cups chicken broth
2 tablespoons butter
2 tablespoons flour

1 teaspoon salt
⅛ teaspoon mace or nutmeg
2 cups milk
2 cups light cream
Scant ¼ teaspoon Tabasco

Cook broccoli and onion in broth about 6 minutes. Melt butter in large saucepan. Add flour, salt and mace or nutmeg. Heat until bubbly. Stir in milk, cream and Tabasco. Cook, stirring constantly, until creamy. Mix broccoli mixture in blender until smooth. Add to cream sauce. Heat to serving temperature. This can be frozen.

Mrs. Royce Kelly (Charlotte Smith)

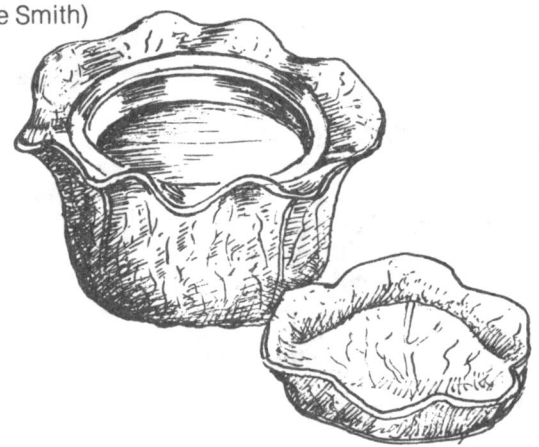

CHEESE SOUP

Serves 8

¼ cup butter
½ cup finely diced onions
½ cup finely diced carrots
½ cup finely diced celery
¼ cup flour
1 ½ tablespoons cornstarch

1 quart chicken stock
1 quart milk
⅛ teaspoon soda
1 cup grated processed Cheddar cheese
Salt and pepper
2 tablespoons finely chopped parsley

Melt butter in large soup pot; combine with onions, carrots, celery and sauté over low heat until soft. Add flour and cornstarch and cook until it bubbles. Add stock and milk stirring until smooth. Stir in soda and the cheese, season with salt and pepper. Garnish with parsley a few minutes before serving.

Mrs. Tom Cambridge (Norma Taggart)

NEW ENGLAND CLAM CHOWDER

Serves 8

1 piece of salt pork,
   2-inch square, cubed
1 large onion, chopped
2–3 stalks celery,
   chopped
¼ cup butter
1 tablespoon flour
1 cup diced potatoes

1 pint clams, strain
   and reserve liquid
1 quart milk or
   half and half
1 tablespoon chopped
   parsley
½ teaspoon paprika

Fry pork over low heat until crisp. Drain. Sauté onion and celery in butter in same skillet. Sprinkle with flour. Cook, stirring constantly, for 2 minutes. Simmer potatoes until almost done in clam juice and ½ cup water. Add onion-celery mixture and chopped clams. Simmer for 3 minutes. Do not boil. Scald milk in a double boiler. Add clam mixture. Garnish with parsley, paprika and pork bits.

Mrs. John Baay (Nancy Middlebrook)

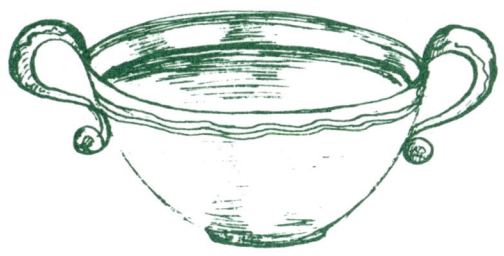

FISH CHOWDER

Serves 8-10

1 cup thinly sliced onion
¼ cup butter
1 cup cubed raw potato
1 cup sliced raw carrot
1 cup water
2 teaspoons salt
⅛ teaspoon pepper

1 package (1 pound) frozen
   haddock, cut in 1-inch cubes
3 cups milk
½ teaspoon rosemary
1 teaspoon salt
1 cup light cream
2 tablespoons flour

Sauté onion slightly in butter. Add potato, carrot, water, 2 teaspoons salt and pepper. Cook until carrots are almost tender. Add fish, milk, rosemary and 1 teaspoon salt. Simmer until fish flakes easily. Blend cream and flour together. Add to chowder and heat thoroughly.

Mrs. J.C. Arthur (Nan Johnson)

COLD SUMMER SOUP

Serves 8-10

2 cups tomato juice
2 cups orange juice
1 cup white wine
  Juice of one lemon
1 teaspoon sugar
1½ teaspoons salt

Cayenne pepper
  to taste
Tabasco to taste
Worcestershire sauce
  to taste
Chopped parsley

Mix first nine ingredients. Chill. Sprinkle with parsley before serving. I like to serve in demitasse cups before brunch or dinner, after cocktails.

Mrs. H. Fred Johnson (Olla Carter)

CRAB BISQUE

Yields 1½ Quarts

½ cup butter
1 cup chopped celery
1 cup chopped shallots
1 teaspoon chopped garlic
¼-½ cup flour
6 cups half & half

1 pound frozen crabmeat,
  thawed
2 bay leaves
2 dashes Tabasco
1 teaspoon McCormick's
  seafood seasoning
  Salt, pepper and paprika

Melt butter in a large saucepan. Sauté onions, celery and garlic, until tender. Make a roux by blending flour with sautéed vegetables. Do not brown. Add cream gradually, stirring constantly. Add remaining ingredients. Cover and simmer 20 minutes over low heat. Remove bay leaves. Good served with garlic toast.

Mrs. Ken McCarty (Sue Sheriff)

CRAB BISQUE

Serves 4-6

3 tablespoons butter
1½ tablespoons
  finely chopped onion
¼ teaspoon dry mustard
1 tablespoon flour
1 cup crabmeat

3 cups milk
1 hard cooked egg, sieved
1 teaspoon salt
  Pepper
1 teaspoon parsley
  Dash of Tabasco

Sauté onion in melted butter. Add mustard, flour and crabmeat. Cook until well blended. Add milk, bring to a boil and add egg and seasonings. Add parsley just before serving.

Mrs. Royce Kelly (Charlotte Smith)

HOT OR COLD CUCUMBER SOUP

Serves 4

2 tablespoons butter
¼ cup chopped onions
2 cups diced,
   unpeeled cucumber
1 cup watercress
   or parsley
½ cup diced
   raw potato
2 cups chicken broth

½ teaspoon salt
¼ teaspoon pepper
¼ teaspoon dry
   mustard
1 cup heavy cream
   Chopped chives
   radishes or
   cucumbers, optional
   garnish

Sauté onion in butter, until transparent. Add next seven ingredients. Bring to a boil and simmer, until potatoes are tender. Purée mixture in blender. Correct seasonings and chill several hours. Serve cold or warm. Add cream and garnish, before serving.

Mrs. Jerold Gormley (Amelia Dickgiesser)

GAZPACHO

Serves 6

1 bottle (24 ounces) Mr. &
   Mrs. T Bloody Mary Mix
4 teaspoons granulated
   beef bouillon
1 tablespoon
   Worcestershire sauce
   Dash Tabasco
4 tablespoons
   wine vinegar
2 tablespoons olive oil

½ green pepper,
   seeded, chopped
2 tablespoons
   chopped onion
½ medium cucumber,
   peeled, seeded, chopped
3 medium tomatoes,
   peeled, seeded, chopped
1 avocado, chopped (optional)
   croutons (optional)

Pour Bloody Mary mix in a saucepan. Add bouillon and bring slowly to a boil. Remove from heat and add remaining ingredients. Put in glass or ceramic bowl. Let mixture stand on counter for one hour. Refrigerate at least 3 hours before serving. Add croutons just before serving, if desired. This is a good food processor recipe using the shredding blade. Drain excess liquid from vegetables before adding to tomato-bouillon mixture.

Mrs. John Kelleher (Cindy Leiphart)

GLADYS' GAZPACHO
Serves 6

3 cans (4 ounces each)
   Snappy Tom tomato juice
1 cucumber, chopped
2 tomatoes, chopped

1 tablespoon sugar
¼ cup vinegar
¼ cup salad oil
1 small onion, finely chopped

Place in blender, one can Snappy Tom, half the cucumber, one tomato, sugar, vinegar and salad oil. Blend for a few seconds. Add remaining ingredients. Serve cold.

Mrs. Stan Morris, Jr. (Kathleen Boyd)

TOBY'S GAZPACHO
Serves 8-12

1 clove garlic
2 teaspoons salt
⅓ cup chopped
   mushrooms
3 tablespoons olive oil
1 cup finely chopped onions
2 cups finely chopped
   tomatoes
1¼ cup finely chopped
   green peppers
1 cup finely chopped
   cucumbers

2 teaspoons chopped chives
1 teaspoon chopped
   fresh parsley
1 teaspoon freshly ground
   black pepper
⅛ – ¼ teaspoon Tabasco
1 teaspoon
   Worcestershire sauce
½ cup tarragon vinegar
2 cups tomato juice
2 cups chicken broth

Crush garlic in salt. Sauté mushrooms in olive oil until lightly browned. Combine mushrooms and garlic salt with remaining ingredients in a 4 quart stainless steel or glass container. Cover and chill at least 3 hours.

Mrs. Benny Lawrence (Ellen Yows)

LULA'S
HEARTY SOUP
Serves 8

2 medium onions, chopped
½ stick butter
1⅓ quarts boiling water
1½ cups potato buds

1 German sausage
1 Polish sausage
½ jalapeño pepper
1 medium head cabbage,
   shredded

Sauté onions in butter until limp. Place in boiling water and add potato buds. Peel and slice sausages into bite size pieces and add to water. Simmer about 30 minutes. Add cabbage and jalapeño. Simmer another 30 minutes. Salt and pepper to taste.

This soup is good served with sliced tomatoes and cornbread or French garlic bread.

Mrs. Jay Taylor (Imogene Herring)

MINESTRONE SOUP

Serves 12

¼ cup each:
Dried lentils
Dried green split peas
Dried blackeyed peas
Dried Great Northern beans
Dried chili beans
Dried pinto beans
Dried barley
Dried speckled
lima beans
¾ cup canned
garbanzo beans
¾ cup canned black beans
3 quarts water or 2 quarts
water and 1 quart chicken
broth

2 pounds stew meat
2 cans (16 ounces each)
tomatoes
2 onions, diced
2-3 cloves garlic, minced
salt to taste
⅛ teaspoon pepper
1 rounded teaspoon
Greek oregano
1 rounded teaspoon basil
Handful thin spaghetti
Parmesan cheese

Rinse beans and soak overnight. Drain. Add water, stew meat, tomatoes, onion, and garlic. Cover. Simmer at least 3 hours. Half hour before serving, add salt, pepper, oregano, basil and spaghetti. Sprinkle each serving with Parmesan cheese.

Mrs. Royce Kelly (Charlotte Smith)

Fun to serve on a cold, cold night, with bread and red wine.

MUSHROOM SOUP

Serves 6-8

3 cups boiling water
4 beef bouillon cubes
2 medium sized onions, diced
1 stick butter, divided
1 pound fresh mushrooms,
diced

3 medium sized Irish
potatoes, diced
Salt and pepper to taste
3 cups milk

Combine water and bouillon cubes. Set aside. Saute' onion in 4 tablespoons butter. Add mushrooms, remaining butter and potatoes into onion mixture. Cook for 10 minutes. Add bouillon, salt and pepper. Cover and simmer for 45 minutes. Add more water occasionally. Before serving, add milk; bring to boil. Serve immediately. Good with Parmesan cheese or croutons on top.

Mrs. Frank B. White, III (Lynn Blackburn)

MUSHROOM SOUP

Serves 4-6

1 stick butter
1 medium onion, chopped
1 pound fresh mushrooms, sliced
1 can (13¾ ounces) chicken broth
1 teaspon curry powder
1 teaspoon Worcestershire sauce
Dash Tabasco
¼ cup sherry
1 pint half and half
Seasoned salt

Sauté onions in butter, until tender. Add mushrooms. Sauté 5 minutes. Stir in the chicken broth, add the curry powder, Worcestershire, and Tabasco. Simmer 10 minutes. Stir in the sherry and the half and half. Simmer until hot, but do not let boil. Correct seasoning.

Mrs. James D. Man (Cordelia Harris)

NAVY BEAN AND CABBAGE SOUP

Serves 6-8

1 pound small white beans (sorted and washed)
3 quarts rich chicken stock
1 large ham hock or part of butt-end ham
1 large onion, chopped
1 small head cabbage, chopped
3 carrots, chopped
Salt
Pepper

Cover beans with chicken stock. Add ham and onion. Simmer 3 hours, or until beans reach the mushy stage. Add cabbage and carrots and simmer additional hour, adding water if needed. Remove ham from bone and return to soup. Season with salt and pepper to taste. Skim off excess fat. Yields approximately 3 quarts.

Mrs. James E. Herring (Margaret Johnson)

OKRA GUMBO

Serves 4-6

½ cup chopped onion
1 green pepper, chopped (approximately 1 cup)
4 slices bacon, cooked until crisp, and crumbled
1 tablespoon oil
2 cups sliced fresh raw okra
1 tablespoon flour
1 can (16 ounces) tomatoes

Sauté onion and pepper in oil. When slightly browned, add bacon and okra. Let okra brown slightly. Add the flour and stir. Add tomatoes and stir. Cover and simmer for 30 minutes; more if desired.

This freezes beautifully and is also good refrigerated and reheated. During the summer when okra is delicious the gumbo can be made in large quantities and frozen to be used during the winter.

Mrs. Jim Walker (Patsy Roberts)

EASY ONION SOUP

Serves 4

1 onion, thinly sliced
Butter
1 package dry onion
soup mix

½ cup water or
½ cup sherry
Mozzarella cheese,
shredded
Croutons

Sauté onion in butter. Prepare soup according to directions. You may substitute ½ cup sherry for ½ cup of the water. Add sautéed onions to soup. Place cheese in the bottom of each bowl. Pour soup over cheese. Top with croutons.

Mrs. Jairl R. Dowell (Lynn Ficke)

ONION SOUP

Serves 6-8

4 cups thinly
sliced onions
½ cup melted butter
2 tablespoons flour

2 cans (10½ ounces each)
beef broth
1 can (10¾ ounces)
chicken broth
1 soup can water

Sauté onions in butter until they are limp, but not brown. Blend in flour. Add broths and water and stir until smooth. Simmer about 30 minutes. Serve with slices of French bread sprinkled with grated Cheddar or Parmesan cheese. Place under broiler to melt cheeses.

Mrs. Jay Taylor (Imogene Herring)

CHUCK BONJEAN'S SPLIT PEA SOUP

1 ham bone with meat or
4 or 5 ham hocks
2 quarts water
1 quart canned
chicken broth
1¼ quart of split peas that
have been rinsed
1 bay leaf

1 large onion, chopped
3 tablespoons chives,
chopped
2 carrots, sliced
3 stalks celery with leaves,
chopped
1 medium potato, peeled
and cut up

Place first seven ingredients in a 5 quart Dutch oven and simmer for 1½ hours. Add carrots and celery and simmer another ½ hour. Add potato and simmer 20 minutes. Remove ham bone and bay leaf. Return meat to mixture. Serve.

61

SPLIT PEA SOUP

Serves 6-8

2 cups dried split peas
4 cups homemade
   chicken stock
4 cups water
2 medium onions,
   peeled and quartered

3 stalks celery, halved
1 pound precooked ham
   (preferably sugar cured
   without nitrate or nitrite)
Pepper to taste

In heavy kettle combine all ingredients, and simmer covered for 2 hours. Remove ham, julienne, and reserve. Purée remaining liquid in blender. Return to kettle, stir in ham, and simmer 5 minutes more. Freezing Tips: Freezes well. May be frozen in milk cartons after soup has cooled completely. Reheat slowly stirring as soup melts.

Mrs. Robert H. Smith (Sally Allen)

POSOLE

Serves 6-8

1 small pork roast
1 onion, diced
2 cups canned tomatoes
   (cut in pieces)
2 cans (15 ounces each)
   hominy

Garlic powder to taste
2 or 3 cans (4 ounces each)
   chopped green chilies
Salt
2 cups water

Cut meat off roast and brown in deep kettle. Sauté onion. Add remaining ingredients and simmer for several hours. Freezes well.

Mrs. Robert L. Bass (Allee Curtis)

POTATO SOUP

Serves 8

½ cup diced onion
4 to 6 slices bacon, cooked
   crisp and diced
   (reserve drippings)
2 tablespoons flour
4 cans (10 ounces each)
   chicken broth

3 potatoes, diced
2 egg yolks, beaten
1 cup sour cream
1 tablespoon
   chopped parsley

Saute' onions in bacon drippings. Drain. Add flour and stir until smooth. Add chicken broth and potatoes. Cook until potatoes are done. Combine sour cream and egg yolks. Add bacon bits to sour cream mixture. Stir mixture into soup just before serving. Top with chopped parsley.

Mrs. Royce Kelly (Charlotte Smith)

CHEESY POTATO SOUP

Serves 6

4 cups boiling water
2 teaspoons salt
6 cups chopped potatoes
3 tablespoons
  chopped onion

¼ cup butter
1 tablespoon flour
4 cups milk
3 cups Old English
  cheese, grated

Cook potatoes and onions in salted water until tender, approximately 45 minutes. Remove from heat, mash slightly. Set aside. In a skillet melt butter, add flour and stir until smooth. Add milk and cook until slightly thick, then add to potatoes. Add cheese and cook until melted. Never let soup boil after cheese is added. Serve with fresh pepper or parsley.

Mrs. Danny Conklin (Carolyn Kerns)

GENE McCARTT'S SHRIMP AND CRAB GUMBO

Serves 8

⅔ cup chopped onions
2 cloves chopped garlic
1 can chicken soup
½ cup chopped celery
2 cups sliced okra
1 can (16 ounces) tomatoes
1 can (4 ounces) chopped
  green chilies
3 tablespoons
  Worcestershire sauce
1 teaspoon salt

1 teaspoon pepper
1 teaspoon Tabasco
1 tablespoon thyme
2 bay leaves
1 tablespoon filé powder
¾ cup bacon grease
⅔ cup flour
3 pounds shelled shrimp
2 pounds shelled crab
  Rice, cooked

Combine first fourteen ingredients in a large pot. Simmer one hour. Make a roux* of bacon grease and flour. Combine vegetables, roux and fish. Simmer 40 minutes. Serve over rice.

*Roux — Melt bacon grease. Add flour and brown. Stir in 1¾ cups hot water. Cook 40 minutes, stirring constantly. Let cool.

SPINACH SOUP

Serves 6-8

2-3 packages (10 ounces each)
   frozen spinach
2 white onions, chopped
½ stalk celery, chopped
4 tablespoons butter
   Salt and pepper

Chervil, to taste
Garlic, to taste
½ cup flour
1 pint half and half
2 quarts milk

Cook spinach. Drain well. Sauté onions and celery in butter. Add salt, pepper, chervil, and garlic to taste. Stir in flour and simmer. Add half and half and milk, Add spinach. Cook on medium high heat until it boils. Let boil until it thickens.

Mrs. Jim Whitlock (Sue Smith)

TOMATO SOUP

Serves 4

4 slices bacon, cooked
   and crumbled
2 tablespoons bacon drippings
½ cup sliced celery
¼ cup chopped onion
3½ cups (1 pound, 12 ounces)
   canned tomatoes
1 can (14 ounces)
   Swanson's chicken broth

½ teaspoon salt
¼ teaspoon pepper
½ teaspoon curry powder
2 tablespoons cornstarch
¼ cup water
   Kraft Parmesan
   cheese, grated

Cook celery and onion in bacon drippings. Cut tomatoes into small pieces. Add tomatoes, juice from tomatoes, chicken broth and seasonings. Combine cornstarch with water. Add to tomato mixture and simmer 15-20 minutes. Stir in crumbled bacon and top with Parmesan cheese.

Mrs. William A. Anthony (Katie Billman)

SPICY TOMATO SOUP

Serves 10

½ cup diced onion
½ cup diced celery
½ cup diced carrots
4 tablespoons butter
4 sprigs of parsley
1 can (46 ounces)
   tomato juice

1 teaspoon white pepper
12 whole cloves
2 bay leaves
2 teaspoons salt
¼ teaspoon thyme
2 cans beef consommé,
   undiluted

Sauté onion, celery and carrots in butter for 5 minutes. Add next seven ingredients and bring to a boil. Cover and simmer over low heat for 1 hour. Strain and add beef consommé; reheat and serve hot.

Mrs. Alan Roberson (Sandie Davis)

TORTILLA SOUP

Serves 6-8

1 onion, chopped
2 cloves garlic, chopped
½ cup chopped bell pepper
2 tablespoons olive oil
1 can (14½ ounces)
   beef broth

1 can (14½ ounces)
   chicken broth
2 cans (13½ ounces each)
   Hunt's tomato juice
   Tortillas

Sauté onions, garlic, and pepper in olive oil until clear. Drain. Combine sautéed vegetables, broth, and tomato juice. Simmer slowly several hours. Serve over broken tortilla chips.

This can be made early in the day, refrigerated, and reheated.

Mrs. Ed Fancher (Shirley Feierabend)

You may add 1 can (4 ounces) green chilies, ⅛ teaspoon cumin, 1½ teaspoons oregano, and 1 can (10 ounces) Rotel tomatoes.

MOM'S HOMEMADE VEGETABLE SOUP

Yields About 6 Quarts

1½ pounds stew meat
3 quarts water
2½ tablespoons salt
½ teaspoon pepper
   Celery leaves
1 large onion, chopped
2 bay leaves
¼ teaspoon oregano
¼ teaspoon thyme
1 package Lipton's
   Onion Soup Mix (dry)
   Parsley

4 beef bouillon cubes
2 medium potatoes, cubed
5 large carrots, sliced
⅓ pound fresh green beans
2 cans (28 ounces each)
   tomatoes
1 package (10 ounces)
   frozen corn
1 package (10 ounces)
   frozen green peas
2 cups shredded cabbage
1 tablespoon sugar

Place meat in large pot with water. Add next ten ingredients. Cover and simmer at least 3 hours. Add vegetables and sugar. Simmer at least one hour.

Mrs. James Herring (Margaret Johnson)

VEGETABLE BEEF SOUP

Serves 4

1 pound lean stew meat
   in one inch cubes
4 tablespoons oil
1 small soup bone
4 cups water
1 can (28 ounces)
   tomatoes
1 package (10 ounces)
   frozen mixed vegetables
3 stalks celery,
   cut in medium pieces
¾ cup carrots,
   cut in medium slices
3 sprigs parsley

1½ cups diced
   raw potatoes
1½ cups shredded cabbage
1 bay leaf
1 tablespoon salt
¼ teaspoon
   marjoram
¼ teaspoon thyme
¼ teaspoon pepper
1 tablespoon
   wine vinegar
   Lawry's seasoned salt
   to taste

Flour, salt and pepper beef cubes. Brown in oil in large Dutch oven until dark brown. Add soup bone, water; simmer covered for 3 hours. Do not boil. Add rest of ingredients and simmer for 45 minutes.

Best served next day. Skim off excess fat and reheat for 30 minutes.

Mrs. William A. Anthony (Katie Billman)

HOT CORNED BEEF SANDWICHES

Serves 4

½ head cabbage, shredded
¼ cup vinegar
¼ cup water
1 teaspoon caraway seed
½ teaspoon salt
1 teaspoon sugar

Dark rye bread
1 pound corned beef, sliced
Sour cream, for each ⅓ cup
of sour cream, add
½ teaspoon prepared
horseradish and a dash
of salt

Combine cabbage, vinegar, water, caraway seed, salt and sugar. Bring to a boil. Cover and simmer for 5 minutes. Toast dark rye bread. Top with corned beef, hot slaw and sour cream.

Mrs. Carter Kelly (Sue Whitney)

CRABMEAT SANDWICH

Serves 6-10

½ cup butter
2 cans (6½ ounces each)
crabmeat
1 pound Velveeta cheese,
cubed
1 jar (2 ounces)
chopped pimientos

2 ounces Ortega
chopped chilies
Dash of
Worcestershire sauce
3 English muffins, halved,
buttered and toasted
Dash of paprika

Combine first six ingredients in double boiler. Heat 20 minutes. Let cool until thickened. Spoon meat mixture over muffins. Broil until hot. Top with paprika.

Mrs. J. Lee Johnson, III (Betty Knight)

CUCUMBER SANDWICH FILLING

12 to 18 Sandwiches

2 packages (8 ounces each)
cream cheese, softened
1 package Good Seasons
Italian Dressing Mix

1 large cucumber
Chopped onion (optional)

Grate cucumber and drain. Mix all ingredients together. Chill several hours to blend flavors. Soften to spread.

Mrs. John Mozola (Jo Rush)

FRENCH DIP SANDWICHES

Serves 8

1 brisket, 4—5 pounds
1 can (10½ ounces) consommé
¼ cup soy sauce
Juice of 1 lemon

1 tablespoon liquid smoke
1 teaspoon garlic powder
¼ – ½ cup red wine
1 package French rolls

Mix consommé, soy sauce, lemon juice, liquid smoke and garlic powder in a 9½ x 13 x 2 inch baking pan. Add brisket. Cover and bake in liquid for 3 hours at 300°. Remove brisket from pan and slice. Add wine to liquid in pan. Place sliced brisket back in pan and heat 5 minutes. Use the liquid in pan for delicious French dip sandwiches.

Mrs. Robert F. Jolley (Soeurette Seay)

GANDOLF SANDWICH

Yield 2

2 slices whole wheat bread
Butter
1 avocado
Mayonnaise
Lemon Juice
Salt and pepper

Fresh mushrooms
Onion, chopped
Tomato, sliced
Monterrey Jack cheese, sliced
Sprouts

Butter one side of bread and warm slightly. Peel and mash avocado. Add mayonnaise and lemon juice to spreadable consistency. Salt and pepper to taste. Spoon half of mixture onto each slice of bread. Chop and sauté mushrooms and onion in butter. Top avocado mixture with sliced tomato, cheese, mushrooms and onion. Place under broiler until cheese melts. Top with sprouts.

Variation: Add jalapeño sauce to avocado mixture and top with 2 slices bacon.

Mrs. Dan Moreland (Catherine Pierce)

OOIEE OOIEE

1 package (8 ounces) cream cheese, softened
½ cup chopped pecans

½ cup chopped green salad olives

Mix all the above.

Originally a celery filling, also good on crackers, other raw vegetables, or as a sandwich spread. Very good grilled or as a cheese ball.

Mrs. Daniel Greener (Shirley Hall)

PIMIENTO CHEESE SPREAD

1 package (10 ounces)
  Cracker Barrel cheese
  (sharp, mellow, or mild)
1 jar (7 ounces) pimiento,
  with juice

2 tablespoons finely
  chopped onion
1 cup mayonnaise
  Salt and pepper
  to taste

Grate cheese. Chop or mash pimiento and onion. Add mayonnaise, salt and pepper. Mix well.

Mrs. David Patton (Gladys Jones)

For appetizer add — Tabasco, additional onion, and serve on crackers.

PITTAS
Serves 6-8

2 tablespoons butter
1 large onion, chopped
2 medium potatoes, cubed
5 carrots, sliced
4 tablespoons parsley
½ pound mushrooms, sliced
½ head of cabbage

1 package green peas, thawed
1½ pounds ground meat
3 tablespoons Cavender's
  Greek Seasoning
8 pocket breads
  Salt and pepper
  to taste

Sauté onion in butter. Add potatoes, carrots, parsley, mushrooms, cabbage and peas. In separate skillet brown meat, drain and add to vegetables with salt and pepper, to taste, and Greek seasoning. Simmer vegetables till tender. Stuff in heated pocket bread and serve.

Mrs. David Kritser, III (Sally Simpson)

CORN DOGS
Serves 6-8

½ cup cornbread mix
½ cup flour
¼ teaspoon pepper
1 egg, beaten

½ cup milk
2 tablespoons
  vegetable oil
1 pound wieners (8–10)

Combine mix, flour and pepper. Mix well with egg, milk and oil. Roll each wiener in dry cornbread mix left over from package. Dip into batter. Fry in deep fat, 375°, until brown and crisp. Drain on paper towels. Serve with plenty of mustard.

Sally Bivins

CHEESE ROLLS

Serves 18

3 dozen hard rolls
1½ pounds sharp
  cheddar cheese, grated
8 fresh green onions, chopped
2 cans (8 ounces each)
  tomato sauce
1¼ teaspoons salt
1½ teaspoons sugar

2 tablespoons
  Worcestershire sauce
1 tablespoon chili powder
1 tablespoon parsley
4 hard boiled eggs,
  chopped
1 can (7½ ounces) pitted
  ripe olives, sliced

Slice tops off rolls and scoop out insides. Let stand to dry or toast in oven. Combine next eight ingredients and cook over low heat until melted. Remove from heat and add eggs and olives. Stuff rolls with mixture and replace tops. Bake in 325° oven for 30 minutes. May be prepared ahead, but stuff just before baking.

Mrs. Tom Cambridge (Norma Taggart)

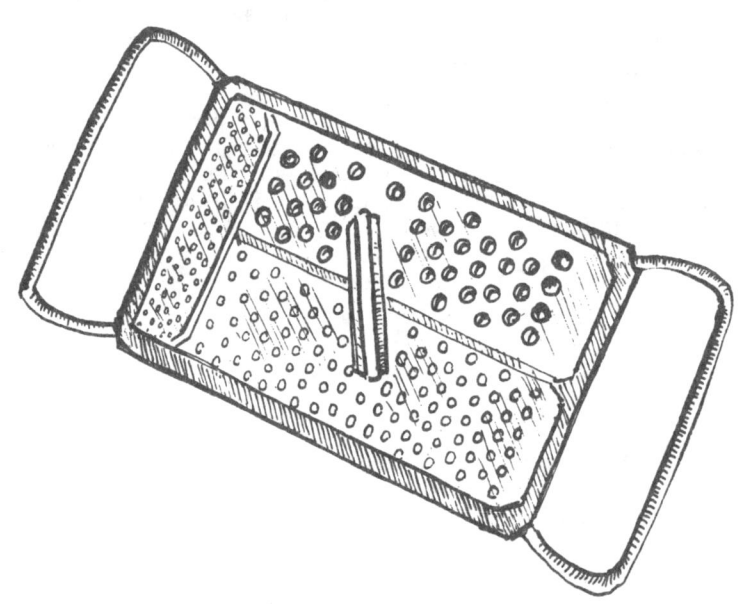

CRANBERRY SALAD

Serves 8-12

2 cups bottled cranberry juice
2 packages (3 ounces each) lemon flavored gelatin
2 cups orange juice
Red food coloring

2 cups seedless grapes or seeded Tokay grapes
½ cup diced celery
½ cup coarsely chopped pecans

Bring cranberry juice to a boil. Add gelatin and stir until dissolved. Add orange juice. Tint with red food coloring. Chill until mixture begins to set. Stir in grapes, celery and pecans. Pour into lightly oiled 6-6½ cup mold or individual molds. Chill until firm. Unmold and serve with frosted grape garnish.

Mrs. George Caufield (Mildred Kirk)

Canned spiced grapes can be used when fresh ones can't be found.

CRANBERRY-SOUR CREAM SALAD

Serves 12

1 package (6 ounces) cherry Jello
2 cups boiling water
1 can (16 ounces) whole berry cranberry sauce

2 cups sour cream
1 cup chopped celery
1 cup chopped pecans
1 cup miniature marshmallows

Dissolve Jello in boiling water. Add cranberry sauce, beating well. Chill until slightly thickened. Thin the sour cream with some of the Jello mixture. Fold sour cream into Jello mixture, mixing thoroughly but gently. Add remaining ingredients. Pour into oiled 2 quart mold. Chill until firm.

Mrs. Horace Wilson (Kathrine Kirk)

GREEN GAGE PLUM SALAD

Serves 5-6

1 can (17 ounces) Green Gage plums, drained and liquid reserved
1 package (3 ounces) lime Jello

2 cups boiling liquid, plum juice and water
⅓ teaspoon salt
1 package (3 ounces) cream cheese, softened

Combine Jello with boiling liquid and salt. Stir until Jello is dissolved. Crumble cream cheese and dissolve in Jello. Place in refrigerator. Put plums through a sieve. When Jello begins to set, add plums and mix thoroughly. Pour into a mold. Serve with mayonnaise or a mixture of mayonnaise and cream.

Mrs. Richard Bivins (Nancy Teel)

73

RED, WHITE, AND BLUE SALAD

Serves 8-10

1 package (3 ounces)
  strawberry Jello
2 cups hot water
1 package unflavored gelatin
½ cup cold water
1 cup light cream
1 cup sugar

1 tablespoon vanilla
2 cups sour cream
1 package (3 ounces)
  raspberry Jello
1 cup hot water
1 can (15 ounces)
  blueberries, drained

Dissolve strawberry Jello in 2 cups hot water. Pour into a rectangular 2-quart pan. Refrigerate to set. Soak gelatin in cold water. Combine cream and sugar in small sauce pan. Heat until sugar dissolves, stirring constantly. Remove from heat and add gelatin. Fold in vanilla and sour cream. Pour over first layer. Return to refrigerator. Dissolve raspberry Jello in 1 cup hot water. Let cool. Fold in blueberries and pour over second layer. Refrigerate.

Mrs. Scott Sutphen (Jean Watson)

SALADE ROUGE

Serves 12-15

2 oranges
1½ cups fresh cranberries
3 packages (3½ ounces each)
  orange Jello
3 cups boiling water
2 tablespoons lemon juice

1 cup sugar
Pinch of salt
1½ cups celery,
  finely chopped
1 cup crushed pineapple
  undrained

Peel oranges. Put peeling and cranberries through food grinder. Remove white membrane from oranges and section them, breaking each section into four pieces. Dissolve Jello in boiling water. Add lemon juice, sugar and salt. Stir until dissolved. Add orange pieces, the ground mixture, celery and pineapple. Pour into mold and chill until set. This salad should be made at least two days before serving.

Mrs. John C. Maynard (Virginia Irwin)

Served at 1977 Symphony Ball.

SHIRLEY SKELTON'S MOLDED WALDORF SALAD

Serves 12

1 package (6 ounces) lemon Jello
1 cup boiling water
½ cup cold water
1½ cups chopped apples, about 3 apples
2 tablespoons sugar
2 tablespoons lemon juice
½ cup chopped nuts
1 cup chopped celery

Dissolve Jello in boiling water. Add cold water and chill until slightly thickened. Mix remaining ingredients and fold into thickened gelatin. Pour into a 3½ cup mold and chill until firm.

May be served with a dressing of sour cream, mayonnaise and lemon juice.

Variation: Use cherry Jello instead of lemon. Dissolve ⅓ cup red hots with boiling water instead of sugar and lemon juice.

ASPARAGUS MOLD

Serves 10-12

2 cans (10½ ounces each) cut asparagus
1 tablespoon unflavored gelatin softened in
¼ cup cold water
2 tablespoons minced onion
2 tablespoons lemon juice
½ teaspoon Tabasco
½ teaspoon Accent
½ teaspoon garlic salt
2 teaspoons salt
1 teaspoon tarragon flakes
1 tablespoon dried parsley
½ cup sour cream
½ cup mayonnaise
1 cup chopped celery
4 hard cooked eggs, chopped

Drain asparagus. Reserve 1 cup juice. Heat juice and dissolve softened gelatin. Mix in next eight ingredients. Blend sour cream and mayonnaise together and slowly pour into asparagus mixture. Add cut asparagus, celery and eggs. Pour into a 2-quart greased mold. Let set in refrigerator at least 12 hours.

Mrs. Hugh L. Umphres, Jr. (Carlie Barnes)

75

EMERALD SALAD

Serves 6

1 package (3 ounces)
  lime gelatin
¾ cup hot water
¾ cup shredded cucumber
2 tablespoons grated onion

1 cup cream style
  cottage cheese
⅓ cup slivered almonds
1 cup mayonnaise

Dissolve gelatin in water and chill until slightly thick. Combine cucumber and onion. Drain well and mix with remaining ingredients. Add to gelatin and pour into oiled mold or an 8-inch pan. Chill until firm.

Mrs. Rolla Cartwright (Margaret Kerr)

BLUE CHEESE ASPIC

Serves 6

1 envelope plain gelatin
1½ cups tomato juice
½ teaspoon garlic salt
½ teaspoon celery salt

½ cup Roquefort or
  blue cheese dressing
1 large avocado
  Mayonnaise
  Salad greens

Soften gelatin in ½ cup tomato juice. Heat remaining juice. Add softened gelatin and stir to dissolve. Add salts. Blend in dressing. Chill until mixture begins to set. Peel and cube avocado. Fold into aspic. Pour into six individual or one large mold. Unmold on salad greens and garnish with mayonnaise.

Mrs. George Caufield (Mildred Kirk)

MOLDED GAZPACHO

Serves 8-10

2 packages unflavored gelatin
3 cups tomato juice
¼ cup wine vinegar
1 clove garlic, crushed
2 teaspoons salt
¼ teaspoon pepper

Dash cayenne
2 large tomatoes,
  chopped and drained
½ cup chopped onion
¾ cup chopped green pepper
¾ cup chopped cucumber
¼ cup chopped pimiento

Soften gelatin in 1 cup cold tomato juice. Bring to a boil. Add remaining ingredients. Place in a greased bundt pan (ring mold is not large enough). Refrigerate. Unmold to serve.

SAUCE

¼ cup mayonnaise
¼ cup sour cream

1 teaspoon horseradish

Combine all ingredients.

Mrs. Virgil Pate (Mary Graham)

76

TOMATO ASPIC

Serves 10

2 packages Knox gelatin
½ cup cold water
2 tablespoons vinegar
3½ cups tomato juice
½ onion, chopped

½ bay leaf
4 whole cloves
¼ teaspoon salt
Cayenne to taste

Soak gelatin in water for 5 minutes. Heat vinegar over hot water. Combine tomato juice, onion, bay leaf, cloves, salt and cayenne. Simmer 45 minutes. Strain. Add gelatin to vinegar when cool. Combine with tomato mixture and pour into molds. Chill.

Do not freeze, but keeps for at least 5 days.

An artichoke heart or cream cheese ball may be added to the mold before chilling aspic.

CHEESE BALL

1 package (3 ounces)
  Philadelphia cream cheese
1 tablespoon grated green onion

Mayonnaise
Parsley

Mix all ingredients together. Shape into ball.

Mrs. J. Lee Johnson, III (Betty Knight)

TOMATO ASPIC WITH SHRIMP MAYONNAISE

Serves 6-8

2 tablespoons gelatin
½ cup water
4 cups tomato juice
  Juice of one small lemon
3 tablespoons sugar

2 ribs celery
1 small onion, sliced
1 bay leaf
  Salt and red pepper

Soften gelatin in water. Combine remaining ingredients in saucepan. Cook over medium heat 10-15 minutes. Pour tomato mixture over softened gelatin. Stir. Strain. Pour into mold and chill. Top with shrimp mayonnaise to serve.

SHRIMP MAYONNAISE

1 cup cooked shrimp,
  cut into pieces
½ cup mayonnaise

Lemon juice
Tabasco to taste

Combine ingredients and chill.

Mrs. David Kennedy (Kay Lewis)

TOMATO ASPIC AND VEGETABLE SALAD

Serves 4-6

2 cups V-8 juice
1 package (3 ounces) lemon Jello
1 tablespoon lemon juice
⅛ teaspoon Tabasco
Salt
Pepper
1 can (16 ounces) artichoke hearts
Tomatoes, quartered

Eggs, hard cooked
Avocado, sliced
Cucumber, sliced
Asparagus spears
½ pint cottage cheese
3 tablespoons grated bleu cheese
Mayonnaise
Heavy cream

Bring 1 cup V-8 juice to a boil. Combine with Jello and stir until Jello is melted. Add remaining V-8, lemon juice, Tabasco, salt and pepper. Arrange artichoke hearts in bottom of 1 quart ring mold. Pour in mixture and chill until firm. Unmold on lettuce leaves and surround with tomatoes, eggs, avocado, cucumbers and asparagus. Blend together cottage cheese and bleu cheese. Fill center with cheeses. Serve with mayonnaise thinned with cream.

Mrs. Warren Freeman, Jr. (Celine Seay)

PINEAPPLE-BANANA SALAD

Serves 6-8

3 tablespoons flour
1 cup sugar
3 eggs, beaten

1 can (14½ ounces) pineapple chunks, drained, reserve juice
1 tablespoon butter
6 bananas, sliced

Mix flour, sugar, eggs and juice of pineapple in top of double boiler. Cook until mixture thickens. Add butter and cool. Just before serving, add chilled pineapple and chilled banana slices. Custard may be made several hours or the night before. If the crowd is large, add a few more bananas.

Mrs. Don L. Patterson (Dorothy McReynolds)
78

SPECIAL FRUIT SALAD

Serves 4-6

- 1 apple, unpeeled
- 1 banana
- ½ cup chopped pecans
- ¼ cup Marachino cherries, reserve liquid
- 1 cup pineapple chunks, reserve liquid
- Grapes

Cut fruit and combine.

DRESSING

- 2 tablespoons butter
- 1 tablespoon flour
- ½ cup pineapple juice
- ½ cup Marachino cherry juice
- Dash of salt
- ½ teaspoon mustard
- Juice of 1 lemon
- 1 egg yolk

Cook butter and flour until bubbly. Slowly add pineapple and cherry juice. Add salt, mustard, and lemon juice. Cook until thick. Remove from heat. Add egg yolk. Beat with a fork until smooth. Cover and let cool.

Pour cooled dressing over salad.

Mrs. Carter Kelly (Sue Whitney)

MAÑANA SALAD

Serves 6-8

- ½ pound Tokay grapes, cut in half and seeded
- ½ pound marshmallows, quartered
- ½ cup chopped walnuts or pecans
- 1 can (8 ounces) pineapple, drained and cubed

Mix the above ingredients and set aside.

DRESSING

- Juice of one lemon
- ¼ cup sugar
- 2 egg yolks
- ½ pint heavy cream, whipped

Cook juice, sugar and egg yolks until creamy and thick. Cool and fold into the cream. Mix in fruit. Let stand until mañana (12-24) hours in refrigerator.

Mrs. Vance Suffield (Martha Bowman)

BROCCOLI SALAD

Serves 4-6

1 head cauliflower
1 bunch broccoli
(about 2 pounds)
2 tablespoons sesame seeds
3 tablespoons vinegar

½ cup chopped onion
2 tablespoons sugar
1 cup Hellmann's mayonnaise

Discard stems and shred cauliflower and broccoli. Combine with remaining ingredients. Marinate 24 hours for extra good flavor or eat it now if you can't wait.

Mrs. Joe B. Wells (Brenda Breece)

SHIRLEY SKELTON'S PICKLED CABBAGE SLAW

Serves 10

1 medium head cabbage,
shredded
1 medium onion, chopped
1 medium green bell pepper,
chopped

1 tablespoon salt
1 cup vinegar
1½ cup sugar
1 teaspoon celery seed
1 teaspoon mustard seed

Cover cabbage, onion, green pepper and salt with boiling water and let stand 1 hour. Drain. Mix remaining ingredients and pour over cabbage mixture. Mix and store in refrigerator. This keeps 4 weeks.

OLD FASHIONED CABBAGE SALAD

Serves 6

1 teaspoon salt
¼ teaspoon pepper
½ teaspoon dry mustard
½ teaspoon celery seed
2 tablespoons sugar
¼ cup chopped
green bell pepper
1 tablespoon
chopped pimiento

1 teaspoon instant
minced onion
3 tablespoons salad oil
⅓ cup white vinegar
4 cups finely shredded
cabbage
watercress, sliced pimiento,
stuffed olives (garnish)

Combine first ten ingredients. Mix well. Cover and refrigerate at least 3 hours. Just before serving, drain cabbage Toss with other mixture. If desired, garnish with watercress, sliced pimiento or stuffed olives.

Mrs. Jack D. Waller (Sandy Johnson)

SIX WEEKS COLE SLAW

Serves 8

1 quart chopped cabbage
2 carrots, diced
1 teaspoon diced pimiento
1 green pepper, diced

2 cups water
2 tablespoons salt
2 stalks celery, chopped

Soak first four ingredients in water and salt for 30 minutes. Drain and add celery.

SYRUP

1 cup sugar
½ cup vinegar

½ cup water
1 tablespoon mustard seed

Combine sugar, vinegar, water and seeds in a saucepan. Bring to a boil and cool. Pour over cabbage mixture. Let set in refrigerator for 2 days before serving.

Mrs. Jerold Gormley (Amelia Deguiser)

RED CABBAGE SALAD WITH POPPY SEED DRESSING

Serves 10-12

1 head red cabbage
3–4 avocados, thinly sliced

1½ pounds green seedless grapes,
cut in half

Finely shred cabbage. Place in a large bowl and cover with ice water. Refrigerate for 1½-2 hours. Drain thoroughly on paper towels or in salad spinner. Add avocados and grapes. Coat with dressing as desired just before serving.

DRESSING

1½ cups powdered sugar
2 teaspoons dry mustard
2 teaspoons salt

⅔ cup vinegar
2 cups Wesson oil
3 tablespoons poppy seeds

Mix sugar, mustard, salt and vinegar in blender. *Slowly* add oil and continue beating until thick. Add poppy seeds and beat a few more minutes.

May be made ahead and stored in refrigerator. Do not freeze.

Mrs. Walter A. Henderson, Jr. (Nell Gunn)

CUCUMBERS IN SOUR CREAM

Serves 10

2 large or 3 medium
  cucumbers, peeled and
  thinly sliced
2 teaspoons salt

1 cup sour cream
2 tablespoons cider vinegar
¼ teaspoon paprika
1 large onion, thinly sliced

Put cucumbers in bowl and sprinkle with salt. Let stand in refrigerator several hours to draw out moisture. Rinse thoroughly in cold water to remove salt. It is best if cucumbers stand overnight or all day before adding sour cream. Blend sour cream, vinegar and paprika. Add cucumbers and onion slices. Place in 1½ to 2 quart casserole or bowl and return to refrigerator until serving time. Can be prepared the day before.

Mrs. William G. Landess (Claudette Leachman)

WILTED CUCUMBERS WITH DILL

Serves 12

4 slender cucumbers,
  peeled and sliced
4 green onions, minced
  Minced fresh dill or
  dried dill weed

Salt
Mayonnaise

Arrange a layer of cucumbers in a bowl. Sprinkle with some of the onion, the dill and a little salt. Spread with a layer of mayonnaise, about ¼ inch thick. Repeat until all ingredients are used. Cover and chill overnight. Before serving, mix gently.

Mrs. Tom Kritser (Barbara Boxwell)

GREEN BEAN-ONION SALAD

Serves 8

2 cans vertical packed green beans, drained

1 white onion, sliced thin

Make alternate layers of beans and onions in a 3-quart container with cover.

MARINADE

1 cup vinegar
1 cup sugar
2 tablespoons salad oil

1 teaspoon Accent
Salt and pepper

OPTIONAL

1 teaspoon celery seed
1 teaspoon whole cloves

3 cinnamon sticks

Bring vinegar, sugar, oil, Accent, salt and pepper to a boil. Optional spices may be added to boiling liquid. Pour liquid over beans and onions. Cover and marinate several hours or overnight. Drain before serving. This will keep for 2 weeks in refrigerator.

Mrs. Gene Edwards (Elaine Johnson)

HOT GREEN BEAN SALAD

Serves 15-20

4 cans (16 ounces each) French cut green beans, drained
1 medium onion, sliced thin
1 large bottle Wishbone Italian dressing

1 can (8½ ounces) water chestnuts — drained and sliced
Slivered almonds
7–10 slices crisp bacon, crumbled

Grease large Pyrex casserole. Put 2 cans of beans in casserole. Cover with onion slices. Spread rest of beans on top. Pour dressing over all and refrigerate overnight. When ready to serve, sprinkle almonds and water chestnuts on top. Be sure to set dish out 20-30 minutes before baking. Cover casserole and bake in preheated 325° oven for 30 minutes. Top with bacon. Return uncovered to oven for an additional 10 minutes.

Mrs. W.C. Turner, Jr. (Nancy Carmichall)

FRENCH-STYLE BEAN SALAD

Serves 6

1 can (16 ounces) French style green beans
1 can (16 ounces) LeSueur English peas
1 onion, sliced

1 green pepper, chopped
2 stalks celery, chopped
1 can (2 ounces) pimientos, chopped

Drain beans well. Add remaining ingredients.

MARINADE

1 cup sugar
1 cup vinegar

½ cup oil
Salt and pepper

Mix marinade. Pour over beans. Refrigerate, covered, 12 hours or longer.

Mrs. Ken McCarty (Sue Sheriff)

PARSLEY, SWISS CHEESE AND CELERY SALAD

Serves 8-12

2 pounds celery hearts
2 pounds Swiss cheese

2 bunches fresh parsley
Bibb lettuce

Cut celery and Swiss cheese into Julienne strips, 1½ inches long. Soak celery strips in ice water for ½ hour. Tear apart parsley blossoms in bite size servings. Marinate cheese strips in dressing 1 hour in refrigerator. Combine celery and parsley with Swiss cheese and vinaigrette, coat well. Drain vinaigrette and reserve. Add salt and white pepper to taste. Nestle salad on Bibb lettuce leaves or in individual Bibb lettuce heads. Add extra vinaigrette if desired. Garnish with fresh parsley. Sprinkle paprika overall.

BASIC VINAIGRETTE DRESSING

½ cup white wine vinegar
¾ teaspoon salt

¼ teaspoon ground pepper
1½ cups olive oil or safflower oil

Combine vinegar, salt, and pepper, stir well with fork and add oil. Beat the mixture with fork until well blended. Lemon juice may be substituted for vinegar.

Mrs. Thomas Herrick (Ann Elliott)

PEA SALAD WITH DILL Serves 6

1 cup sour cream
½ cup mayonnaise
½ cups finely chopped
   scallions
1-2 teaspoons dill weed

3 cups fresh green peas or
3 cups frozen peas,
   partially cooked
   Salt, pepper and cayenne
    to taste

Combine sour cream, mayonnaise, scallions and dill. Toss with cooled peas and season to taste. Cover and chill.

Mrs. Richard Reeves (Louise Coe)

POTATO SALAD Serves 10-12

8 large white potatoes, boiled
   in jackets then peeled
   and diced
17 eggs, hard cooked, peeled,
   and diced (reserve one
   for garnish)
1 large red onion, chopped
1½ cups chopped sweet pickle
   or pickle relish

1 jar (2 ounces)
   pimientos, chopped
1 tablespoon celery seed
   Salt and pepper
    to taste
   Equal amounts of boiled
   dressing and mayonnaise
   Paprika

Combine first seven ingredients. Add enough dressing to moisten and mix well. Slice remaining egg. Garnish with egg and paprika.

Homemade boiled dressing is the key to this recipe's success. Salad tastes better when made a bit in advance.

BOILED DRESSING Makes 3 Cups

½ cup sugar
1 teaspoon dry mustard
¼ teaspoon salt
4 eggs, beaten
3 tablespoons flour

½ cup vinegar
1½ cups water
1 tablespoon butter
1 can (5.33 ounces)
   condensed milk

Mix dry ingredients. In another container, mix eggs, vinegar, and water. Combine and cook, stirring constantly over low heat until mixture boils and thickens. Remove from heat. Add butter and milk. Place in covered container and cool.

Add whipped cream for a fruit salad dressing.

Mrs. Harry Phillips (Nancy Boxwell)

GERMAN POTATO SALAD

Serves 8-10

6 potatoes
2 tablespoons vinegar
6 slices bacon
6 green onions, sliced

1½ teaspoons celery seed
Salt and pepper
    to taste
Fresh parsley

Boil potatoes and let cool. Cut potatoes in approximately one inch cubes. Sprinkle vinegar over potatoes and stir to coat. Fry bacon and crumble (reserve grease). Sprinkle bacon, onion, celery seed, salt and pepper over potatoes.

DRESSING

2 eggs
2 tablespoons sugar

6 tablespoons vinegar
1 tablespoon dry mustard

Beat eggs. Add sugar, vinegar and dry mustard. Add to bacon grease in skillet and simmer until thick. Pour the dressing over the potatoes. Stir until evenly coated. Cool and garnish with parsley before serving. This dish lasts well when refrigerated.

Mrs. Herb Greiner (Kay Thomson)

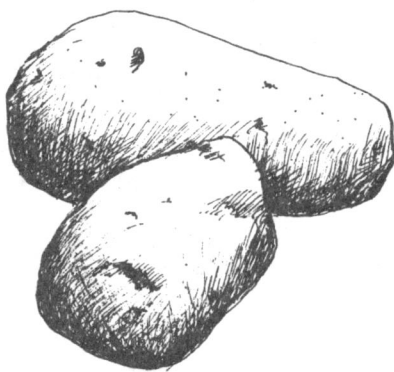

CLAIRE'S POTATO SALAD

Serves 8-10

6 large baking potatoes
   with skin, washed, cut in
   bite size pieces, boiled
   in salt water, drained
   Italian dressing
1 cup chopped green onions
   (include green tops)

1 cup chopped celery
1 can (8 ounces)
   water chestnuts, sliced
1 cup sliced black olives
   Mayonnaise
   (to hold together)
   Lemon juice, to taste
   Salt and pepper

While potatoes are warm moisten with Italian dressing and chill. Add remaining ingredients and refrigerate.

Mrs. Bivins Childers (Betty Bivins)

SOUR CREAM POTATO SALAD

Serves 6-8

6 medium potatoes,
   boiled and cubed
6 green onions, thinly sliced
   with some tops
1 teaspoon salt

½ teaspoon black pepper
1 cup mayonnaise
1 cup sour cream
3 tablespoons milk
   Bacon bits

Toss potatoes, onions, salt and pepper. Add more salt until slightly oversalted. Combine mayonnaise, sour cream and milk. Fold into potato mixture. Cover and refrigerate overnight. Serve with bacon bits.

Mrs. Walter S. Berry (Mary Knupp)

COLD RICE SALAD

Serves 6

1 cup raw rice
2 tablespoons wine vinegar
2 tablespoons salad oil
   Salt and pepper to taste
¼ cup minced parsley
¼ cup minced onion

1 can (8 ounces) water
   chestnuts, chopped
1 jar (7 ounces) olives,
   chopped
   Mayonnaise

Cook rice. Add oil, vinegar, salt and pepper. Cool in refrigerator. Add parsley, onion, water chestnuts, and olives. Chill. Add mayonnaise to taste at serving time.

Mrs. William Ford (Moselle Alden)

TOMATO ROSÉ

Serves 6

4 large tomatoes, peeled
   and thinly sliced
¼ cup finely chopped celery
¼ cup finely sliced green onion
1 envelope Italian
   salad dressing mix

3 tablespoons wine vinegar
⅓ cup salad oil
½ cup red wine
   Lettuce leaves for garnish
   Celery leaves for garnish

Put tomatoes in shallow dish or deep bowl. Combine remaining ingredients and pour over tomatoes. Cover. Chill several hours. Serve on lettuce leaves. Garnish with celery leaves.

Mrs. John Mozola (Jo Rush)

SYLVIA NUGENT'S CAESAR SALAD

Serves 4-6

Garlic clove
3 anchovy fillets
½ teaspoon Dijon mustard
½ cup salad oil
Juice of one lemon
2 egg yolks
Dash of
Worcestershire sauce

Freshly ground black pepper
1 head romaine lettuce
6 green onions
½–1 cup croutons
1 cup grated
Parmesan cheese
½ pound crumbled bacon

Rub a large wooden salad bowl with a clove of garlic. Add the anchovy fillets, mustard, salad oil, lemon juice, egg yolks, Worcestershire, pepper and mix thoroughly. Just before serving, add lettuce, onions, croutons, Parmesan, and bacon. Toss and serve.

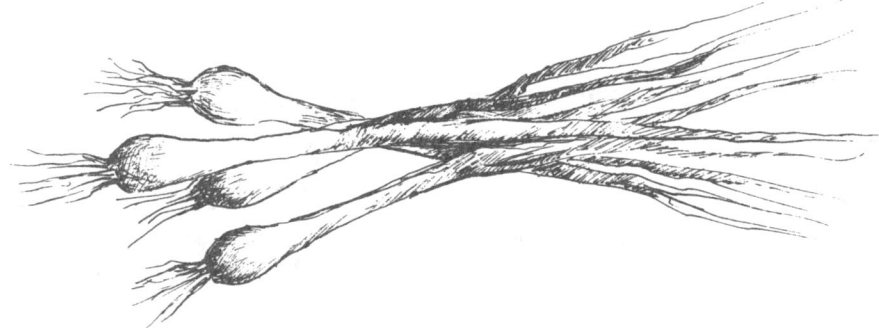

FOO YUNG SALAD

Serves 8

1 small head lettuce
1 large bunch spinach
1 can (16 ounces)
   bean sprouts, drained
10 slices bacon,
   cooked and crumbled

3 hard cooked eggs, chopped
Onions and slivered
almonds (optional)
Foo Yung Dressing

Tear lettuce and spinach into bite size pieces. Combine with remaining ingredients, reserving a few pieces of egg and bacon for garnish. Just before serving, toss well with Foo Yung Dressing.

FOO YUNG DRESSING

1 cup oil
¼ cup sugar
⅓ cup catsup
¼ cup vinegar

2 tablespoons chopped onion
2 teaspoons
   Worcestershire sauce
1 teaspoon salt

Blend all ingredients in a blender.

Mrs. Scott Sutphen (Jean Watson)

LAYERED
GREEN PEA SALAD　Serves 8-12

1 head crisp lettuce, torn in
　　bite size pieces
2 onions, sliced thin
1 can (16 ounces) green peas,
　　drained or
1 package frozen peas

1 cup mayonnaise, thinned
　　with vinegar
¼ pound Julienne
　　Swiss cheese
8–10 pieces bacon,
　　fried and crumbled

Layer first five ingredients in glass salad bowl. Repeat once. Do not toss! Top with bacon. Chill 4-6 hours.

Mrs. Merrill Winsett (Catherine Monning)

For a variation, use frozen peas, grated Cheddar cheese and mayonnaise thinned with fresh lemon juice.

MAJESTIC
LAYERED SALAD　Serves 10

1 quart shredded lettuce
2 cups mushroom slices
1½ cups red onion rings
2 packages (10 ounces each)
　　frozen peas, cooked
　　and drained

1 cup real mayonnaise
½ teaspoon sugar
½ teaspoon curry powder
2 slices bacon, cooked crisp
　　and crumbled

In 2½ quart bowl layer first four ingredients in order. Combine mayonnaise, sugar and curry powder. Spread over salad to seal. Do not toss. Cover and refrigerate overnight. Top with bacon before serving.

Mrs. Robert Ringo (Carolyn Huseman)

THE ORIGINAL
COUNTRY SALAD　Serves 1
From the Amarillo Country Club

¼ head Iceburg lettuce,
　　chopped
½ tomato, chopped
¼ cup diced celery
2 tablespoons grated carrot

Paprika
Onion salt
Garlic salt
Beau Monde
　(secret ingredient)
1 slice bacon, diced and
　　cooked, reserve drippings

Combine first four ingredients. Sprinkle seasonings over the salad according to taste. Fry bacon and pour with hot drippings over the salad.

Mrs. Russell Smith (Louise Russell)

HOT SALAD

Serves 4

2 tablespoons bacon fat
1 medium onion, diced
3 tablespoons water
2 tablespoons mild vinegar
1 tablespoon brown sugar
1 tablespoon sugar

½ teaspoon salt
1 bunch leaf greens, washed
   drained and torn in
   bite size pieces
6 slices bacon,
   cooked and crumbled

Combine first seven ingredients in a saucepan and bring to a boil. Pour this mixture over leaf greens. Sprinkle with bacon. Serve immediately.

Mrs. Lee T. Bivins (Betty Teel)

SPINACH AND CRAB SALAD

Serves 4

1 package fresh spinach
2 cans (6½ ounces each)
   crab meat
3 hard cooked eggs,
   sliced and diced
1 bunch green onions
   and tops, chopped

1 cup chopped celery
¼ cup capers
1 cup chopped lettuce
1 bunch radishes, chopped,
   if desired
1 small can anchovies,
   if desired

Wash and tear spinach, remove veins. Combine all other ingredients in bowl and toss with spinach. Cover with Remoulade dressing (page 96). Toss again.

Mrs. Dottie Francis (Dottie Cherry)

SPINACH SALAD

Serves 6-8

1¼ pounds fresh spinach
½ pound bacon, cooked
   crisp and crumbled
2 hard cooked eggs, sliced
1 small purple or white onion,
   sliced

¾ cup garlic croutons
   (optional)
   Salt and pepper to taste
½ cup sour cream
¼ cup mayonnaise —
   no substitutions
   Pinch of sugar

Wash spinach leaves and dry well. Tear leaves into bite-sized pieces, and place half of them in bowl. Arrange one-half of egg slices, bacon bits, onions and croutons over spinach. Salt and pepper to taste. Combine sour cream, mayonnaise, and sugar. Mix well. Spread half of sour cream mixture over top. Repeat. Chill or serve immediately.

Remove croutons from any left-over salad. Cover well and refrigerate.

Mrs. Don Babcock (Caron Sramek)

SPINACH SALAD

Serves 6-8

1 package fresh spinach
1 red onion, sliced
3 hard cooked eggs, sliced
¼ pound bacon,
  cooked and crumbled

Wash spinach and tear into bite sized pieces. Combine with remaining ingredients. Toss.

DRESSING

¼ cup sugar
¼ cup red wine garlic vinegar

Salt and pepper to taste

Mix all ingredients and serve over salad.

Mrs. James A. Hedgecoke, Jr. (Sallye Dees)

DRESSING

½ cup mayonnaise
1 hard cooked egg, mashed
  Salt and pepper

Red wine vinegar, enough to
thin mixture to desired
consistency

Mix all ingredients well. For this dressing omit eggs in salad.

Mrs. Jim Whitlock (Sue Smith)

ORANGE-AVOCADO TOSS

Serves 6-8

1 medium head lettuce, torn in
  bite-size pieces
1 small cucumber,
  thinly sliced (optional)
1 large avocado,
  peeled and sliced
1 can (11 ounces) mandarin
  oranges, drained
2 tablespoons chopped
  green onions

Combine lettuce, avocado, mandarin oranges and onion in large salad bowl.

DRESSING

½ teaspoon grated
  orange peel
¼ cup orange juice
½ cup salad oil
2 tablespoons sugar
2 tablespoons
  red wine vinegar
1 tablespoon lemon juice
¼ teaspoon salt

Combine orange peel, juices, salad oil, sugar, vinegar and salt in a jar and shake well. Just before serving, pour over salad and toss lightly.

Mrs. Tommy York (Linda Neal)

ORANGE SALAD BOWL   Serves 8

8 cups torn salad greens
2 cups orange sections or
2 cans (11 ounces each)
   mandarin oranges

1 cup sunflower seeds,
   chopped pecans or peanuts
1 onion, sliced and
   separated into rings

Combine all salad ingredients, and toss gently with celery seed dressing.

CELERY SEED DRESSING

⅓ cup sugar
1 teaspoon salt
1 teaspoon dry mustard
⅓ cup vinegar

1 small onion, chopped
1 cup salad oil
1 tablespoon celery seeds

Combine all ingredients, mixing well. Chill thoroughly before serving.

Mrs. Stephen Cowan (Terry Baum)

WILTED LEAF SALAD   Serves 6

6 slices bacon
½ cup sliced green onion
¼ cup vinegar
¼ cup water
4 teaspoons sugar

½ teaspoon salt
½ teaspoon pepper
8 cups leaf lettuce, torn
6 radishes, sliced thinly
1 hard cooked egg, chopped

In skillet, cook bacon until crisp. Remove bacon, drain and crumble. Add onion to drippings in skillet, cook over low heat until onion is tender. Add vinegar, water, sugar, salt and bacon. Cook and stir until boiling. Place lettuce in large salad bowl, pour hot dressing over lettuce. Toss until well coated. Garnish with radish and egg. Serve immediately.

Mrs. Stephen Curtis (Jerre Lewis)

DANA'S WATERCRESS SALAD   Serves 4-6

2 bunches watercress
10–12 fresh mushrooms,
   sliced
8 bacon slices
   cooked and crumbled
3 tablespoons sesame seeds,
   toasted

½ cup Hellmann's mayonnaise
2 tablespoons lemon
   or lime juice
1 tablespoon sugar

Wash watercress. Discard stems. Wash and slice mushrooms. Combine watercress, mushrooms, bacon and sesame seeds. To make dressing thin mayonnaise with lemon or lime juice. Add sugar. Toss with the salad.

Mrs. Glen Brosier (Kay Wagner)

BUFFET
CHICKEN SALAD
Serves 6-8

2 cups cooked chicken,
  cut in chunks
2 cups chopped celery
3 tablespoons minced onion
3 tablespoons lemon juice
½ teaspoon salt
½ teaspoon black pepper

½ cup pecans
¾ cup mayonnaise
1 can (4 ounces)
  sliced mushrooms
1 can cream of chicken soup
  Potato chips

Mix first nine ingredients and pour into a 2 quart casserole. Pour soup on top and cover with crushed potato chips. Bake in 300° oven for 30-45 minutes. May be frozen without soup and chips.

Mrs. Barton C. Grooms (Suzanne Simmons)

CHICKEN SALAD
Serves 8

2½ cups cooked chicken
  breasts, diced
1 cup chopped celery
1 cup white grapes, sliced
½ cup slivered almonds,
  toasted

2 tablespoons minced parsley
  Salt to taste
1 cup mayonnaise
  Capers to garnish

Mix all ingredients. Serve chicken salad in tomato cups on a bed of lettuce on sliced fresh pineapple. Top with spoonful of mayonnaise and a dab of capers.

Mrs. David Kennedy (Kay Lewis)

MOLDED CHICKEN SALAD (DIET)

Serves 6-8

2 envelopes unflavored gelatin
3 tablespoons lemon juice
   Tabasco
1 avocado, peeled and diced
1¼ teaspoons instant
   chicken broth
½ teaspoon dill weed

½ teaspoon salt
½ cup Kraft salad dressing
2 cups diced cooked chicken
1 cup diced water chestnuts
½ cup diced celery

For top layer, soften 1 envelope of gelatin in 1 cup water. Stir constantly over low heat until dissolved. Add ¾ cup cold water, lemon juice, and 3 drops Tabasco. Chill until mixture starts to thicken. Add avocado. Pour into a 3½-4 cup mold and chill until firm. For second layer, combine remaining gelatin, broth, dill weed, salt, 4 drops Tabasco, and ¾ cup water. Heat, stirring constantly until gelatin dissolves. Stir in salad dressing and mix until smooth. Add chicken, celery, and water chestnuts. Cool. Pour on top of firm first layer. Chill until all is firm.

267 calories per serving.

Mrs. Thomas A. Bunkley, Jr. (Myra Anne Stanley)

MRS. GUS ROBERTS' CRAB MEAT SALAD

Serves 6-8

1 whole cooked crab

Remove meat from crab. Break in small pieces.

DRESSING

2 tablespoons Remoulade
   Seafood Sauce
1 cup mayonnaise
1 hard cooked egg, chopped

1 tablespoon chopped parsley
1 tablespoon chopped onion
1 tablespoon capers
1 teaspoon honey

Combine all ingredients. Toss with crab.

SHRIMP MOLD

Serves 8-10

1 can tomato soup
3 packages (3 ounces each)
  cream cheese
1½ tablespoons gelatin
¼ cup water

1 cup mayonnaise
¾ cup chopped onion
2 cups small shrimp

Bring undiluted soup to a boil. Add cream cheese. Dissolve gelatin in water and add to soup mixture. Mix and cool. Stir in mayonnaise, onion and shrimp. Pour into mold. Refrigerate for several hours until firm. Unmold. Slice and serve with crackers.

Mrs. Frank B. White, III (Lynn Blackburn)

SHRIMP SALAD

Serves 12

2 boxes (3 ounces each)
  lemon gelatin
2 cups boiling water
1 can tomato soup, undiluted
8 ounces cream cheese
1 cup mayonnaise

1 cup chopped onion
1 cup chopped celery
½ cup chopped
  green bell pepper
2 cups cooked shrimp

Dissolve gelatin in boiling water. Let cool. Heat soup and dissolve cream cheese in it. Let cool. Mix gelatin, soup, mayonnaise, onion, celery, green pepper and shrimp. Pour into 9x13 inch pan. Refrigerate until set (approximately 4 hours).

Mrs. Ed Harrell (Carol Flynn)

COLORADO TACO SALAD

Serves 2-4

1 head lettuce
1-2 tomatoes, chopped
1 large onion, sliced
1 avocado, cubed
½-1 pound ground beef,
  browned and drained
  (keep warm)

2 cups favorite cheese, melted
  in double boiler
  (keep warm)
Jalapeño peppers, chopped
  (optional)
Doritos
Hot sauce

Keep all ingredients separate until ready to assemble. Toss lettuce, tomatoes, onion and avocado together. Place on individual serving plates. Generously spoon on ground beef. Top with melted cheese. Sprinkle with peppers. Serve with Doritos and hot sauce.

Miss Susan E. Roach

REMOULADE SALAD DRESSING

Yields Approximately 3 Cups

1½ cups mayonnaise
2 cloves garlic, chopped
1½ tablespoons mustard
1 tablespoon paprika
1½ tablespoons vinegar

Dash Tabasco
½ cup olive oil
2 tablespoons horseradish
1 tablespoon Worcestershire sauce

Combine all ingredients and mix thoroughly. Place in a covered jar and refrigerate for 24 hours before serving.

Mrs. Dottie Francis (Dottie Cherry)

FRENCH DRESSING

Yields About 2 Cups

½ cup oil
⅔ cup catsup
2 teaspoons minced onion
½ teaspoon paprika

1 cup sugar
⅓ cup vinegar
1 teaspoon salt

Combine all ingredients in a jar and shake well. Let stand several hours before serving.

Mrs. Stan Morris, Jr. (Kathleen Boyd)

FRENCH DRESSING

Yields 4 Cups

1 can tomato soup
½ cup sugar
1 cup cider vinegar
1 cup Wesson oil
1 tablespoon Worcestershire sauce

3 teaspoons salt
1 teaspoon prepared mustard
1 teaspoon paprika
1 medium onion, grated

Combine all ingredients and mix well.

Mrs. Jim Whitlock (Sue Smith)

WHITE DRESSING

Yields 1 Quart

½ pound Roquefort or bleu cheese, crumbled
⅓ cup chopped chives or onion tops
½ cup finely chopped parsley
2 tablespoons anchovy paste

2 tablespoons lemon juice
1 cup sour cream
2 cups Hellmann's mayonnaise
2 cloves garlic, pressed
Dash of cayenne pepper

Mix all ingredients. This will store in refrigerator for one month.

Mrs. Joe B. Wells (Brenda Breece)

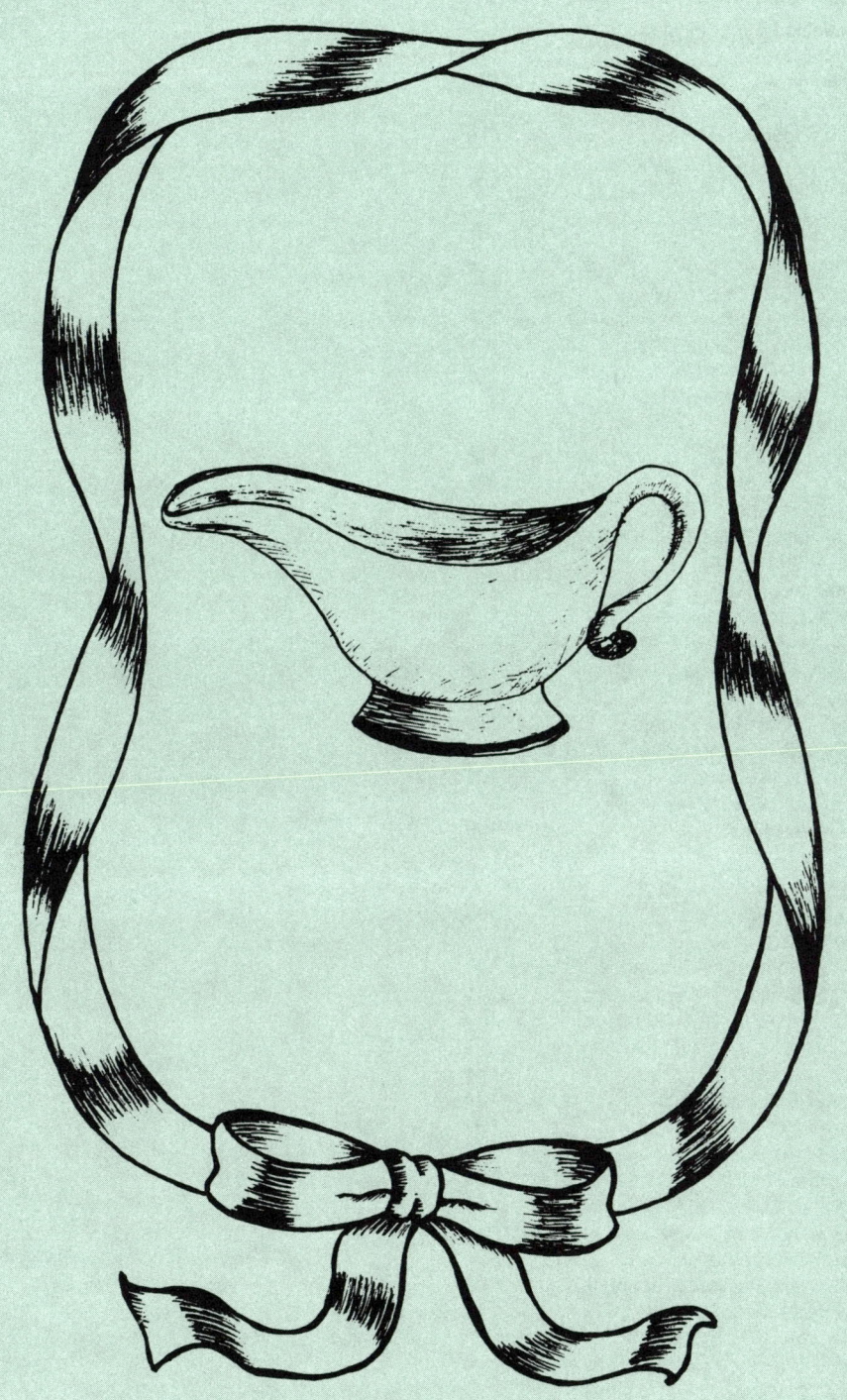

Accompaniments, Pickles, and Relishes

Fruits

Marinades for Meats and Vegetables

Sauces

ORANGE BUTTER

Yields ¾ Cup

1 tablespoon frozen orange
  juice, concentrate
½ cup powdered sugar

1 teaspoon grated orange rind
1 stick butter, softened

Combine first three ingredients and blend to a smooth paste. Add butter and blend thoroughly. Pack in jar, cover and chill. Delicious on hot rolls, biscuits, toast or pancakes.

Mrs. William Comerford (Pat Nunley)

BEARNAISE SAUCE

Yields 1 Cup

3 egg yolks
1 teaspoon powdered
  chicken bouillon
1 tablespoon unsalted butter
  Juice of 1 lemon
½ rounded teaspoon Arrowroot

⅛ teaspoon cayenne pepper
1 teaspoon tarragon
1 teaspoon shallots
2 tablespoons red wine
  Hot water

Put egg yolks, chicken bouillon, butter, lemon juice and arrowroot in food processor and blend 10-15 seconds. Boil tarragon, shallots and red wine until nearly all the liquid is gone. Add hot water as needed to make ⅓ cup of liquid. With food processor running add this to first mixture. Pour into a pan. Heat, stirring constantly, until thickened.

Mrs. Don T. Curtis (Suzanne Stokes)

GLEN BROSIER'S BAR B Q SAUCE

Yields 1 Quart

3½ cups catsup
¾ cup molasses
½ cup and 3 tablespoons
  prepared mustard
2½ cups vinegar

1 tablespoon Tabasco
3 tablespoons soy sauce
1 tablespoon coarse
  ground pepper
  Worcestershire sauce
  to taste

Combine all ingredients. Heat to dissolve mustard.

For pork ribs, baste on both sides for last 20 minutes of cooking. For chicken, baste on both sides for last 10 minutes of cooking.

This sauce was used on ribs cooked by Jim Man and Glen for the Junior League party at Houghton ranch.

SCOTT'S BARBEQUE SAUCE

1 pound butter
1 onion, finely chopped
1 clove garlic, minced
  Juice of 6 lemons
2 tablespoons salt

2 tablespoons sugar
1 tablespoon black pepper
1 tablespoon dry mustard
2 ounces
  Worcestershire sauce

Melt butter over low heat. Sauté onion and garlic in butter. Add lemon juice and mix well. Add seasonings. Stir until smooth and even. Reheat as necessary to use later.

Mrs. Mike Montgomery (Suzanne Stafford)

BARBEQUE SAUCE   Yields 3 Cups

2 tablespoons
  bacon drippings
1 medium onion, chopped
1 clove garlic, minced
1 bottle (14 ounces) catsup
¼ cup beer

½ cup
  Worcestershire sauce
2 tablespoons brown sugar
¼ teaspoon salt
½ teaspoon dry mustard
  Tabasco, to taste

Melt bacon drippings in a saucepan and sauté the onion and garlic until limp. Add remaining ingredients. Bring to a boil then simmer gently for 15 minutes. Remove from heat and let cool; then pour into a jar and refrigerate. It will keep for weeks. Good on ribs, chicken, pork or beef.

Mrs. Lee T. Bivins (Betty Teel)

CABALLERO'S
BAR-B-QUE SAUCE

¾ cup chopped onion
½ cup corn oil
¾ cup catsup
¾ cup water
⅓ cup lemon juice
3 tablespoons sugar

3 tablespoons
  Worcestershire sauce
2 tablespoons prepared
  mustard
2 teaspoons salt
½ teaspoon black pepper

Cook onion in oil until soft. Add remaining ingredients and simmer 15 minutes. Especially good on ribs.

This sauce keeps well in refrigerator or may be frozen.

Mrs. James B. Austin, III (Ann Franklin)

QUICK BLENDER HOLLANDAISE SAUCE

4 egg yolks
2 tablespoons lemon juice

Pinch cayenne pepper
1 cup butter, melted

OR

3 egg yolks
1 tablespoon lemon juice

Pinch cayenne pepper
½ cup butter, melted

Warm blender with hot water. Add yolks, lemon juice and cayenne. Turn on low. Add hot butter in a steady stream. Serve immediately or keep warm over hot water. Store in refrigerator or freezer.

This is good on broccoli, seafood, meat, openfaced mushroom sandwiches, etc.

Mrs. John Mozola (Jo Rush)

HOLLANDAISE, IN FOOD PROCESSOR

1 pound butter
2 large lemons
12 egg yolks

½ teaspoon white pepper
Pinch of salt

Melt butter until bubbling, but not brown. While melting, squeeze lemons through a strainer into processor bowl. Add yolks, pepper and salt, process with steel blade until creamy. While still processing, pour bubbling butter quickly into egg mixture. Process for 1 minute. Sauce will be half cooked. Pour amount to be used into top of double boiler. Save remaining sauce in a quart jar in the refrigerator.

This keeps well. Any amount can be warmed over hot, but not boiling water. Stir while heating. Sauce may be thinned with a little hot water. Save egg whites for meringue or angel food cake.

Mrs. Ray C. Johnson, Jr. (Joan McCormick)

CHUCK BONJEAN'S MAYONNAISE

1 egg
1 tablespoon oil
1 tablespoon lemon juice

1 teaspoon Dijon mustard
1 cup oil

Mix first 4 ingredients in a food processor using the plastic blade. Then slowly pour in 1 cup oil and continue mixing until desired thickness is reached.

MARINADE FOR FUNFEST STEAK ON A STICK

1 cup water
¼ cup red wine vinegar
1 tablespoon tomato paste
1 teaspoon garlic salt
1 teaspoon lemon pepper

1 bay leaf
½ cup chopped
  jalapeño peppers
2 pounds top loin beef
  cut in 1 inch cubes

Mix together all ingredients. Marinate beef overnight in refrigerator. Drain and grill. Use sauce to baste while cooking. Soak wooden skewers several hours in water before use to prevent burning over fire.

Mrs. Robert D. Forrester (Carol Tate)

DADDY'S STEAK MARINADE

Approx. 1¾ Cups

2 sticks corn oil margarine
½ cup tarragon wine vinegar
1 tablespoon lemon juice

3 tablespoons
  Worcestershire sauce
Salt and pepper
Seasoning salt

Melt margarine. Add vinegar, lemon juice and Worcestershire sauce. Stir to even mixture. Dip 6-8 steaks in marinade to completely cover. Add salt, pepper and seasoned salt. Let stand in refrigerator several hours before broiling.

Mrs. Paul Fields (Barry Beck)

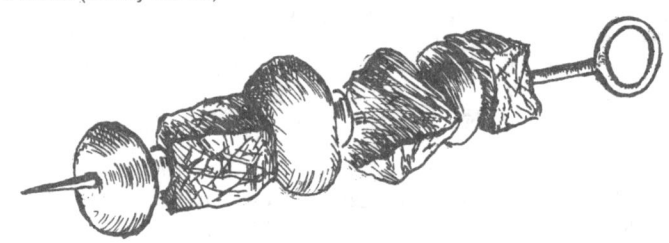

MARINADE FOR BEEF KABOB

Yields About 1⅓ Cups

½ cup salad oil
¼ cup soy sauce
½ cup dry red wine
1½ teaspoons ground ginger

2 tablespoons catsup
¼ teaspoon coarse pepper
½ clove garlic, diced
2 teaspoons curry powder

Mix all ingredients together. Any meat used should marinate at least 4 hours or overnight. This is enough marinade for 2-3 pounds cubed sirloin.

Mrs. James B. Austin III (Ann Franklin)

MONTEPLIER SAUCE

1 cup sour cream
1 cup mayonnaise
1 tablespoon heavy cream or evaporated milk
1 tablespoon finely chopped mushrooms
1 tablespoon capers
1 teaspoon minced onion
2 teaspoons lemon juice
½ teaspoon salt
½ teaspoon dill weed
¼ teaspoon cracked black pepper

Mix ingredients as listed in glass or stainless steel bowl. Cover and refrigerate for at least 2 hours before serving. This is an accompaniment for fish and is especially good with fresh salmon steaks.

Mrs. Ronald E. Walker (Mary Stevens)

MUSTARD SAUCE FOR HAM

Yields 1⅓ Cups

1 cup currant jelly
⅓ cup prepared mustard
3 tablespoons prepared horseradish

Combine ingredients in a saucepan and boil rapidly, stirring constantly for 3 minutes.

Keeps well in a jar in the refrigerator.

Mrs. John Baay (Nancy Middlebrook)

MUSTARD SAUCE

Yields Approximately 1½ Cups

1 tablespoon butter
1 egg
¼ cup light brown sugar, firmly packed
3 tablespoons granulated sugar
1 teaspoon paprika
3 tablespoons prepared mustard
½ cup cider vinegar

Melt butter in small saucepan. Set aside. In small bowl using rotary beater, beat egg, sugars, mustard and paprika. Add vinegar and beat. Blend into cooled butter. Cook over low heat, stirring just until thickened (4-5 minutes). Cool. Very good with ham and pork.

Mrs. Jim Southern (Linda Ann Duke)

LUKE'S HOT MUSTARD   Yields 3-4 Cups

1 cup white vinegar   1 cup sugar
1 cup hot powdered mustard   3 eggs, beaten

Combine vinegar, mustard and sugar in large saucepan. Simmer over low heat. Gradually add eggs, stirring constantly until thickened.

Mrs. Benny Lawrence (Ellen Yows)

HOT MUSTARD

1 cup dry mustard   1 cup sugar
½ cup vinegar   1 beaten egg

Mix dry mustard and vinegar and let stand overnight. Mix sugar and egg together and add to other ingredients. Cook over very low heat until thick. Stir constantly.

Mrs. Robert Green (Kathryn Pitts)

SWEET SOUR MUSTARD

½ cup dry mustard   1 tablespoon water
½ cup vinegar   ½ cup sugar
1 egg   Pinch of salt

Mix mustard and vinegar well. Let stand overnight in covered container. Beat egg with water. Add sugar and salt. Combine with mustard mixture. Cook in double boiler until thick and smooth. Cool and refrigerate in covered jar.

Mrs. Tom Cambridge (Norma Taggart)

JIM'S
RÉMOULADE SAUCE   Serves 8-10

2 cups mayonnaise   1 tablespoon parsley
4 tablespoons catsup   1 tablespoon chives
2 tablespoons tarragon   2 teaspoons
  vinegar   Worcestershire sauce
½ cup chili sauce   Salt and pepper
4 tablespoons chopped onion   to taste

Combine all ingredients and mix well. Chill and serve with shrimp or other seafood. (Cannot freeze).

Mrs. James D. Man (Cordelia Harris)

104

STEAK AND CHICKEN LIVER SAUCE

Serves 2-3

4 ounces (½ cup)
  chicken livers, sliced
2 tablespoons butter
¼ cup chopped green onions

1 cup sliced fresh mushrooms
½ cup dry white wine
¼ teaspoon salt
  Dash of pepper

Cook livers in butter and remove from pan. Add onions and cook until almost tender. Add mushrooms and cook 1-2 minutes more. Return livers to skillet. Stir in wine, salt and pepper. Heat, but do not boil. Serve over steak.

Mrs. Jim Whitlock (Sue Smith)

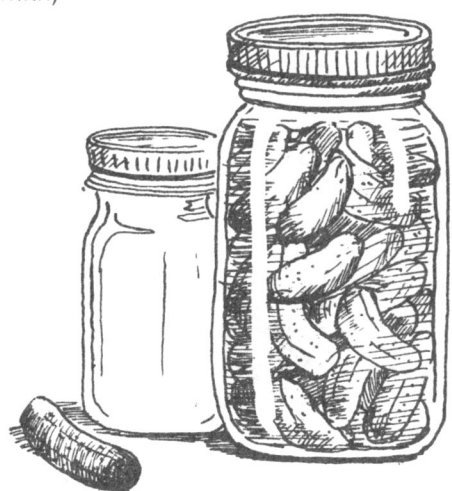

BREAD AND BUTTER PICKLES

Yields 5-6 Quarts

25–30 medium cucumbers
 8 large white onions,
   chopped

2 large green bell
   peppers, chopped
½ cup salt

Combine and let stand 3 hours. Drain and rinse.

5 cups vinegar
5 cups sugar
2 tablespoons mustard seed

½ teaspoon cloves
1 teaspoon tumeric

Combine and bring to boil. Add drained cucumbers and heat thoroughly, but do not boil. Pack in hot sterilized jars.

Mrs. Danny Conklin (Carolyn Kerns)

CINNAMON CUCUMBER RINGS

Yields 12 Half-Pint Jars

7 large cucumbers, peeled and
  sliced ½ inch thick
1 cup slack lime
1 gallon water
3 cups vinegar
1 bottle (2 ounces)
  red food coloring

1 tablespoon alum
2 cups water
10 cups sugar
8 sticks cinnamon
1 package (8 ounces)
  red hot candies

Soak cucumber slices overnight in lime and gallon of water. Drain and soak for 4 hours in clear water. Remove centers from slices. Combine slices, 1 cup vinegar, food coloring, alum and water to cover. Simmer for 2 hours. Drain and wash slices. Combine 2 cups vinegar, 2 cups water, sugar, cinnamon and red hots. Bring to a boil. Pour over rings and soak for 3 days. On third day, bring to a boil and seal in sterilized jars.

Mrs. Charles Cathcart (Pat Hill)

PICKLED CARROTS

Serves 10-12

1 medium onion, sliced
1 bell pepper, sliced
1 can tomato soup
1 cup sugar
¾ cup vinegar
¼ cup oil

2 pounds carrots, sliced
Water
1 teaspoon
  Worcestershire sauce
Salt
Pepper

Mix onion, pepper, soup, sugar, vinegar and oil. Bring to a boil. Cook carrots in water until almost tender. Add Worcestershire to boiled mixture with salt and pepper to taste. Pour over carrots. Let stand at least 2 days in refrigerator. Sauce is better when used more than once. When carrots are gone, just add more carrots.

Mrs. Neely Legacy (Susan Neely)

LIZ WRIGHT'S PICKLED OKRA

Yields 11 Quarts

7-8 pounds okra
    Peppers, fresno or
    chili petiné

22 cloves of garlic,
    peeled
1 bunch fresh dill

Wash okra and discard any that are soft, rough, broken or have an open end. Wash peppers and make a slit in the side of each. Pack in sterlized jars.

PINT JAR

Okra
1 clove garlic
1 pepper
1 small stem dill

QUART JAR

Okra
2 cloves garlic
2 peppers
1-1½ stems dill

BRINE SOLUTION

1 gallon white vinegar
4 cups water

1 cup salt (pickling or plain
    table salt, not iodized)

Combine all ingredients. Bring to a boil. Pour into filled jars leaving ½ inch head room. Seal. Allow jars to cool 24 hours before moving them.

OKRA PICKLES

Yields 6 Pints

6 garlic cloves
6 teaspoons dill seed
4 pounds small okra

1 quart water
1 pint white vinegar
½ cup salt

Place 1 garlic clove and 1 teaspoon dill seed in a sterilized pint jar. Pack washed okra into jars. Bring liquid and salt to a boil. Pour over okra immediately. Seal jars with sterilized hot lids.

Mrs. Michael Musick (Sharon Prater)

CRANBERRY RELISH

Serves 6-8

1 pound cranberries, washed
2 cups sugar
½ cup orange juice

½ cup water
2 teaspoons grated
    orange rind
½ cup blanched
    slivered almonds

Combine first five ingredients in a saucepan and cook until cranberries pop (about 10 minutes). Skim-off foam. Add almonds. Chill and serve.

Mrs. Mack Gordon (Dixie Conley)

DILLY ONION RINGS   Serves 4-6

2 large mild onions
⅓ cup sugar
2 teaspoons salt

1 teaspoon dried dill weed
½ cup white vinegar
¼ cup water

Cut the onions into thin slices, separate into rings and pack them into a quart jar. Combine the sugar, salt, dill weed, vinegar and water; stir until the sugar dissolves. Pour the liquid over the onion rings. Cover and refrigerate at least 5 hours, shaking the jar occasionally so that the marinade mixture covers the rings.

The marinade mixture can be brought to a boil before it is poured over the onion rings. This insures that the sugar is completely dissolved. These onion rings complement all kinds of beef and they keep well for several weeks.

Mrs. Richard Bittman (Agnes Leachman)

MARINATED VEGETABLES   Serves 12-15

1 cup celery
2 bunches carrots
3–4 zucchini, unpeeled

1 large head cauliflower
1 green pepper
1 large red onion

Chop celery, cut carrots and zucchini crosswise and cut cauliflower into flowerets. Slice green pepper and onions into rings. Boil all vegetables except onions, until done but still crunchy.

MARINADE

¾ cup white vinegar
1 teaspoon salt
½ teaspoon pepper
1 teaspoon dry mustard

1 cup corn oil
1 cup sugar
1 cup canned tomato soup, undiluted

Mix a little vinegar with salt, pepper and dry mustard until dissolved. Add remaining vinegar and other ingredients. Stir well. Pour over well drained vegetables and refrigerate at least 24 hours. This keeps well under refrigeration about 2-3 weeks. Other vegetables may be added.

The preparation time may be cut by using a food processor.

Mrs. Hollis Russell (Beth Knox)

MARINATED VEGETABLES

Serves 10-12

1 can (16 ounces) French
   style green beans
1 can (16 ounces) peas
1 cup chopped celery
1 green pepper, chopped

1 jar (2 ounces) pimientos
1 medium onion, chopped
1 cup sugar
1 cup vinegar
½ cup oil

Place first six ingredients in a bowl. Mix remaining ingredients together. Pour over the vegetables. Let marinate 24 hours in refrigerator. Keeps 2 weeks.

Mrs. Barton Grooms (Suzanne Simmons)

VEGETABLE MEDLEY

Serves 6

1 cup cider vinegar
1 tablespoon sugar
1 tablespoon dill weed
1 tablespoon Accent
1 teaspoon salt

1 teaspoon pepper
1 teaspoon garlic salt
1½ cups olive oil
1 tablespoon fresh
   lemon juice

Place the above ingredients in a blender and blend for 1 minute. Pour over 4 cups of one or a combination of any of the following raw vegetables:

broccoli flowers
carrot slices
whole mushrooms
yellow squash slices
cucumber slices

cauliflower flowers
zucchini slices
radishes
celery pieces

Marinate at least 12 hours in refrigerator, turning often. Remove vegetables from liquid. Liquid may be reused. A good combination of vegetables is broccoli, carrots, mushrooms and yellow squash.

Mrs. Anne Ansley Reid (Anne Ansley)

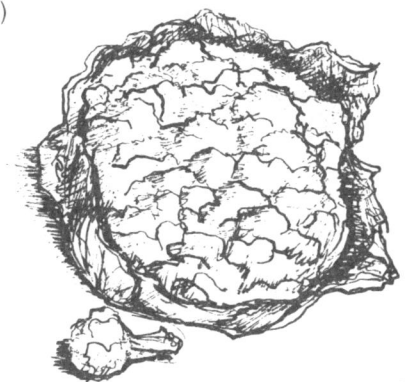

MEXICAN HOT PICKLES

Yields 12 Quarts

½ bushel cucumbers
1 gallon cider vinegar
⅓ gallon water
6¾ cups sugar
1¾ cups salt
½ (1.5 ounce box) celery seed
½ (2⅜ ounce box) mustard seed
24 small whole dried red chilies
⅛ teaspoon red pepper
48 large garlic buds
12 large slices of onion

Slice and soak cucumbers in ice for 3 hours. Boil together for 10 minutes vinegar, water, sugar, salt, celery seed, mustard seed, red chilies and red pepper. Place 4 large garlic buds in each hot quart jar, pack pickles and place onion slice on top. Pour boiling mixture over cucumbers. (When pouring mixture be sure that 2 red chilies go into each jar.) Seal.

Mrs. Jim Whitlock (Sue Smith)

CHOW CHOW (SOUR)

Yields 10-12 Pints

8 quarts green tomatoes, ground
1 head cabbage, ground (more if desired)
3 sweet bell peppers, ground
8 large onions, ground
1 cup salt (less if desired)
2 quarts dark cider vinegar
1 tablespoon powdered mustard
2 tablespoons cinnamon
2 tablespoons black pepper
1 tablespoon allspice
1 tablespoon whole cloves
2 tablespoons ginger
¼ teaspoon cayenne
2-3 jalapeño peppers, ground (optional)

Place vegetables in large deep heavy pot. Add salt, let stand overnight. Next morning drain off the liquid. Add vinegar, spices and jalapeño peppers. Mix well. Cook over medium heat until spices absorb in vegetables (about 30-45 minutes, until color darkens slightly). Watch closely and stir often. Pour chow chow into clean sterilized jars and seal. (This is not a food processor recipe.)

Mrs. Fred Dodson (Joyce Caraway)

TOM DAWKINS' SAUERKRAUT

Makes 24 Pints

10 gallon glazed crock
1 clean lint-free cloth
1 hardwood board, circular cut to cover the mouth of the crock is best.
(Do not use softwood like pine). A heavy plate may be used instead of the board.

1 brick to be used as a weight
50 pounds field fresh cabbage, DO NOT WASH
1 box (26 ounces) table salt
1 box (1½ ounces) caraway seed
1 bottle (one-fifth) white Rhine wine

Peel and discard outer leaves of cabbage heads. Cut into quarters. Remove and discard cores. Finely shred the quarters. Now you are ready to fill the crock. Using a dasher or other suitable utensil, firmly tamp the cabbage down into the crock until a firmly compressed layer about 4 inches thick is formed. Continue tamping the cabbage until a layer of moisture appears on top. Sprinkle this layer with a generous amount of salt and caraway seed. Dash wine over the salt and caraway seed. (This one bottle of wine will be used for the entire 50 pounds of cabbage, so calculate the number of four-inch layers and divide accordingly.) Repeat the cabbage, salt, caraway seed and wine in tightly compressed four-inch layers until crock is full. Be sure to continue tamping each layer until the moisture appears on top of the cabbage.

Cover the crock with the cloth and board. Weight down with the brick. Store in a cool place, approximately 60°, for fermentation. Once fermentation sets in, remove the scum and clean the cover cloth daily. Kraut will be ready in about 30 days.

To store the kraut, the mouth of the crock may be sealed with parafin. It may also be stored in jars by heating the kraut to 200°. Pour into hot jars.

If you drink while you work — get two bottles of wine.

HOT PEPPER JELLY

Yields 6-7 Half Pint Jars

¼ cup finely chopped or ground hot red peppers
¾ cup chopped or ground bell peppers

6 cups sugar
1½ cups apple cider vinegar
1 bottle (6 ounces) Certo

Use rubber gloves to work with hot peppers — don't rub eyes.

Mix peppers, sugar and vinegar. Bring to a rolling boil. Boil for 1 minute, stirring constantly. Remove from heat. Add Certo and boil until 220°. Alternately skim and stir for 5 minutes before pouring into half pint jelly jars.

Do not refrigerate or it will turn to sugar. Makes attractive Christmas gifts.

Mrs. R.G. Morrison, Jr. (Esther Jones)

HOT TOMATO RELISH OR SAUCE

Yields 1 Gallon

1 gallon tomatoes, fresh or canned, peeled
2 cans (16 ounces each) tomatoes
2 cups ground jalapeño peppers
2 cups ground bell peppers
2 cups vinegar
1¾ cups sugar
3 pounds onions, chopped
2 tablespoons salt

Mash tomatoes lightly with a potato masher. Add peppers, vinegar, sugar, onions and salt. Cook over medium heat, stirring often. Bring to a boil gradually increasing heat. Cook a minimum of 10 minutes or until desired thickness is obtained.

This sticks easily, so stir often. The longer the mixture cooks the stronger the jalapeño pepper will flavor the sauce. Use a stainless steel pan or jalapeños will eat the finish.

Mrs. Neely Legacy (Susan Neely)

WALDEMAR APPLES

Serves 6

1 cup sugar
1 can (18 ounces) pineapple juice
3 tablespoons butter
Red food coloring or enough red hots to give a rosy color
6 large or 7 small firm apples, cored

Make a syrup of sugar and juice. Boil until it makes big beads. Add coloring, butter and apples. Simmer, basting frequently, until apples are tender and transparent. Can be used to garnish pork or ham.

Mrs. Jay Taylor (Imogene Herring)

BAKED APRICOTS

Serves 8

2 cans (28 ounces each) apricot halves, drained
1 pound light brown sugar
1 box (12 ounces) Ritz crackers, crumbled
1 stick butter

Grease a 2 quart casserole. Divide all ingredients in half. Layer in order and repeat. Bake in a 300° oven for 1 hour.

Amounts can be varied to suit taste.

Mrs. James B. Austin, III (Ann Franklin)

BAKED RUM FRUIT

Serves 8

1 can (1 pound 4 ounces)
  cling peaches
1 can (1 pound 4 ounces)
  pineapple chunks
1 can (1 pound 1 ounce)
  sweet pitted cherries

1 can (1 pound 1 ounce)
  unpeeled apricot halves
1 cup brown sugar
1⅓ cups light rum
1 pint sour cream

Drain peaches, pineapple and cherries. Arrange in a large glass baking dish. Add apricot halves *with* juice. Mix brown sugar and 1 cup rum. Pour over fruit. Bake 1½ hours uncovered in 350° oven. Stir once. Remove from oven and pour in remaining ⅓ cup rum. Top with sour cream and serve warm or cold.

Mrs. Robert Sanders (Bonnie Hier)

PINEAPPLE CHEESE DISH

Serves 6

1 can (14½ ounces) chunk
  pineapple, drained,
  reserving juice
⅓ cup sugar
⅓ cup flour

8 ounces New York
  Cheddar cheese, grated
  Butter

Place half of pineapple in 9x12 inch buttered dish. Sift flour and sugar together and put one half of mixture over pineapple. Cover with one half of grated cheese. Repeat. Dot with butter and pour one half of pineapple juice over all. Bake in 350° oven for 45 minutes.

Mrs. Mack Gordon (Dixie Conley)

SCALLOPED PINEAPPLE

Serves 12

2 sticks butter
1½ cups brown sugar
3 eggs

1 can (16 ounces) crushed
  pineapple, drained
1 quart cubed day old bread
  crumbs, toasted

Cream butter and sugar. Add eggs, pineapple, sugar and bread cubes. Mix well. Bake in 9x13 inch Pyrex casserole for 1 hour at 350°.

Mrs. E.W. Williams (Mary Anne Morrison)

SWEET PICKLED FRUIT
Serves 4-6

1 cup sugar
¼ cup vinegar
4 sticks cinnamon
12 cloves

2½ cups fruit — any mixture
   of canned fruits or juices:
   apricots, peaches, pears,
   pineapple slices or chunks,
   figs or soaked prunes.
   Peaches and pears are best.
½ cup juices from canned fruit

Mix sugar, vinegar, spices and fruit juice together. Simmer 10 minutes. Add as many pieces of fruit as can be put into the syrup without crowding. Simmer 10 minutes. Remove fruit to bowl or jar. Repeat until all of fruit is cooked. Put spices with syrup in the jar. Refrigerate 24 hours before serving.

Mrs. R.G. Morrison (Esther Jones)

SHERBET FOR CHICKEN OR GAME

1 package (10 ounces) frozen
   boysenberries or raspberries

¼ cup fresh lemon juice
1 quart pineapple sherbet

Thaw frozen berries. Add berries along with lemon juice to softened sherbet. Fold in carefully avoiding crushing berries. Fill scalloped orange shells or individual ramekins and freeze. Take out a few minutes before serving. Also beautiful in large crystal bowl.

Right flavor for game dinners!

Mrs. Ed Fancher (Shirley Feierabend)

VIRGINIA SAUCIER'S CRANBERRY ICE
Serves 8-10

4 cups cranberries
2 cups boiling water
1 teaspoon unflavored gelatin,
   dissolved in ¼ cup
   cold water

2 cups sugar
1 pint ginger ale
Orange rind, grated to taste

Cook cranberries in boiling water until skins pop. Press through strainer. Add gelatin and sugar. Stir until dissolved. Cool. Add ginger ale and orange rind. Freeze until mushy. Empty into mixing bowl and beat with rotary beater until fluffy. Freeze until firm.

Delightful as an accompaniment to turkey, chicken, all fowl or may be served as a dessert.

Eggs

Cheese

BAKED EGGS

Serves 1

2 thin slices ham
1 slice Mozzarella cheese

1 egg poached
Grated cheese

In individual dishes put two slices ham, slice of cheese and place in warm oven. Place poached egg on ham and cheese. Cover with grated cheese. Warm to melt.

Mrs. Clifford J. Roberts (Jane Ann Hodges)

CREOLE EGGS

Serves 6

9 hard cooked eggs,
sliced thin

CREOLE SAUCE

1 large bell pepper, chopped
1 large onion, chopped
4 ribs celery, chopped
2 tablespoons butter
1 can (1½ pounds) tomatoes
2 tablespoons
Worcestershire sauce

1 can (3 ounces)
tomato paste
1 teaspoon sugar
2 tablespoons horseradish
Salt and pepper

Place eggs in bottom of Pyrex dish in single layer. Make creole sauce by cooking pepper, onion and celery in butter until soft. Add tomatoes, Worcestershire sauce, tomato paste, sugar, horseradish, salt and pepper. Simmer until thick.

Cover eggs with a white sauce then creole sauce. Sprinkle with buttered bread crumbs and bake long enough to heat.

Mrs. David Kennedy (Kay Lewis)

MICROWAVE WHITE SAUCE

Yields 1 Cup

Thin
1 tablespoon butter
1 tablespoon flour
½ teaspoon salt
1 cup milk

Medium
2 tablespoons butter
2 tablespoons flour
½ teaspoon salt
1 cup milk

Melt butter in 1 quart casserole. Add flour and salt, blend to a smooth paste. Add milk gradually, stirring all the time. Cook 4 minutes or until thick. After the first 2 minutes, stir at end of each 30 seconds.

Mrs. Larry D. Williams (Sharon Stevenson)

EGGS FLORENTINE

Serves 8

- 2 packages (10 ounces each) frozen chopped spinach, cooked and well drained
- 2 tablespoons minced onion
- 2 tablespoons lemon juice
- ½ cup grated Cheddar cheese
- 6 hard cooked eggs, sliced
- 3 tablespoons butter
- 3 tablespoons flour
- ½ teaspoon dry mustard
- ½ teaspoon salt
- ¼ teaspoon pepper
- 2½ cups milk
- ½ cup bread crumbs
- 1 tablespoon butter, melted

Combine spinach, onion and lemon juice. Spread in baking dish. Sprinkle with cheese. Top with eggs. Combine 3 tablespoons butter, flour, mustard, salt and pepper in a saucepan. Cook until smooth and bubbly. Add milk, stirring constantly. Pour sauce over eggs. Toss bread crumbs in 1 tablespoon butter. Sprinkle over sauce. Bake in 400° oven for 20 minutes.

Mrs. Phillip Brent (Nancy Fellers)

GOLD RUSH BRUNCH

Serves 8

- 1 package (10 ounces) dry hash brown potatoes, with onions, if available
- 4 tablespoons margarine
- ¼ cup flour
- ½ teaspoon salt
- ⅛ teaspoon pepper
- 2 cups milk
- 1 cup sour cream
- 2 tablespoons parsley
- 8 slices Canadian bacon
- 8 eggs

Prepare potatoes according to package directions and set aside. Melt butter in 3 quart saucepan. Blend in flour, salt and pepper. Add milk all at once. Cook, stirring until thick and bubbly. Remove from heat. Stir in sour cream, parsley and hash browns. Put in 13x9x2 inch casserole. Arrange bacon on top. Bake uncovered for 20 minutes in 300° oven. Place eggs in depressed areas made with a spoon. Salt and pepper to taste. Bake for 15-25 minutes until eggs are set.

Mrs. Frank B. White, III (Lynn Blackburn)

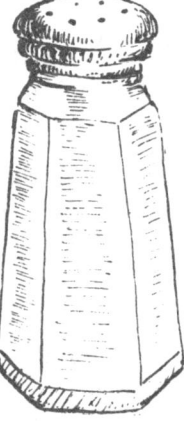

EGGS LORRAINE

Serves 4

4 slices Canadian bacon
2 thin slices cheese, halved
(Swiss, Raclette,
or Appenzeller)
4 eggs

½ teaspoon salt
¼ teaspoon white pepper
¼ cup sour cream

In baking dish, place bacon, top each slice with cheese. Place an egg on top of cheese. Salt and pepper to taste. Top each egg with sour cream. Bake in a 400° oven for 15 minutes or until whites are set.

Heat the sour cream slightly so that it won't slide off.

Mrs. Ed Fancher (Shirley Feierabend)

SCOTCH EGGS

Serves 8

8 hard cooked eggs,
cooled and shelled
1 pound bulk pork sausage
½ cup bread crumbs
¼ teaspoon paprika

1 egg, slightly beaten
6 tablespoons drippings
6 tablespoons flour
2–3 cups milk
Seasoning

On lightly floured surface, flatten sausage into an 8x8 inch square. Cut into 8 pieces and cover eggs carefully. Combine crumbs and paprika. Dip sausage covered eggs in beaten egg and roll in crumbs. Bake in square Pyrex dish in 350° over for 30 minutes. Put drippings in skillet and add flour. Blend together. Slowly add milk. Stir constantly until thick. Season. Serve over eggs.

Sausage will work easier if it isn't too cold.

Mrs. Robert L. Bass (Allee Curtis)

EGG-SPINACH-CHEESE CASSEROLE

Serves 12-24

2 tablespoons butter
3 tablespoons flour
½ teaspoon salt
2 cups milk
1 cup grated Cheddar cheese

1 dozen hard cooked eggs,
cut in half
1½ pounds spinach cooked,
drained and chopped
6 slices bacon

Melt butter, add flour and salt, stirring until thickened. Add milk gradually, stirring constantly. Cook until sauce is thick and creamy. Add cheese, stirring until melted. Add egg yolks and spinach, mixing well. Stuff egg whites with spinach mixture. Place eggs in baking dish, place remainder of spinach mixture over eggs, and cover with bacon. Bake in 350° oven for 20 minutes.

Mrs. Scott Sutphen (Jean Watson)

CRABMEAT AND SHRIMP QUICHE

Serves 8

1 unbaked 10 inch pie shell
½ pound Swiss cheese, cut into ¼ inch slices
1 cup crabmeat
½ cup small cooked shrimp
1½ cups light cream
4 eggs, beaten

1 tablespoon flour
½ teaspoon salt
Dash of pepper and cayenne
¼ teaspoon nutmeg
2 tablespoons butter, melted
2 tablespoons dry sherry

Line unbaked pie shell with Swiss cheese. Cover with layer of crabmeat and shrimp. Combine cream, eggs, flour, salt, pepper, cayenne and nutmeg. Stir in melted butter and sherry. Beat well. Pour over seafood. Refrigerate or freeze. When ready to serve bring to room temperature and bake in 375° oven for 40 minutes or until browned. Let stand for 20 minutes before serving.

Mrs. Stanley Mandel (Patti Jo Solnick)

SUGGESTED PIE CRUST

1 cup flour
2 tablespoons sugar

1 teaspoon baking powder
½ cup butter

Mix together with hands for warmth. Roll out with rolling pin and place in pie pan.

Mrs. James M. Goforth (Brenda Lee)

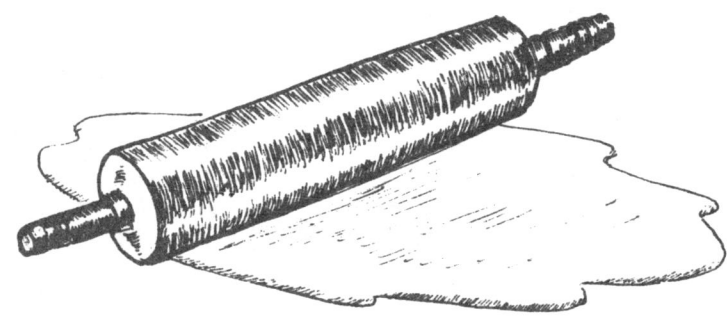

EASY QUICHE

Serves 4-6

8 ounces Monterey Jack
  cheese, grated
2 cans (4 ounces each)
  diced green chilies

4 eggs, beaten
  Favorite spices or salt
  and pepper, to taste

Line bottom and sides of quiche or pie pan, with half the cheese. Add the chilies and another layer of cheese. Combine eggs and your favorite spices. Mix carefully into cheese mixture, poking beaten eggs into cheese. Bake in 275° oven for 45 minutes.

Mrs. Richard Reeves (Louise Coe)

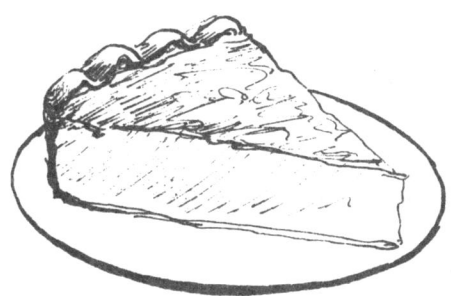

QUICHE LORRAINE

Serves 6-8

1⅓ cups plus 1 tablespoon flour
  Pinch of salt
¼ pound margarine
3 ounces cream cheese or
  ¼ cup water
8 thin slices of cooked ham

8 ounces Swiss cheese,
  thinly sliced
2 cups milk or sour cream
3 eggs plus one yolk
½ teaspoon salt
1 tablespoon melted butter
2 tablespoons minced onions
  Nutmeg (optional)

Sift flour and salt. Add margarine and cream cheese. Mixture is crumbly, but eventually forms ball. Set aside for 30 minutes to an hour. Roll out and line a deep pie dish. Cut ham and cheese into 1x1½ inch pieces and place on the bottom of pie crust. Combine remaining ingredients and pour over ham and cheese. Sprinkle with nutmeg. Bake in 375° oven for 35-40 minutes or until set.

Mrs. Mack Gordon (Dixie Conley)

SPINACH QUICHE

Serves 8-10

PASTRY

1 ¼ cups flour
6 tablespoons cold butter, cut into bits

2 tablespoons vegetable shortening
¼ teaspoon salt
3 tablespoons ice water

In a large bowl cut flour, butter, shortening and salt until the mixture resembles meal. Add ice water and toss until mixed. Form the dough into a ball. Knead the dough lightly with the heel of the hand against a smooth surface for a few seconds to distribute the fat evenly. Reform it into a ball. Dust the dough with flour and chill it, wrapped in wax paper, for 1 hour. Roll out dough ⅛ inch thick on a floured surface. Drape it over the rolling pin and fit it into a 9-inch flan pan with a removeable fluted ring. Press the dough firmly into the pan and trim off the excess, leaving a ½ inch overhang. Fold the overhang over the rim, pressing it onto the sides of the shell with a fork. Chill the shell 1 hour. Line the shell with wax paper, fill the paper with raw rice and bake the shell in preheated 400° oven for 10 minutes. Carefully remove the rice and paper, and bake the shell for 10-15 minutes more, or until it is lightly colored. Remove the shell from the pan. Transfer it to a rack and let it cool to room temperature.

FILLING

3 tablespoons minced green onions
2 tablespoons butter
1 ½ cups cooked, drained and chopped spinach (fresh or frozen)
¼ teaspoon nutmeg
¼ teaspoon salt

¼ teaspoon pepper
¼ pound cream cheese, softened
¼ pound Gruyère cheese
4 eggs, separated
½ cup heavy cream
⅓ cup bread crumbs

In a skillet, sauté onion in butter until soft. Stir in spinach and seasonings. Cook mixture for five minutes. Transfer to a large bowl and add cheeses. Add 4 egg yolks, 1 at a time. Add ½ cup heavy cream and combine mixture well. In a separate bowl, beat 4 egg whites with a pinch of salt until they hold stiff peaks. Fold them into the spinach mixture. Return the pastry shell to the pan, pour in the spinach mixture and dot the top with 1 tablespoon softened butter. Sprinkle with bread crumbs and bake in 375° oven for 30 minutes or until top is puffed and brown. Remove the quiche from the pan, transfer it to a rack and let cool.

Mrs. Elayne Shults (Elayne Steele)

TOMATO-CHEESE PIE
Serves 6-8

1 pastry shell, 8-or 9-inch
2 or 3 large tomatoes,
  cut in ½-inch slices
1 pound Gruyere cheese,
  cut in thin slices
  Salt

Freshly ground black pepper
1 teaspoon dried basil, or
1 tablespoon fresh basil
2 tablespoons grated
  Parmesan cheese
2 tablespoons butter, melted

Bake pastry shell and let cool. Sprinkle the tomato slices generously with salt; put on cake rack to drain about ½ hour. Preheat oven to 375°. Arrange cheese slices, slightly overlapping, in the bottom of pastry shell, and place drained tomato slices side by side on top. Sprinkle with a little black pepper, basil, and Parmesan cheese. Dribble butter over tomatoes and bake in upper third of oven for 25 minutes, or until cheese has melted and top slightly browned. An 8-inch square baking dish may be used. Bake in 375° oven for 25 minutes.

Mrs. Lee T. Bivins (Betty Teel)

EGG AND ARTICHOKE CASSEROLE
Serves 4-6

1 bunch green onions
2 jars (6½ ounces each)
  marinated artichoke hearts
1 clove garlic

4 eggs, beaten
8 ounces medium
  Cheddar cheese, grated
6 crackers, crushed

Mince onions, using half of tops. Cut drained artichokes in thirds and reserve oil. Combine all ingredients. Place in a greased 9x9 inch Pyrex dish. Bake in a 350° oven for 40 minutes.

May be prepared a day ahead and refrigerated. Also may be frozen. To serve after freezing, thaw and heat in 350° oven for 15-20 minutes. Does not have to be served warm.

Tripled and cut into 2 inch squares, this serves 30 for brunch.

Mrs. George W. Morris (Biddy Eckhart)

GREEN CHILI SOUFFLE   Serves 8-10

4 cans (4 ounces each)
  chopped green chilies
1 pound Cheddar cheese,
  grated

3 cups milk
1 cup flour
1 tablespoon salt
3 eggs

Grease 9x13 inch casserole. Alternate layers of chilies and cheese. Mix thoroughly eggs, milk, flour and salt. This mixture should be beaten just before gently pouring over chili-cheese mixture. Bake in 350° oven for 1½ hours. Allow 15 minutes to set before serving.

The two mixtures can be prepared a day ahead and combined right before baking.

Mrs. T. Boone Pickens, Jr. (Bea Carr)

ROQUEFORT SOUFFLE   Serves 8

6 eggs
½ cup heavy cream
1 teaspoon
  Worcestershire sauce
  Dash Tabasco

¼ teaspoon pepper
½ pound Roquefort
  or blue cheese
11 ounces cream cheese
1 tablespoon butter

Blend eggs, cream, Worcestershire, Tabasco and pepper in blender until smooth. Break cheese into chunks and add to egg mixture while blender is running. Blend on high speed 5-10 seconds. Butter a 6-cup souffle dish. Pour mixture into dish and bake in 400° oven for 45-50 minutes. May be prepared 24 hours in advance, but return to room temperature before baking.

Mrs. James A. Hedgecoke, Jr. (Sallye Dees)

WELSH RAREBIT   Serves 4

2 tablespoons butter
3 cups grated sharp
  cheddar cheese
½ teaspoon dry mustard
½ teaspoon salt
  Dash cayenne

1 teaspoon
  Worcestershire sauce
2 egg yolks, lightly beaten
  with ½ cup beer
4 slices hot buttered toast

Combine butter and cheese in double boiler. Cook, stirring constantly with a wooden spoon in one direction only. Add seasonings and continue stirring until mixture is thick and creamy. Add egg yolk mixture. Keep hot, but do not boil. Pour generously over toast.

This is good served over broiled sliced tomatoes, or over sliced tomatoes, ham, and asparagus placed over toast.

Mrs. James C. Ballard (Barbara Lloyd)

124

HUEVOS RANCHEROS   Serves 6

5 slices bacon
1 can (16 ounces) tomatoes
1 tablespoon green chilies, chopped
1 clove garlic, crushed

6 eggs
½ teaspoon salt
⅛ teaspoon pepper
6 soft corn tortillas

Cut bacon into small pieces and fry in 10-inch skillet until crisp. Drain off fat. Add tomatoes, chilies and garlic to bacon in skillet and heat until bubbly. Carefully slip eggs onto hot tomato mixture. Sprinkle eggs with salt and pepper. Cover and continue cooking over medium-low heat for 5-8 minutes, or until eggs are set. Serve on soft, warm corn tortillas.

Mrs. Paul E. Cizon (Laurie Gray)

RED ENCHILADAS   Yields 24 Enchiladas

24 corn tortillas
Grated cheese
Onion, sauteed
1 package (1.5 ounces) Shilling enchilada sauce mix
1 can (10 ounces) green enchilada sauce

1 can (10 ounces) tomatoes and green chilies
2 cans (8 ounces each) Mountain Pass tomato sauce
Cumin to taste
1 pound ground beef, cooked and drained (optional for filling)

Soften tortillas in hot oil. Fill with cheese and onion. Roll. Place in large casserole. Combine remaining ingredients in large saucepan and bring to a boil. Pour over tortillas. Heat until bubbly.

If meat is used add to cheese and onion for filling.

This freezes well.

Mrs. James C. Boyce (Anne Dryden)

SOUR CREAM ENCHILADAS

Serves 8-10

16–20 corn tortillas
3 cartons (8 ounces each) sour cream
2 cans cream of chicken soup
2 cans (4 ounces) chopped green chilies

1½ pounds grated Cheddar cheese (Longhorn, Colby)
2–3 bunches (about 1 cup) green onions, thinly sliced

Soften corn tortillas by dipping them in hot shortening for only 2 or 3 *seconds*. Drain on paper towels to cool. Make a sauce with the sour cream, soup and green chilies. Spread a thin layer of sauce (about 1 cup) over bottom of 13x9x2 inch pan. Place a handful of cheese and onion to taste on each tortilla and roll snuggly. Place rolled enchiladas side by side in pan and pour remaining sauce over all. Top with any remaining onion and cheese. Bake in 350° oven for 30-40 minutes until bubbly. Good when reheated. If you prefer a meat dish, you can add diced chicken to filling ingredients.

Serve with garnish of shredded lettuce and diced tomatoes.

Mrs. Daniel Greener (Shirley Hall)

VERY BEST CHILI RELLENOS

Serves 6-12

12 large green chilies with stems
⅓ pound Longhorn cheese, cut in 12 strips

⅓ pound Monterey Jack cheese, cut in 12 strips
⅓ pound cream cheese, cut in 12 strips

BATTER

1 cup flour
1 teaspoon baking powder
½ teaspoon salt

¾ cup cornmeal
1 cup milk
2 eggs

Wash and dry chilies. Grease and pierce several times with ice pick. Put under broiler until skin is light brown and pops, turn on all sides. Remove from broiler. Cover with cool, damp cloth until cooled. Peel off skins. Make slit in side and carefully remove all seeds. Stuff chilies with slices of all three cheeses. Place on foil covered baking sheet and freeze. Use in several hours or package and keep for later. Combine batter ingredients in blender. This can also be frozen for later use. Dip frozen chilies in batter. Fry in deep fat in deep fat fryer or electric skillet at 425°-450°. Turn when golden brown. Serve immediately with hot sauce or cheese sauce.

This is a lot of work, but well worth it.

Mrs. W.C. Turner, Jr. (Nancy Carmichall)

CLOUD BISCUITS

Yields 1 Dozen

2 cups flour
1 tablespoon sugar
4 teaspoons baking powder
¼ teaspoon soda

½ teaspoon salt
½ cup shortening
1 egg, beaten
1 cup buttermilk

Sift first five ingredients. Cut in shortening. Combine egg and buttermilk and add to dry ingredients. Stir until dough follows fork around bowl. Pinch off dough the size of biscuit desired, mold with floured hands. Place on greased pan and bake in 450° oven for 10-14 minutes.

Mrs. Robert Sanders (Bonnie Hier)

COCKTAIL BISCUITS IN FOOD PROCESSOR

Yields 2-3 Dozen

1¾ cups unbleached flour
¼ cup Gluten flour
¼ teaspoon baking powder
1 teaspoon salt

1½ teaspoons sugar
6 tablespoons margarine
½ cup milk

Preheat oven to 350°. Combine first six ingredients in processor bowl. Blend until mixture resembles very fine cornmeal. Scrape sides and bottom of bowl several times. With the motor running, dribble milk into dough until a ball forms in the center. Roll on a board until smooth and thin. Cut with a small biscuit cutter (as small as bite size, if desired). Place on lightly buttered or Teflon baking sheet. Pierce each biscuit with fork. Bake in 350° oven 12 minutes. Biscuits may be flavored with grated cheese, sesame seeds, caraway seeds, herbs, bacon bits, or whatever the host desires. Freezes well.

Mrs. Ray C. Johnson, Jr. (Joan McCormick)

QUEEN VICTORIA'S CHEESE BISQUITS

Yields 4 Dozen

1 stick butter, softened
1 cup flour
4 ounces freshly grated
   Parmesan cheese

Pinch of salt
Pinch of white pepper

Preheat oven to 350°. Cut butter into flour. Add remaining ingredients. Mix well. Roll out on a well-floured board. Cut in 1½—2 inch circles. Bake on ungreased cookie sheet 10 to 15 minutes or until barely brown.

Mrs. Robert Patterson (Rosemary Cherry)

BEER BREAD

Serves 12

1 cup dark beer
2 tablespoons butter
1 package hot roll mix
2 tablespoons brown sugar

½ teaspoon salt
1 egg, beaten
½ cup wheat germ

Heat beer to boiling point. Add butter, let melt. Cool to room temperature; dissolve yeast in beer mixture; stir in brown sugar, salt, egg, wheat germ and hot roll mix. Blend well. Cover and let rise until double in bulk, (1-1½ hours). Knead dough, 5-7 minutes, on floured board. Put in 9x5x3 inch greased loaf pan and let rise again. Butter top. Bake at 375° for 30-40 minutes. This bread will be quite brown on top before done. Never fear, it is delicious.

Mrs. Donald Bagot (Elna Ruth Beck)

JAY TAYLOR'S CORN DODGERS

Yields 1-1½ Dozen

1 cup yellow cornmeal
1½ cups boiling water

⅛ teaspoon salt
4 egg whites, beaten until stiff

Scald cornmeal in salted boiling water. Cool in refrigerator. Fold in egg whites. Pour into well buttered iron pans and bake in 350° oven for 45 minutes.

CORN FRITTERS

Yields 4 Servings

1⅓ cups flour, sifted
1½ teaspoons baking powder
¾ teaspoon salt
⅔ cup milk if using whole kernel corn

½ cup milk if using cream style corn
1 egg, well beaten
1½ cups whole kernel corn, drained or
1½ cups cream style corn

Sift together flour, baking powder and salt. Blend the milk and egg and add them gradually to the dry ingredients. Stir in the corn. The batter should be stiff. Drop from tablespoons into hot deep fat, 365°-375°. Fry 2-5 minutes or until golden. Drain on a paper towel.

Mrs. Tom Cambridge (Norma Taggart)

MEXICAN CORNBREAD

Serves 8-10

1 cup corn meal
1 tablespoon flour
½ teaspoon soda
1 teaspoon salt
2 eggs
¾ cup milk
2 tablespoons
  bacon drippings
1 can (8¾ ounces)
  cream style corn
1 can (2 ounces)
  chopped pimientos
½ teaspoon onion powder
1 can (4 ounces) Ortega
  chopped green chilies
1½ cups grated Cheddar cheese
  either Old English Deluxe
  or Kraft

Mix all ingredients thoroughly. Bake in a 9x9 inch greased pan for one hour in a 350° oven. It is good hot and cold.

Mrs. R.G. Rogers (Linda Rogers)

MRS. CUSTARD'S CORN BREAD

Serves 4

2 tablespoons butter
¾ cup white corn meal
¼ cup flour, sifted
1–2 tablespoons sugar
½ teaspoon salt
1 teaspoon baking powder
1 cup plus 2 tablespoons milk
1 egg, well beaten
½ cup milk

Melt butter in 9-inch square pan. Combine next seven ingredients. Pour mixture into hot pan. Float ½ cup milk over top of batter (do not stir). Bake in 400° oven for 30 minutes or until done.

Mrs. C.D. Hoover, Jr. (Jane Skillman)

SPOON BREAD

Serves 6-8

1½ cups boiling water
1 cup corn meal
1 tablespoon butter
3 egg yolks
1 cup buttermilk
  or sour cream
1 teaspoon salt
1 teaspoon sugar
1 teaspoon baking powder
¼ teaspoon soda
3 egg whites, beaten
  to hold soft peaks

Pour water over cornmeal. Stir until cool to keep from lumping. Add butter and egg yolks, stirring until eggs are thoroughly blended. Stir in buttermilk. Blend in salt, sugar, baking powder and soda. Fold in egg whites. Pour into a greased 9 inch square baking pan. Bake in 375° oven for 45-50 minutes. Serve immediately.

Mrs. Phillip Brent (Nancy Fellers)

APPLESAUCE MUFFINS

Serves 4-6

- 2 cups biscuit mix
- ¼ cup sugar
- 1 tablespoon cinnamon
- ½ cup applesauce
- ¼ cup milk
- 1 egg, slightly beaten
- 2 tablespoons oil

Combine first seven ingredients and beat 30 seconds. Fill small muffin tin ⅔ full. Bake in 400° oven for 12 minutes.

TOPPING

- 4 tablespoons butter, melted
- ½ cup sugar
- ½ teaspoon cinnamon

Cool muffins slightly. Remove and dip in butter. Roll in cinnamon mixture.

Freezes well.

Mrs. Oth Miller (Cheryl Collins)

ICE BOX MUFFINS

Makes 10 Dozen Tiny Muffins

- 1 cup Crisco or butter
- 2 cups sugar
- 4 eggs, beaten
- 3 cups flour
- 2 teaspoons baking powder
- ¼ teaspoon salt
- 1 cup milk
- 1 teaspoon vanilla
- 1 cup chopped nuts (optional)
- ½ teaspoon lemon extract (optional)

Cream butter and sugar. Stir in eggs. Combine flour, baking powder and salt. Add alternately with milk. Stir in vanilla. Add nuts and lemon extract if desired. Fill greased muffin cups ½ full. Bake in 400° oven for 20 minutes. If tiny muffin pans are used, bake 12-15 minutes.

This batter will keep two weeks under refrigeration if kept in a covered container.

Mrs. Jim Walker (Patsy Roberts)

MONEKA STIDHAM'S ICE BOX GINGERBREAD MUFFINS   Yields 3 Dozen

1 cup margarine
1 cup sugar
1 cup molasses
4 eggs
4 cups flour
½ teaspoon baking powder
2 teaspoons ground ginger
¾ teaspoon salt
¼ teaspoon allspice
1 teaspoon soda
½ teaspoon cinnamon
1 cup buttermilk
White raisins
English walnuts

Cream first three ingredients together. Add eggs 1 at a time, beating thoroughly after each addition. Sift dry ingredients together. Add alternately with buttermilk. Add as many raisins and nuts as desired with last addition of flour. Spoon into muffin tins. Bake in a 400° oven until muffin bounces back to touch.

This dough may be kept in covered bowl in refrigerator as long as 3 weeks.

RAISIN BRAN MUFFINS

4 eggs, beaten
1 cup Wesson oil
3 cups sugar
5 teaspoons baking soda
2 teaspoons salt
5 cups flour
1 quart buttermilk
1 package (15 ounces) Post Raisin Bran
1 cup raisins (optional)

Stir ingredients together in order. Place in muffin tin. Bake in 400° oven for 15 minutes.

Batter will keep in refrigerator for 2 weeks or will freeze. Baked muffins reheat well in microwave.

Mrs. William K. Irwin (Shirley Neely)

CRÊPES

Yields 10-15

¾ cup flour
1 teaspoon baking powder
½ teaspoon salt
2 tablespoons
  powdered sugar

2 eggs, beaten
⅔ cup milk
⅓ cup water
½ teaspoon lemon rind
  or vanilla

Sift together the flour, baking powder, salt and powdered sugar. In a separate bowl combine eggs, milk, water and flavoring. Beat well. Combine the two mixtures and store in refrigerator overnight. Heat skillet and add butter while skillet is hot. Add a little batter; tip skillet until batter is well spread. Cook over fairly high heat. Peek under and flip when a little brown. Serve with sugar or jelly, folding crêpe into quarters.

Crêpes may be frozen and used later for chicken crêpes or other fillings.

Mrs. Stanley Marsh, 3 (Wendy O'Brien)

BONNIE'S PANCAKES

Serves 8

2½ cups flour
1 teaspoon soda
4 teaspoons baking powder
4 teaspoons sugar
1 teaspoon salt

Dash cinnamon
4 eggs, well beaten
2½ cups buttermilk
1 stick melted butter

Sift dry ingredients into mixing bowl. Combine eggs and buttermilk. Add dry ingredients to egg mixture and mix well, but do not beat. Add butter and blend well. Cook pancakes on hot griddle. Keeps well in refrigerator if tightly sealed.

Mrs. Hugh Gilmour (Michele Lamarca)

GERMAN PANCAKES

Serves 4

4 eggs, beaten
½ cup sifted flour
½ teaspoon salt

½ cup milk
2 tablespoons margarine

Mix eggs, flour, salt and milk in a blender. Melt margarine in 10 inch oven proof skillet. Add batter. Bake on middle rack in 450° oven for 15 minutes. Serve with butter and syrup.

May top with powdered sugar and lemon juice or fruit, if desired.

Mrs. Alan Roberson (Sandie Davis)

HOLIDAY PANCAKES

2 eggs, separated
7 tablespoons oil
1 cup flour
1 teaspoon salt

2 teaspoons baking powder
1 tablespoon sugar
1 cup milk
½ teaspoon vanilla

Beat egg whites until stiff. Mix the remaining ingredients and beat with a mixer. Fold egg whites into batter.

Mrs. Robert C. Hill (Betty McComb)

YOGURT PANCAKES WITH ORANGE SYRUP   Serves 4

1 cup flour
¼ teaspoon salt
1 tablespoon sugar
1 tablespoon baking powder
1 cup milk

1 egg
2 rounded tablespoons
   plain yogurt
2 tablespoons melted butter

Blend flour with salt, sugar, and baking powder. Mix milk with egg; add to flour mixture. Add remaining ingredients. Cook on hot griddle turning once. Batter will keep overnight.

ORANGE SYRUP

1 cup sugar
⅓ cup orange juice
   concentrate

½ cup butter

Mix all ingredients together. Bring to a boil. Serve hot over pancakes.

Mrs. Don T. Curtis (Suzanne Stokes)

SOUR CREAM WAFFLES   Serves 4-6

1½ cups flour
2 teaspoons baking powder
½ teaspoon soda
¼ teaspoon salt
1 tablespoon sugar
3 eggs, separated

¾ cup sour cream
¾ cup milk
¼ cup shortening,
   melted or corn oil
¼ cup margarine, melted

Sift dry ingredients together into large bowl. Beat egg yolks, sour cream and milk. Add to dry ingredients alternately with cooled fats. Stir until batter is smooth. In another bowl beat egg whites until stiff. Fold into batter until well blended. Bake on hot waffle iron. These can be frozen and reheated in oven.

Mrs. Stan Morris, Jr. (Kathleen Boyd)

DAY BEFORE
FRENCH TOAST

Serves 3-4

6 slices Italian or
French bread,
¾ to 1 inch thick
4 eggs
1 cup milk

3 tablespoons sugar
¼ teaspoon salt
1 teaspoon vanilla
3 tablespoons butter

Arrange bread in single layer, in a 13x9 inch pan. Blend eggs, milk, sugar, salt and vanilla in blender. Pour over bread. Turn bread to coat evenly. Cover and refrigerate overnight. Sauté bread in hot butter, in a skillet until golden on both sides; about 4-5 minutes per side. These can be frozen after they are cooked and reheated in your oven.

Mrs. Stan Morris, Jr. (Kathleen Boyd)

BUBBLE CAKE

3 cans biscuits, quartered
½ cup sugar
1 teaspoon cinnamon
1½ sticks butter

½ teaspoon cinnamon
1 cup sugar
1 cup pecans

Shake biscuit quarters in sack filled with ½ cup sugar and 1 teaspoon cinnamon. Bring butter, ½ teaspoon cinnamon, and 1 cup of sugar to a boil. Layer biscuits and pecans in a buttered bundt pan. Pour the butter mixture over the biscuits. Bake in a 325° oven for 40 minutes.

Mrs. Scott Gilmour (Nancee Parker)

SOUR CREAM
COFFEE CAKE

2 cups sugar
2 eggs
2 sticks margarine
1 cup sour cream
1 teaspoon vanilla
2 cups flour

1 teaspoon baking powder
¼ teaspoon salt
1 teaspoon cinnamon
4 tablespoons brown sugar
1 cup chopped pecans

Cream sugar, eggs and margarine. Add sour cream and vanilla. Sift dry ingredients together and add to creamed mixture. Fill greased and floured bundt pan with one half of the batter. Combine cinnamon, brown sugar and pecans for the topping. Sprinkle half of the topping over the batter. Add remaining batter. Sprinkle with the remaining topping. Bake in 350° oven for 50-60 minutes. Cool 10 minutes. This freezes well.

Mrs. Victor W. Shawgo (Mary Kaye Dolan)

BANANA BREAD

Yields 2 Loaves

½ cup butter
1 cup sugar
2 eggs

2 cups flour, sifted
1 teaspoon soda
4 ripe bananas, mashed

Cream butter and sugar together. Add eggs and flour, 1 cup at a time. Mix in soda and bananas. Divide mixture in half and pour into 2 loaf pans. Bake in 350° preheated oven for 40 minutes. Add one cup of nuts if desired. This bread freezes well. Check for doneness with a toothpick. Toothpick comes out clean if loaf is done.

Mrs. Walter Dickinson (Marilee Akerly)

BANANA NUT BREAD

1½ cups sugar
½ cup margarine
2 eggs
1 cup mashed bananas
1¾ cups flour

1 teaspoon soda
¼ cup sour milk or
½ cup mashed bananas
1 teaspoon vanilla
1 cup chopped pecans

Mix all ingredients together and put in greased, floured loaf pan. Bake in 325° oven for 1 hour. It is very moist.

Mrs. James H. Simms (Freeda Daugherty)

FAVORITE BANANA BREAD

Yields 1 Loaf

3 ripe or overripe bananas
(4 if small), mashed
1 cup sugar
1 egg

1½ cups flour
¼ cup butter, melted
1 teaspoon soda
1 teaspoon salt

Combine all ingredients. Pour into Teflon or buttered 8½x4½x2½ inch loaf pan. Bake in 325° oven for 1 hour.

Mrs. Douglas Easley (Hilda Steven)

GRANDMOTHER BECK'S BANANA NUT CAKE

½ cup butter
1½ cups sugar
2 eggs, separated
3 well-ripened bananas, mashed
½ cup nuts

¼ cup milk
1 teaspoon vanilla
2 cups flour
1½ teaspoons baking powder

Cream butter and sugar; add unbeaten egg yolks, bananas and nuts. Add milk, vanilla, flour and baking powder. Fold in egg whites beaten stiffly. Pour into a floured and greased large loaf pan. Bake in 300° oven for 1 hour or a little less.

Mrs. Paul Fields (Barry Beck)

CRANBERRY BREAD

2 cups flour
½ teaspoon salt
1½ teaspoons baking powder
½ teaspoon soda
1 cup sugar
2 tablespoons Wesson oil

Grated peel and juice of 1 orange with boiling water to make ¾ cups
1 egg, well beaten
1 cup chopped nuts
1 cup chopped cranberries

Sift first four ingredients. Add sugar, oil and liquid. Fold in egg. Add nuts and cranberries. Pour in greased 9x5x3 inch pan. Bake in 325° oven for 1 hour. Cool and store for 24 hours before cutting.

Very cold or frozen cranberries are easier to chop.

Mrs. James A. Johnston (Harriet Buie)

PUMPKIN BREAD   Yields 3-4 Loaves

3 cups sugar
4 eggs
1 teaspoon ginger
2 teaspoons cinnamon
2 teaspoons soda
1 cup oil

1 cup canned pumpkin
3⅓ cups flour (reserve ⅓ cup)
⅔ cup water
1 cup chopped pecans
1 cup golden raisins

Mix sugar, eggs, spices and oil with mixer. Add pumpkin. Add 3 cups flour alternately with water, beginning and ending with flour. Combine ⅓ cup flour with nuts and raisins. Stir into pumpkin mixture. Pour into 3 or 4 greased and floured one pound coffee cans. Bake in 350° oven for 1 hour. These can be frozen. They make super gifts.

Mrs. Ben Bynum (Penny Brooks)

CARAWAY-RYE CRACKERS

Yields 3½-4 Dozen

1⅓ cups flour
⅔ cup rye flour
⅓ cup oil
1½ teaspoons caraway seed

1 teaspoon salt
½ teaspoon soda
2 tablespoons vinegar
¼ cup water

Mix all ingredients with a pastry cutter and roll thin. Cut into desired shape. Place on ungreased cookie sheet. Prick with a fork. Salt each cracker if desired. Bake in 375° oven for 12-15 minutes.

Mrs. Danny Conklin (Carolyn Kerns)

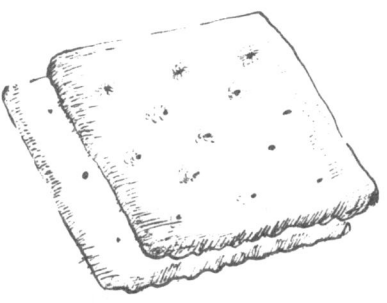

GARLIC BREAD STICKS

1 pound butter, melted
½ teaspoon garlic powder

1 package hot dog buns
Parmesan cheese

Melt butter in saucepan. Add garlic. Slice buns lengthwise in at least fourths. Roll each "stick" in butter and put on cookie sheet. Sprinkle generously with cheese. Bake 1 hour in 250° oven, or until crispy. Keeps indefinitely in tightly sealed container. Good with soup.

Mrs. Ken McCarty (Sue Sheriff)

VELMA HARRIS' YEAST BISCUITS

Yields 5 Dozen

1 package dry yeast
½ cup lukewarm water
5 cups flour
1 teaspoon salt
1 teaspoon soda

3 teaspoons baking powder
3 tablespoons sugar
¾ cup shortening
2 cups buttermilk

Dissolve yeast in lukewarm water and set aside. Sift together flour, salt, soda, baking powder and sugar. Cut the shortening into the dry ingredients. Add buttermilk and the yeast mixture. Mix well and knead. Put in covered bowl in refrigerator and use as needed. Will keep 1 week or longer. When ready to use, roll out on lightly floured board about ½ inch thick. Cut with biscuit cutter. Place on ungreased cookie sheet. Brush top of biscuits with melted shortening. Bake in 450° oven for 12-15 minutes or until brown.

BATTER RISING BREAD

Yields 4 Loaves

2 packages yeast
⅓ cup water
3 tablespoons sugar
2 cups milk, scalded
9 cups flour (Approx.)

2 eggs, well-beaten
½ cup butter,
   melted and cooled
1 cup sugar

Dissolve yeast in water with sugar. Let bubble. Combine with cooled milk and 4 cups flour. Stir well. Let rise in large bowl until double. Beat eggs, butter and sugar together. Mix well with batter. Add 4 cups flour, 1 cup at a time. Knead with the fifth cup of flour. (Add more flour if needed for a smooth dough.) Knead well. Set in buttered bowl, butter top of dough. Let rise. Knead again and let rise. Split dough into fourths. Roll out ½ inch thick. Spread with butter; sprinkle with sugar and cinnamon. Roll up. Pat into bread pans. Let rise. Cook in 400° oven for 30 minutes or until done.

Mrs. Robert Patterson (Rosemary Cherry)

BLANCHE'S BRAN BREAD

2 packages dry yeast
½ cup warm water
2 cups warm milk
¼ cup sugar
¼ cup melted shortening

1 tablespoon salt
1 cup All-Bran
2 eggs
7–8 cups flour

Dissolve yeast in warm water. Combine next six ingredients in a large bowl. Add yeast mixture and 1 cup flour. Add flour until dough is stiff enough to handle without sticking to fingers. Knead lightly, place in greased bowl, grease top and let rise until doubled in size (about 1½ hours). Punch down and let rise again. Can be made into either rolls or bread. Bake 20-30 minutes in buttered pans in 350° oven. Will make 2 big or 3 small loaves. This freezes well.

Mrs. Ed Notestine (Elaine Folley)

CHEESE PEPPER BREAD   Serves 12

1 ¾ cups milk
½ cup water
3 tablespoons unsalted butter
5 cups all purpose flour
2 teaspoons salt
2 packages dry yeast
2 tablespoons sugar

1 heaping teaspoon black
   pepper (medium grind)
2 cups (½ pound)
   sharp cheese, grated
1 cup flour
   Melted butter
2 tablespoons poppy seeds

Heat milk, water and butter in small pan until very warm (120-130°). Set aside. Combine dry ingredients. Mix well. Add cheese and mix. Add liquid mixture and stir until it clings together. Add 1 cup more flour, ½ cup at a time, until dough is no longer sticky. Knead until smooth and elastic. Place in a greased bowl and grease top of dough. Cover and let rise in a warm place until double (about 45 minutes). Punch down. Divide into 30 balls of equal size. Roll balls until smooth. Arrange 15 balls (that have been dipped in melted butter) into a well buttered tube pan. Sprinkle 1 tablespoon poppy seeds on top. Repeat with next 15 balls. Pour remaining melted butter over top. Sprinkle remaining poppy seeds over top. Let rise again until double (about 45 minutes). Bake in 375° oven for 40 minutes. Remove at once from pan. Cool on rack. Freezes well. Thaw before reheating.

Mrs. Don T. Curtis (Suzanne Stokes)

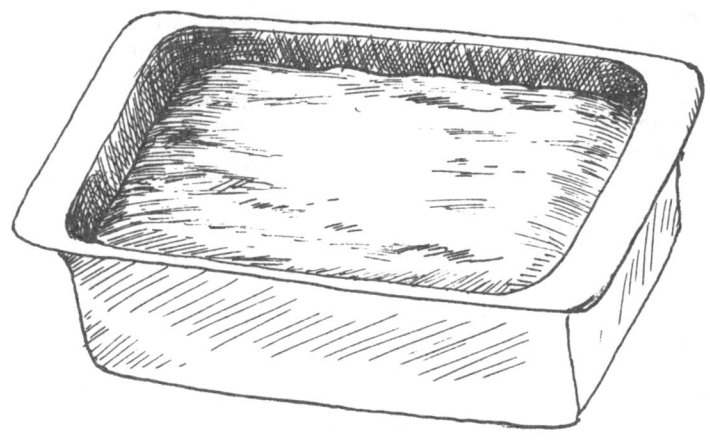

CINNAMON ROLLS
OR COFFEE CAKE

1 cup milk, scalded
1½ packages dry yeast
1 stick butter,
   melted and cooled
¼ cup sugar

1 egg, beaten
3½–4 cups flour
1 stick butter, melted
½ cup sugar
1½–2 teaspoons cinnamon

Cool milk to lukewarm. Add yeast. When it bubbles, mix with one stick butter, ¼ cup sugar and egg. Add flour until it makes a soft dough. Knead on floured board for 10 minutes. Place dough in a greased bowl and grease top of dough. Cover with a damp cloth. Let rise in a warm place for 1 hour. Punch down. Roll out to ¼ inch thickness. Combine ½ cup sugar and cinnamon.

ROLLS

For bite size rolls cut dough with small ½-¾ inch cutter. Dip each piece in butter then roll in sugar-cinnamon mixture. Put each piece in a loaf pan. Fill half full. Let rise 1 hour. When done remove from pan, separate and lay out to cool. (Top pieces will be crisp and the middle soft.)

COFFEE CAKE

Cut with biscuit cutter. Dip each piece in butter then roll in cinnamon and sugar mixture. Stand discs sideways in two rows in bundt pan. Let rise 1 hour. Bake in 350° oven for 35-40 minutes. This can also make 2 small coffee cakes by baking in loaf pans. To reheat, wrap bite size pieces in foil. Dot coffee cake with butter and heat slowly.

Mrs. Robert Patterson (Rosemary Cherry)

CINNA-SWIRLS

Yields 2½-3 Dozen

1½ cups milk, scalded
½ cup sugar
2 teaspoons salt
½ cup oil
2 packages (¼ ounce each) dry yeast

½ cup lukewarm water
2 eggs, beaten
6½ cups unsifted flour
½ cup sugar mixed with
2 teaspoons cinnamon

Combine milk, sugar, salt and oil. Cool to lukewarm. Dissolve yeast in warm water. Add to cooled milk mixture. Add egg and half the flour. Beat until smooth. Stir in remaining flour.

Turn onto lightly floured board. Knead until smooth and elastic. Place in greased bowl and brush with oil. Cover. Let rise until double its bulk, about 1 hour. (For a finer texture: punch down and let rise a second time. About 30 minutes.)

Punch down, turn out on board. Divide dough in half. Roll each half into a 10x14 inch rectangle. Cover each rectangle with the sugar-cinnamon mixture. Roll up jelly roll fashion. Cut individual rolls about 1 inch thick. Place on greased sheets. Cover. Let rise about 30 minutes. Fry in deep fat until golden brown.

GLAZE

2½ cups powdered sugar   5 tablespoons milk

Combine powdered sugar and milk. Beat until smooth. Dip rolls in glaze while warm.

Mrs. Danny Conklin (Carolyn Kerns)

DILLY CASSEROLE BREAD

Serves 8

1 package active dry yeast
¼ cup warm water (110-115°)
2 tablespoons sugar
1 teaspoon salt
¼ teaspoon soda
1 cup cream style cottage cheese, heated to lukewarm
1 tablespoon butter
1 tablespoon instant minced onion
2 teaspoons dill seed
1 egg
2¼–2½ cups flour

Soften yeast in water and let stand 10 minutes.

Combine sugar, salt and soda. In a separate bowl, combine cottage cheese, butter, onion, dill seed, egg and softened yeast. Add dry mixture. Beat well to blend thoroughly. Add flour gradually, beating after each addition. Cover and let rise 1 hour. Stir down dough. Turn into well greased 1½-2 quart casserole. Let rise in a warm place until light (30-40 minutes). Bake in 350° oven for 35-45 minutes or until crust is golden brown. Brush top with soft butter and sprinkle with salt. Cool about 5 minutes in casserole. Remove to cooling rack.

This bread freezes well.

Mrs. Prescott Haralson (Jo Anne Grimm)

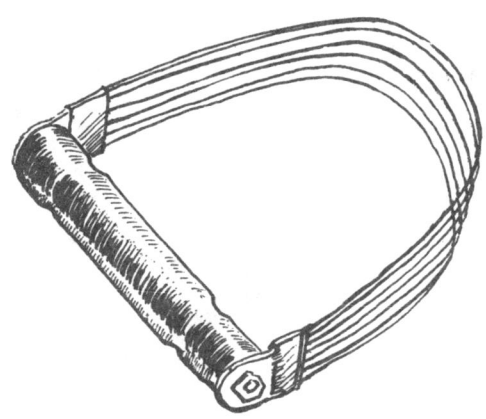

GLEN BROSIER'S DUTCH OVEN BREAD

Serves 12-16

3 cups very hot water (120°)
½ cup butter
½ cup sugar
2½ teaspoons salt

2 packages active dry yeast
9½ cups (approximately) all
    purpose flour, unsifted
Salad oil

Combine water, butter, sugar and salt. Stir until butter melts. Let cool until lukewarm. Stir in yeast. Cover and set in warm place until bubbly; about 15 minutes. Add 5 cups flour. Beat with a wooden spoon to form a thick batter. Stir in enough of the remaining flour (about 3½ cups) to form a stiff dough. Turn dough onto floured board. Knead until smooth, 10 minutes, adding flour as needed to prevent sticking. Turn dough over in a greased bowl, cover and let rise until doubled, about 1½ hours. Punch dough down. Knead on floured board to form a smooth ball. Grease the inside of a 5 quart cast iron Dutch oven and the underside of the lid with salad oil. Cut a circle of foil or brown paper to cover the bottom of the Dutch oven. Grease the paper in the Dutch oven. Place dough in the pot. Cover with lid. Let rise until dough pushes lid up about ½ inch, (1 hour). Watch closely! Bake covered in 375° oven 12-15 minutes. Remove lid; bake another 30-35 minutes or until loaf is golden brown and sounds hollow when tapped. Turn loaf onto rack to cool.

Fun to serve with a big hunk of Longhorn cheese and beer for informal entertaining.

GOOD BREAD

Yields 2 Loaves

2 cups lukewarm water
1 package active dry yeast
1½ tablespoons sugar

1½ tablespoons salt
1 cup stone ground
    whole wheat flour
5 cups all purpose flour

Dissolve yeast with sugar and salt in lukewarm water in large bowl. Add flour 1 cup at a time, stirring until dough is too stiff to stir anymore (usually after fourth cup). Add whole wheat flour while stirring is still possible. Knead in 2 cups of flour for about 10 minutes. Let rise until doubled in a lightly greased large bowl, covered with a damp cloth. Punch dough down and put into two lightly greased loaf pans. Slash tops of loaves with sharp knife diagonally about three times. Let loaves rise about 45 minutes. Bake in 400° oven for 20 minutes. Let cool in pans about 10 minutes. Bread may be frozen in foil. This recipe also makes good little individual French type rolls. It's good also toasted for breakfast and served with your grandmother's best wild plum jelly!

Mrs. Jack Hunt (Diane Pierce)

GRANDMOTHER TAYLOR'S BREAD

Yields 2 Loaves

2 cups milk, scalded
½ cup shortening
½ cup sugar

1 teaspoon salt
1 package active dry yeast
6 cups flour

Stir first four ingredients in large, deep pan until shortening melts. Remove from heat and cool. Sprinkle yeast over cooled mixture and stir rapidly to dissolve. Slowly add 6 cups of flour, stirring with spoon until too stiff to stir. Knead in remaining flour for 8-10 minutes. Grease a large bowl and put dough in it. Turn dough over so greased side is facing up. Place in cold oven on the top rack. On lower rack, place a pan of very hot water and close oven door. *Do not turn on oven and do not open door* for 1 hour. Dough should be doubled in size. Punch down and place dough in 2 greased loaf pans. Let rise again with the same "oven and water" method for 1 hour or until dough has doubled in size. Bake in 350° oven for 30-45 minutes. Top will be golden brown and crusty.

This recipe may be frozen before dough rises or after being baked. This "oven and water" method can be used with any yeast bread recipe and is virtually a foolproof way to get bread to rise.

Mrs. Paul E. Cizon (Laurie Gray)

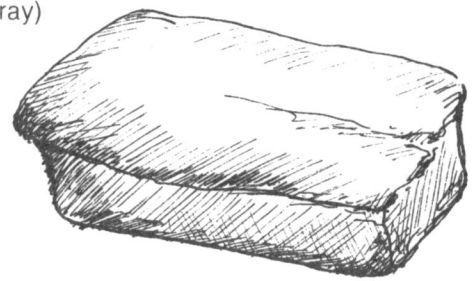

ITALIAN BREAD

Yields 2 Loaves

2½ packages yeast
1 tablespoon sugar
1 cup warm water
½ cup butter
¾ cup hot water

5-6 cups flour
cornmeal
1 egg white, beaten
Salt

Combine yeast, sugar and warm water in a large bowl. (Let bubble). Melt butter in hot water. Let cool and combine with yeast mixture. Add flour 1 cup at a time. Knead on a floured surface for 10 minutes. Let rise until doubled in greased bowl. Knead and let rise again (optional, but better). Roll out until ½ inch thick. Roll up tightly into long loaves. Tuck ends under and pinch seams closed. Place on a cookie sheet that is buttered and sprinkled with cornmeal. Let rise. Brush with salted egg whites. Bake in 425° oven for 40 minutes or until brown.

Mrs. Robert Patterson (Rosemary Cherry)

JACKIE'S
MONKEY BREAD

Yields 3 Loaves

4 cups flour
1 cup sugar
1 teaspoon salt
2 cups milk, scalded
4 eggs, beaten

1 cup margarine, melted
2 packages yeast, dissolved
   in ¼ cup warm water
2 cups flour
1½ sticks margarine, melted

Stir first six ingredients together in a very large bowl. Cool to lukewarm. Add yeast. Let stand covered for 45 minutes at room temperature. Beat in 2 cups of flour. Let rise until doubled in size. Turn dough (it is runny at this stage) out on a well-floured board and pat with hand until about ¾ inch thick.

Pour equal amounts of margarine into three 11x14 inch pans. Cut dough with a biscuit cutter. Dip each side in margarine and place in pans. Let rise in pans until double. Bake in 400° oven for 20-25 minutes.

These are pull-apart rolls. They may be frozen. For best results, freeze them after they are shaped and placed in pans, but before they rise again. Take from freezer 6 hours before baking.

Mrs. Robert Sanders (Bonnie Hier)

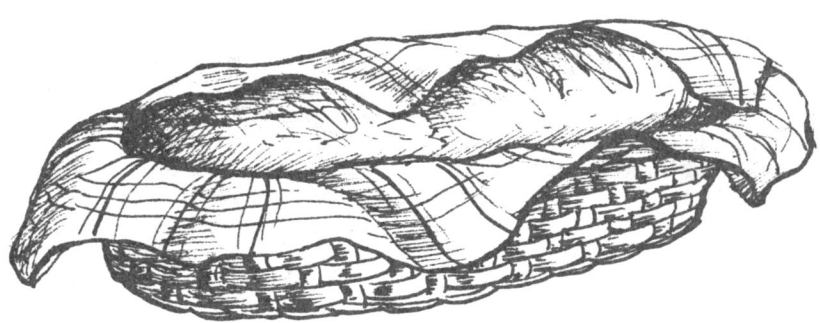

KORPUT
(FINNISH BREAD)

Yields 3 Loaves

2 envelopes active dry yeast
½ cup lukewarm water
(too warm will kill yeast)
2 cups scalded milk
1 cup sugar
1 stick butter, cut into pieces
2 teaspoons salt

¾ teaspoon cardamon
4 eggs
8–9 cups flour
Egg wash (1 egg with
¼ cup milk)
¼ cup sugar
½ teaspoon cardamon

Proof yeast in lukewarm water for 10 minutes. In large bowl combine milk, 1 cup sugar, butter, salt and cardamon until butter is melted. Beat in eggs, yeast mixture and 4 cups flour until the dough is smooth and elastic. Beat in 4 or 5 more cups flour to make stiff dough. Let it rest for 15 minutes. Knead for 15 minutes until smooth and satiny. Put into buttered bowl, turn to coat, let rise 1 hour or until double in bulk. Punch down, let rise again for 30-45 minutes. Turn out on lightly floured surface and divide each third into thirds. Roll each piece into a rope about 16 inches long. With 3 ropes side by side, braid them out from the middle to form straight loaves. Pinch the ends. Roll the rest of the parts and braid. Arrange 3-4 inches apart on buttered baking sheets and let rise, lightly covered with a tea towel 30 minutes or until double. Brush with egg wash. Sprinkle with ¼ cup sugar combined with ½ teaspoon cardamon. Bake in 350° oven for 25 minutes. Do not overbake. They should be golden. Check bread during cooking time. You may need to switch pans (top to bottom) in oven during cooking time to insure even cooking. Bread will keep in refrigerator at least 2 weeks in plastic bag.

Mrs. George L. Biffle (Ruth Ellen Bryant)

POTATO BREAD

Yields 4 Small Loaves

1 large potato, peeled and diced
1 teaspoon salt
1 cup water
½ cup butter
½ cup sugar
½ cup skimmed powdered milk
3 large eggs

2 yeast cakes
¼ cup warm water
1 teaspoon sugar
5–6 cups flour
Canned milk
Poppy seeds or
toasted sesame seeds

Bring potato, salt and water to a boil. Cook until tender. Remove from heat and add butter and sugar. Beat mixture until potato is mashed. Add powdered milk and eggs and beat until well blended. Dissolve yeast in warm water with sugar. Add to the potato mixture. Stir in enough flour to make a soft dough. Knead until smooth and elastic. Place in greased bowl. Cover. Let rise until doubled. Punch down; divide dough into 4 equal portions. Divide 4 portions into 3 pieces and braid into loaves. Place loaves on flat, greased cookie sheet. Brush with canned milk and sprinkle with seeds. Let rise again. Bake in 325° oven for 15-30 minutes until golden. May be frozen after baking.

Mrs. Royce Kelly (Charlotte Smith)

NO EXCUSE BREAD

Yields 2 Loaves

2 packages dry yeast
2 teaspoons salt
⅓ cup oil or margarine
⅓ cup honey or sugar
⅔ cup powdered milk

2 eggs
1 cup wheat germ
2 cups warm water
3 cups white flour
3 cups whole wheat flour

Place salt, oil, honey, powdered milk, eggs, wheat germ, warm water and 3 cups of whole wheat flour into a large mixing bowl. Beat 5-10 minutes at medium speed on electric mixer. By hand, stir in 2 cups white flour (no need to make it smooth). Sprinkle 1 cup of white flour into a 10-inch circle on kneading surface. Pour dough onto surface and knead with fingertips until dough stiffens. Then knead an additional 5-10 minutes until dough is smooth and elastic. Add more flour if necessary. Cover with plastic wrap and a folded towel. Let sit for 20 minutes. Divide into 2 equal portions. Roll each portion with a rolling pin into an 8x12 inch rectangle. Roll up dough toward you in jelly roll fashion and fold over ends, sealing well. Place in greased bread pans. Cover with plastic wrap. Refrigerate 2-24 hours. Take out 10 minutes before baking. Puncture with toothpick. Bake in 350° oven for 35-40 minutes.

Mrs. Ed. Harrell (Carol Flynn)

PIONEER BREAD

Yields 1 Loaf

1 package active dry yeast
¾ cup warm water (105°-115°)
3 tablespoons sugar
2 teaspoons salt
1 egg

3 tablespoons shortening
½ cup yellow cornmeal
2-2½ cups flour
Butter, softened

Dissolve yeast in water in large bowl. Add sugar, salt, egg, shortening, ⅓ cup cornmeal and 1 cup flour. Blend on low speed for ½ minute, scraping bowl constantly. Beat on medium speed for 2 minutes scraping bowl occasionally. Stir in enough remaining flour to make dough easy to handle. Turn dough onto lightly floured surface and knead until smooth and elastic; about 5 minutes. Place in greased bowl. Turn greased side up. Cover and let rise in a warm place until doubled; about 1-1½ hours. Punch down. Roll into 18x9 inch rectangle. Fold crosswise into thirds, overlapping the sides. Roll up, beginning at one of the open ends. Place in greased loaf pan seam side down. Brush lightly with butter. Sprinkle with cornmeal. Let rise until doubled; about 50-60 minutes. Bake in 400° oven for 25-30 minutes. Remove from pan and cool on wire rack.

Mrs. Jacob P. Laeufer (Sue Dye)

SOUR CREAM BREAD

2 cartons (8 ounces each)
    of sour cream
½ cup butter
½ cup sugar
1 teaspoon salt

2 packages yeast
⅓ cup warm water
4½–5 cups sifted flour,
    divided
3 eggs

Heat sour cream being careful not to boil. Pour it over butter, sugar and salt. Cool. Dissolve yeast in warm water and add to sour cream mixture. Add 2 cups of flour. Add eggs, beating well. Then add remaining flour to make dough stiff. Let rise until doubled. Beat the dough. Spoon into 8 greased, 1 pound 4 ounce cans, until each is half full. Let rise again. Bake in 350° oven until tops are brown.

Mrs. Joe Pritchard (Marianne Gerding)

This may be baked in five miniature bread pans.

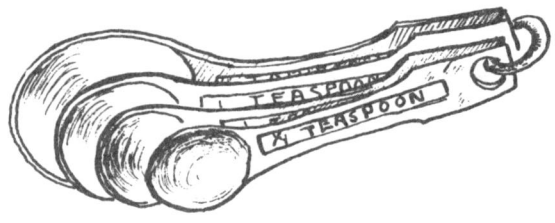

REFRIGERATOR ROLL DOUGH

Yields 2 Dozen

¾ cup hot water
½ cup sugar
1 tablespoon salt
3 tablespoons shortening

1 cup warm water (115°)
2 packages yeast
1 egg, beaten
6 cups flour

Mix hot water, sugar, salt and shortening in the pan used to heat the water and cool to lukewarm. Mix 1 cup warm water and yeast together. Combine mixtures. Add the egg and 3 cups flour to mixture and beat until smooth. Add the remaining 3 cups flour and mix with hands. Place in a greased bowl. Brush top with soft shortening. Cover with foil and store in refrigerator. This will keep one week. Make 2 or 24 rolls at a time. It may be used before it is stored in refrigerator. Let rolls rise about 1 hour if dough is cold; about 30 minutes if not. Shape rolls as pan rolls, Parker House rolls, fan tails, etc. Brush tops with melted butter that has cooled. Cover with dish towel and let rise. Bake in 375-400° oven for 15-20 minutes.

Mrs. Danny Conklin (Carolyn Kerns)

An easy recipe that requires no kneading.

ROLLS

Yields 5-6 Dozen

3 cups milk
5 tablespoons sugar
1 teaspoon salt
⅔ cup butter
2 yeast cakes or 2 packages
   dry yeast

⅓ cup water
1 egg
6½ cups Gold Medal flour

Scald milk. Add sugar, salt and butter. Dissolve yeast in water and add to milk mixture when it is lukewarm. Add egg and flour. Start mixing flour and milk with electric mixer and finish by hand. Let rise once or twice and refrigerate before forming rolls. Shape into Parker House rolls. For cinnamon rolls, roll out dough and sprinkle with cinnamon and sugar. Pour melted butter over the dough. Roll the dough up and cut into small pieces. This is my mother's recipe. The secret of her success is that she uses real butter. She cuts the rolls with a cutter or can, dips them in melted butter on both sides, and folds them over so they are easy to open.

Mrs. Edward Scott (Elizabeth Fields)

WHOLE WHEAT ROLLS

Yields 1-1½ Dozen

½ cup boiling water
½ cup safflower oil
¼ cup honey
1 teaspoon salt
1 package yeast

½ cup warm water
1 egg, well beaten
3 cups stone ground
   whole wheat flour

Pour boiling water over safflower oil, honey and salt. Let stand until lukewarm. Dissolve yeast in warm water. Add yeast, egg and flour to oil mixture. Beat well. Refrigerate 2 hours or longer. Knead on floured board. Roll out to large rectangle (approximately 12x16 inches). Brush with melted butter. Roll up like jelly roll. Slice into rolls ½ inch thick. Lay in buttered Pyrex pan 9x13 inches. Brush tops with butter. Let rise until double. Bake in 400° oven for 20 minutes.

Mrs. Tom Cambridge (Norma Taggart)

YEAST ROLLS (REFRIGERATOR)

Yields 40 Rolls

4 cups warm water
⅔ cup margarine
⅔ cup sugar

1 tablespoon plus
1 teaspoon salt
2 packages dry yeast
11 cups flour (approximately)

Combine water, margarine, sugar and salt in a large bowl. Add yeast. Do not stir. When yeast has dissolved, add flour until smooth. Knead until a smooth ball forms. Place in a bowl and spread margarine over the top to prevent drying. Place in refrigerator to rise. Bake in 400° oven until done. Dough will keep in refrigerator for two weeks. These can be made into crescent rolls, buns, cinnamon rolls or coffee cake. Baking time depends on type of roll.

Mrs. Stidham Reid (Cynthia Stidham)

ALL-BRAN ROLLS

Yields 20 Rolls

1 cup shortening
1 cup boiling water
¾ cup sugar
1 cup All-Bran cereal
2 teaspoons salt

2 cakes yeast
1 cup warm water
1 egg, beaten
5 cups flour

Combine first five ingredients. Stir until shortening is melted. Cool. Dissolve yeast in warm water. Add yeast mixture and egg to cooled All-Bran. Mix thoroughly. Add 2 cups flour and mix. Stir in remaining flour. Cover and place in refrigerator overnight. Shape into rolls and let rise at least 1 hour or until double in bulk. Bake in 400° oven for 10-15 minutes or until brown.

Mrs. William A. Sansing (Betty Ann Troutman)

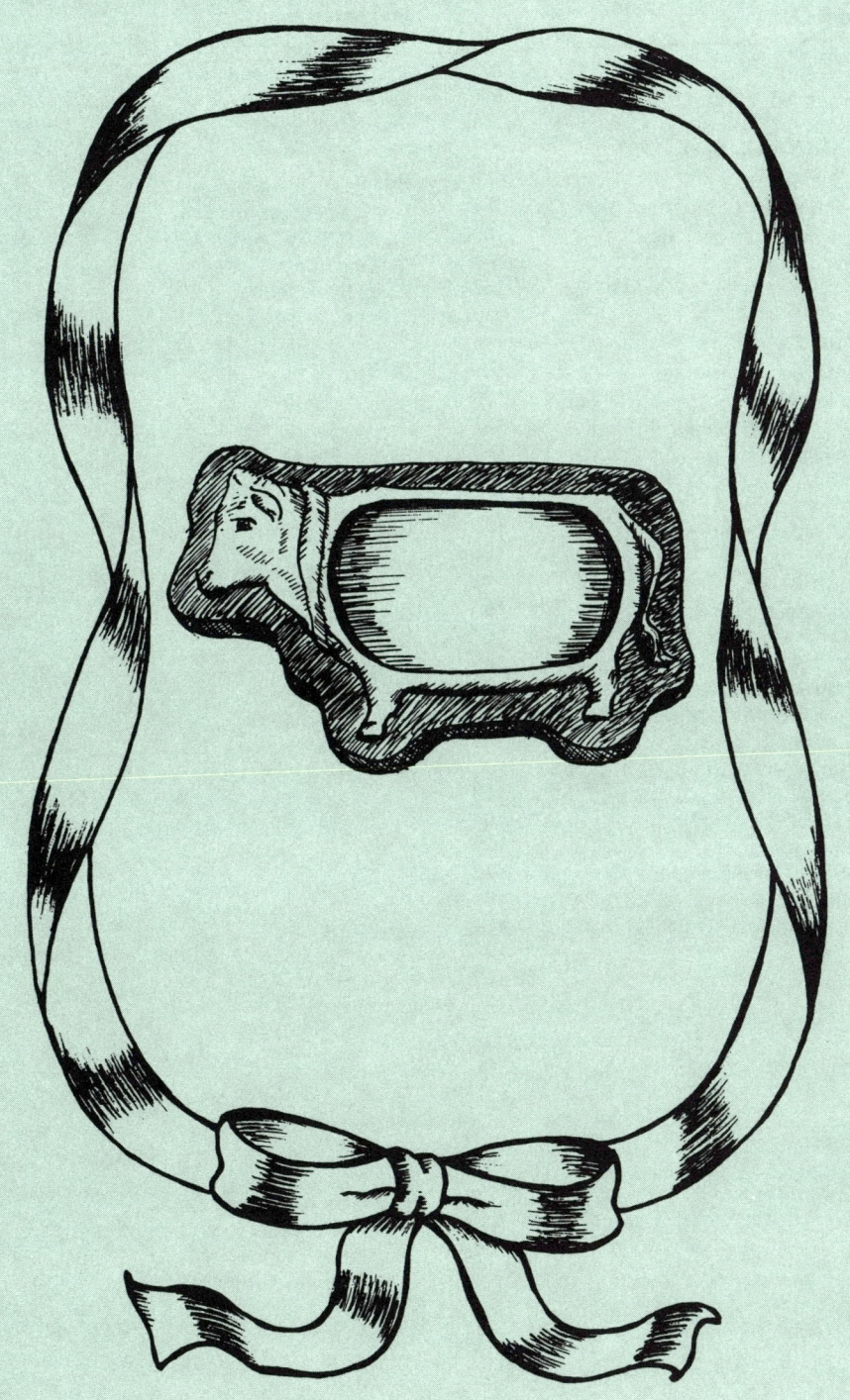

BEEF WELLINGTON

Serves 12

5-6 pound beef tenderloin
3 large pieces suet
2 tablespoons butter
5 chicken livers
½ pound fresh mushrooms,
  finely chopped

¼ pound cooked ham,
  finely ground
1 tablespoon catsup
⅓ cup sherry
1 egg yolk, beaten
  reserve white
2 packages Pepperidge
  Farm patty shells

DAY BEFORE SERVING

Preheat oven to 425°. Place beef on wire rack in shallow, open roasting pan. Place suet over beef. Insert meat thermometer into center of beef. Roast to desired degree of doneness or a little underdone. Remove beef from oven. Remove suet. Cool. Refrigerate. Sauté chicken livers in butter until brown. Chop them finely. Return to skillet and add next four ingredients. Cook 10 minutes stirring occasionally. Cool. Stir in egg yolk. Refrigerate. Place patty shells in refrigerator to thaw.

ONE HOUR BEFORE SERVING

On floured board roll out patty shells into pastry square about 18x18 inches or large enough to enclose beef. Spread chicken liver mixture over entire beef. Enclose beef in pastry. Pinch seam side together with hands wet with water. Place seam side down on greased cookie sheet. Quickly brush pastry with slightly beaten egg white. Bake in a 425° oven for 30 minutes or until pastry is golden brown. Carefully move to serving platter. Garnish & serve.

Mrs. John Chambers (Susie Morris)

RELAXED ROAST

Standing rib roast
at room temperature

Salt and pepper

Place roast, fat side up, in a shallow pan and roast in a pre-heated oven at 425° for 7 minutes a pound. Turn off oven and *do not open* door for 6 hours. Salt and pepper roast which will be very rare throughout.

Reheat for serving if desired

Mrs. Greg E. Mitchell (Julie Bowers)

STEAK AND BACON TOURNEDOS

Serves 4

1-1½ pounds beef flank steak
  Non-seasoned meat
  tenderizer
½ pound bacon
1 teaspoon garlic salt
½ teaspoon freshly ground
  pepper

2 tablespoons parsley
1¾ ounce envelope
  hollandaise sauce mix
  or homemade
¼ teaspoon dried tarragon,
  crushed

Pound flank steak to even thickness, about ½ inch thick. Sprinkle with tenderizer. Meanwhile, cook bacon until almost done, but not crisp. Sprinkle steak with garlic salt and pepper. Score steak diagonally making diamond-shaped cuts. Place bacon strips lengthwise on steak. Sprinkle with parsley. Roll up jelly roll fashion, starting at narrow end. Skewer with wooden picks. Cut in 1 inch slices with serrated knife. Grill over medium coals 15 minutes, turning once, or pan fry. Can be served with prepared hollandaise mixed with tarragon.

Mrs. Stephen Curtis (Jerre Lewis)

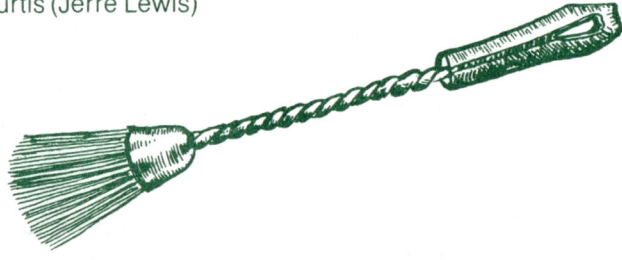

PEPPER STEAK

Serves 6

¼ cup oil
1 clove garlic, crushed
1 teaspoon salt
1 teaspoon ginger
½ teaspoon pepper
1½ pounds sirloin,
  cut in thin strips
2 large green peppers, sliced
4 green onions, cut into
  1 inch pieces
2 large onions, sliced

¼ cup cold water
¼ cup soy sauce
1 tablespoon cornstarch
½ teaspoon sugar
½ cup beef bouillon
1 can (6 ounces)
  water chestnuts, sliced
  Cooked rice

In hot oil, sauté garlic, salt, ginger and pepper until garlic is golden. Add meat and brown 2 minutes. Remove meat. Add green pepper and onions. Cook 3 minutes. Mix water with cornstarch and add to mixture. Return meat to pan and add all remaining ingredients. Simmer until thick. Serve over hot rice.

Mrs. Royce Kelly (Charlotte Smith)

KOREAN STEAK

Serves 4

1 cup Kikkoman soy sauce
½ cup oil
¼ cup sugar
3 green onion tops, chopped

1 tablespoon cracked pepper
5 garlic cloves, split in half
1–1½ pounds steak

Mix together the first six ingredients. Marinate the meat in this mixture for 2-3 hours. Remove the meat and grill on a barbecue pit.

Mrs. Robert F. Jolley (Soeurette Seay)

PRIME RIB
á la DEWEY

Serves 6

1 prime rib roast
(8 pounds)

Salt and pepper to taste

Salt and pepper outside of roast. Place on meat rack in cold oven. Turn oven on to 500°. Cook exactly 1 hour without opening oven door. Turn the heat off and leave roast in tightly closed oven 2 more hours. This will produce a juicy, well-seared very rare roast. Add one more hour "sitting time" for a roast with medium to medium-well meat with a medium-rare to rare center. *Do not open oven door until all time has passed.* This method works well with any large cut of meat you may wish to serve rare, such as tenderloin of beef. This can even be used for less expensive rolled roasts. Sliced very thin, it is delicious!

Mrs. Paul E. Cizon (Laurie Gray)

PEPPER STEAK

Serves 4

1–1½ pounds steak
2 tablespoons cooking oil
  Salt, pepper and garlic salt
  or powder to taste
1 tablespoon sugar
2 tablespoons wine vinegar

3–5 tablespoons soy sauce
1 cup water
1 or 2 green peppers,
  cut in strips
1 or 2 tomatoes cut in wedges
1 can (16 ounces) chunk
  pineapple with juice

Brown steak in cooking oil; season to taste. Add sugar, vinegar, soy sauce and water. Add remaining ingredients. Cook slowly for at least 30 minutes. Tastes better if you cook it for 2 hours.

Good served over rice.

Mrs. Edward Scott (Elizabeth Fields)

JAPANESE KABOB

Yields 4-6

¾ cup soy sauce
¼ cup brown sugar
¼ teaspoon
monosodium glutamate
½ teaspoon salt
½ teaspoon ginger

1 clove garlic, crushed
2 pounds sirloin, cut in
1 inch cubes (or smaller
pieces if for appetizer)
Pineapple chunks

Combine soy sauce, brown sugar, monosodium glutamate, salt, ginger and garlic. Marinate steak cubes for at least 2 hours. Skewer steak cubes and pineapple chunks alternately. Broil in oven or on charcoal grill. Cook to desired doneness.

Mrs. Hugh A. Sticksel (Pan Purdy)

EASY SHERRIED BEEF

Serves 6-8

3 pounds beef stew meat
1 can mushrooms or
½ pound fresh mushrooms
1 can water chestnuts, sliced

2 cans Golden Mushroom
soup
1 cup sherry
1 package onion soup mix
Noodles or rice

Mix all ingredients together, except noodles. Place in tightly covered casserole and bake in 300°-350° oven for 4 hours. A crockpot can be used if desired. This recipe can be cooked at a lower temperature for a longer time to improve the flavor. Serve over noodles or rice.

Mrs. Terry A. Curtis (Melonye Lowe)

BEEF BOURGUIGNONNE OR FRENCH BEEF STEW

Serves 4-6

3 pounds beef, cubed
2 tablespoons butter
Flour
1½ cups red wine
1 can beef consommé
Salt and pepper

2 bay leaves
Pinch of thyme
Parsley, chopped
1 carrot, sliced
1½ cups mushrooms, sliced
6 small white onions

Lightly brown meat in butter in large heavy pot. Remove from heat and drain. Sprinkle meat with flour, stirring and heating until light brown. Add remaining ingredients and simmer several hours until meat is tender and sauce thickens.

Serve with hot crusty French bread and crisp green salad.

Mrs. John Mozola (Jo Rush)

158

EASY BURGUNDY BEEF STEW

Serves 4

1½ pounds chuck roast or stew meat cut in 2 inch cubes
½ cup burgundy, claret or other red dinner wine
1 can (10½ ounces) condensed consommé, undiluted
1 medium onion, sliced

1½ teaspoons salt
¼ teaspoon pepper
¼ cup flour
¼ cup fine dry bread crumbs
½ teaspoon Kitchen Bouquet if desired

Preheat oven to 300°. Combine beef, wine, consommé, onion, Kitchen Bouquet, salt and pepper in 2 quart casserole. No pre-browning necessary. Mix flour with crumbs. Stir into beef mixture. Bake about 3 hours or until beef is tender.

Mrs. E.T. Manning (Sally Manning)

FRANCISCO HUNGARIAN GOULASH

Serves 10-12

3 onions, finely chopped
3 cloves garlic, finely chopped
2 pounds beef, cubed
2 pounds pork, cubed
½ pound butter

2 quarts sauerkraut, washed in hot water
1 can (16 ounces) tomatoes
1 cup sour cream
1 can (4 ounces) mushrooms

Cook onions and garlic in butter for 10 minutes. Add meats and cook for 2 hours. Add kraut and tomatoes and cook an additional hour. Just before serving, add the sour cream and mushrooms. This can be frozen.

Mrs. Greg E. Mitchell (Julie Bowers)

POT ROAST, QUICK AND EASY

Serves 6-8

4-5 pounds boneless beef roast (rump, English or chuck)
1 envelope Lipton Mushroom-Beef or Mushroom Soup mix
¼ teaspoon salt

1 jar (7¾ ounces) junior (baby) apricots with tapioca
2 medium onions, sliced
1 tablespoon lemon juice
2 tablespoons chopped parsley

Place roast on rack in roaster or Dutch oven. Combine next 3 ingredients and pour over roast. Cover tightly and cook in 325° oven for 2 hours. Add onion and lemon juice to liquid in pan. Cover and cook 1 hour longer, until tender.

Remove roast to warm platter. If thicker gravy is desired, combine 2 tablespoons flour and a small amount of warm water and stir into liquid. Top with chopped parsley.

Mrs. Sue Alice Stokes (Sue Alice Simpson)

BAR-B-QUE BEEF

Serves 6-10

1 medium size roast
1 medium onion,
finely chopped
1 tablespoon shortening
or butter
1½ cups chili sauce
3 tablespoons vinegar

3 tablespoons brown sugar
½ teaspoon dry mustard
1 teaspoon chili powder
1 teaspoon Worcestershire
sauce

Cook roast until tender. In saucepan sauté chopped onion in butter or shortening. Add rest of ingredients except roast. Cook sauce for 5 minutes over medium heat. Chop up roast, add sauce and simmer 15-20 minutes. Serve heated on buns for sandwiches. Freezes well.

Mrs. Phil Lee Jordan (Hilda Henderson)

SPICY BEEF BRISKET

Serves 6-8

1 4-5 pound beef brisket
2 tablespoons liquid smoke
1 teaspoon celery salt
1 teaspoon onion salt

1 teaspoon garlic salt
3 tablespoons
Worcestershire sauce
½ teaspoon cracked pepper

Make a paste of liquid smoke, celery, onion and garlic salt. Rub into brisket. Wrap with heavy duty foil and seal tightly. Refrigerate overnight. Next day sprinkle with Worcestershire sauce and pepper. Reseal carefully and bake in 250° oven for 5 hours.

Slice thinly. Serve on rye bread or buns. Good with cole slaw. Reheats well in own sauce.

Mrs. William A. Sansing (Betty Ann Troutman)

BAR-B-QUED BRISKET

Serves 8-10

5–7 pound brisket
2 tablespoons liquid smoke
Garlic salt or onion salt
6 tablespoons butter
1 bottle (14 ounces) catsup
4 tablespoons
Worcestershire sauce

1 tablespoon liquid smoke
Pinch salt and pepper
2 teaspoons celery seed
½ cup water
3 tablespoons brown sugar
3 teaspoons dry mustard

Rub 2 tablespoons liquid smoke over brisket and refrigerate overnight. Season with garlic salt or onion salt and wrap in foil. Bake 5 hours in 300° oven. Refrigerate and slice when cool. Combine remaining ingredients. Bake brisket in sauce for 30 minutes in 350° oven.

Mrs. Dottie Francis (Dottie Cherry)

JAY TAYLOR'S CORNED BEEF BRISKET

Serves 8-10

5 pounds beef brisket
4 quarts water
1½ cups coarse salt
½ ounce saltpeter
1 tablespoon brown sugar

12 bay leaves
2 tablespoons pickling spices
10 cloves garlic, divided
1 onion, sliced
½ cup vinegar

Combine water, salt, saltpeter, brown sugar, 9 bay leaves, 8 cloves garlic and pickling spices. Boil 5 minutes, then cool. Put brisket in stone crock and add above mixture, to cover meat completely. Put weight on meat to hold under. Stretch muslin tightly over top of crock, leaving a small gap for air. Let stand in cool place for two weeks. Rinse meat well and put in Dutch oven. Add fresh water to a level of one inch above meat. Add 3 bay leaves, 2 cloves chopped garlic, onion and vinegar. Bring to a boil, then simmer for 2½-3 hours. Let stand, covered, for 30 minutes. Drain and serve.

BARBEQUED HAMBURGERS

Serves 8-12

2 pounds hamburger
1 small green pepper, chopped
1 large onion, chopped
1 bottle (14 ounces) catsup
1 tablespoon brown sugar

½ – ¾ cup vinegar
1 tablespoon prepared mustard
Salt and pepper
1 teaspoon liquid smoke (optional)

Lightly brown meat. Add green pepper, onion and saute. Add remaining ingredients and simmer one hour. Serve on hamburger buns (particularly good on Roman Meal buns). Freezes well.

Mrs. Alan Roberson (Sandie Davis)

ROAST BEEF PIE

Serves 6

3 cups leftover roast beef cut
　into ¾ inch cubes
3 tablespoons bacon fat
1 clove garlic, mashed
1 large onion, sliced
¼ pound mushrooms, sliced
3 tablespoons flour
2½ cups consommé

½ cup dry red wine
　Salt and pepper to taste
1 teaspoon minced parsley
½ teaspoon marjoram
1 teaspoon Worcestershire
　sauce
　Canned biscuits
2 tablespoons sherry

Cut leftover roast beef in ¾ inch cubes. Melt bacon fat in heavy skillet
and saute garlic, onion, and mushrooms until onion begins to take on
color. Stir in meat and sauté lightly a few minutes. Sprinkle flour over all
and mix well. Pour on consommé and red wine, stirring constantly until
sauce is smooth and thickened. Season to taste. Add parsley, marjoram
and Worcestershire sauce. Pour into a 2-quart casserole and top with
biscuits. Bake at 450 degrees for 10-15 minutes or until biscuits are
golden brown. Before serving, pour sherry into the pie through openings
between biscuits. Serve with rice.

Mrs. Elayne Shults (Elayne Steele)

CHEESEBURGER PIE

Serves 6-8

　Pastry for 9-inch one crust
　pie, unbaked
1 pound ground beef
½ teaspoon ground oregano
½ cup crushed soda crackers

1 can (8 ounces)
　tomato sauce
¼ cup chopped onion
¼ cup chopped green pepper
¾ teaspoon salt
¼ teaspoon pepper

Brown meat. Drain. Stir in remaining ingredients and pour into pastry
shell.

CHEESE TOPPING

1 egg, beaten
¼ cup milk
½ teaspoon salt
½ teaspoon dry mustard

½ teaspoon
　Worcestershire sauce
2 cups grated
　Cheddar cheese

Combine egg and milk. Stir in seasonings and cheese. Spread topping
evenly over filling. Cover edge of pie crust with 2-3 inch strip of aluminum
foil to prevent excessive browning. Remove foil the last 15 minutes of
baking. Bake in 425° oven for 30 minutes.

Mrs. Victor W. Shawgo (Mary Kaye Dolan)

162

JUDY KRACKE'S ITALIAN BEEF PIE

Serves 6-8

1 pound ground beef
1 can (8 ounces) mushrooms, drained
2 packages (10 ounces each) frozen chopped spinach, cooked and drained
1 cup sour cream
1 can condensed celery soup
½ teaspoon garlic salt
½ cup chopped onion
2 unbaked pie shells
  Grated cheese

Brown meat and add mushrooms. Drain. Add remaining ingredients. Pour into pie shells. Cover with cheese. Bake in 350° oven for 35-45 minutes.

HAMBURGER QUICHE

Serves 6-8

1 unbaked 9 inch pastry shell
½ pound ground meat
½ cup real mayonnaise
½ cup milk
2 eggs
1 tablespoon cornstarch
1½ cups (½ pound) grated Cheddar or Swiss cheese
⅓ cup chopped green onion
  Dash pepper

Brown meat in skillet, drain, and set aside. Blend next four ingredients until smooth. Stir in meat, cheese, onion and pepper. Turn into pastry shell and bake in 350° oven for 30-40 minutes (or until a knife comes out clean). This is also good cold. Can also add green chilies.

Mrs. S.T. Curtis (Zallee Williams)

MEATBALLS AND WINE SAUCE

Serves 4

1 pound lean round steak, ground
½ cup milk
½ teaspoon Beau Monde
1 cup soft bread crumbs
  Salt and pepper
  Bacon Drippings
2 rounded tablespoons flour
1 can (10 ounces) consomme
½ cup dry sherry

Mix meat, milk, Beau Monde, crumbs, salt and pepper and shape into small balls. Brown in a small amount of bacon drippings. Place in shallow uncovered casserole. Stir flour into bacon drippings. Add consommé and sherry. Bring to a boil. Pour over meatballs. Bake in 350° oven for 40 minutes. Serve with tiny noodles.

Mrs. Horace Wilson (Kathrine Kirk)

MEAT LOAF

Yields 2 Loaves

2 pounds ground beef
1 onion, chopped
2 eggs

Salt and Pepper
½ (8 ounce can) tomato sauce
1 cup bread crumbs

Mix all ingredients and shape into 2 loaves. Place in 9x13 inch pan. Pour sauce over loaf and bake in a 350° oven for one hour.

SAUCE

½ cup tomato sauce
2 tablespoons mustard
1 tablespoon brown sugar

2 tablespoons vinegar
½ cup water

Mix all ingredients together.

Mrs. Lee Walsh (Phyllis Schupp)

SWEET AND SOUR MEATBALLS

Serves 6

½ cup water
½ cup bread crumbs
1 cup water chestnuts, chopped

1 pound ground chuck
2 egg yolks or
1 whole egg

Combine meatball ingredients and shape into 1 inch balls. Bake in 350° oven for 12 minutes or until done.

SAUCE

⅓ cup orange marmalade
1 clove garlic, minced
¼ cup soy sauce

2 tablespoons lemon juice
⅓ cup water

Combine sauce ingredients in saucepan and heat. Combine meatballs and sauce in chafing dish and serve hot. These can be made ahead and frozen.

Mrs. Robert Green (Kathryn Pitts)

Can be made into smaller balls and served as an appetizer.

ITALIAN STUFFED GREEN PEPPERS

Serves 4

4 green peppers, cut
in half lengthwise
1 pound lean ground beef
1 teaspoon instant onion
¾ cup Pepperidge Farm
Seasoned Stuffing
1 can (8 ounces) tomato sauce
1 teaspoon salt
½ teaspoon pepper
½ teaspoon oregano
½ cup ricotta or
small curd cottage cheese
1 tablespoon dried parsley
1 package (10 ounces)
Mozzarella cheese, sliced
or grated

Remove pepper seeds and membranes and parboil in salted water 5 minutes. Drain. Brown ground beef until it loses its pink color. Drain excess fat. Add onion, stuffing, tomato sauce, salt, pepper, oregano, cottage cheese and parsley. Mix well. Stuff the pepper halves with meat mixture and place in 9x14 inch dish. Bake uncovered in 375° oven for 20 minutes. Top each pepper half with Mozzarella cheese. Bake for 10 minutes longer or until cheese is melted.

Good for both low calorie and low cholesterol diets.

Mrs. William A. Anthony (Katie Billman)

STUFFED GREEN PEPPERS

Serves 6

3 medium green peppers,
halved
¼ cup chopped onion
¾ pound ground beef
1 cup cooked rice
1 can (8 ounces) tomato sauce
¼ cup water
1 egg
1 teaspoon salt
Black pepper to taste

Remove seed section from cut green peppers. Place pepper halves on a paper towel and cook 6 minutes with microwave energy. Cook onions and beef in an 8-inch round glass cake dish about 4 minutes or until all pink has left meat. Stir several times during cooking. Cook rice according to directions on box. Mix tomato sauce with water. Combine onion and beef mixture with cooked rice, half of tomato mixture, egg, salt and black pepper. Stuff pepper halves and place in a 2-quart glass utility dish. Pour remaining tomato sauce over top and place waxed paper over the dish. Cook with microwave energy 10 minutes.

This recipe is also good with chopped black olives and mushrooms added or grated cheese on top.

Mrs. Larry D. Williams (Sharon Stevenson)

BEEF FRITTATA

Serves 8-10

2 tablespoons olive oil
1 onion, diced
1 garlic clove, minced
1½ pounds lean ground beef
¾ teaspoon oregano
½ teaspoon marjoram
½ teaspoon thyme

Salt and pepper to taste
5 eggs
1½ teaspoons cornstarch
4 cups milk
1 cup chopped spinach, cooked and drained

In large skillet, sauté onion and garlic in olive oil. Add ground meat, oregano, marjoram, thyme, salt and pepper. Cook until meat is browned. Pour off excess grease. In large bowl beat eggs with cornstarch. Stir in milk. Add beef mixture and spinach. Stir and season with salt and pepper. Pour mixture into lightly greased 3-quart baking dish. Bake in 350° oven for 55 minutes.

Mrs. H. Boyd Hinton (Maelyn Latham)

Good with green chili salsa.

ITALIAN SPAGHETTI SAUCE

Serves 8

2 pounds ground beef
3 tablespoons olive oil
2 onions, chopped
4 cloves garlic, finely chopped
    Handful chopped parsley
½ teaspoon sweet basil

¼ teaspoon oregano
    Salt
    Pepper
½ teaspoon Italian seasoning
2 cans (16 ounces each) tomatoes
1 can (6 ounces) tomato paste

Sauté meat in olive oil until color is gone. Add remaining ingredients except tomatoes and tomato paste. Sauté until onions are clear, not brown. Add tomatoes and tomato paste. Simmer slowly for 2 hours. Add water if mixture gets too thick.

Serve over spaghetti cooked about 10-12 minutes in boiling salt water. Sprinkle with Parmesan cheese. May be frozen.

Mrs. James E. Herring (Margaret Johnson)

166

ITALIAN CASSEROLE

Serves 6-8

1 pound ground chuck
2 cloves garlic, finely sliced
2 tablespoons cooking oil
1 small onion, finely chopped
1 cup celery, finely chopped
1 can (4 ounces) mushrooms
1 package (6 ounces)
  wide egg noodles

1 can (16 ounces) tomatoes
1 can (6 ounces) tomato paste
½ teaspoon whole oregano
½ teaspoon salt
⅛ teaspoon coarse ground
  black pepper
½ cup burgundy wine
  Grated Parmesan cheese
  Stuffed green olives

Brown ground meat with garlic in oil, drain. Sauté onions, celery and mushrooms over low heat, until vegetables are soft (about 10 minutes). Cook noodles according to package directions; drain and add to meat and vegetables. Add tomatoes, tomato paste, oregano, salt, pepper and wine. Pour into greased 2 quart casserole. Top with grated cheese and dot with sliced olives. Bake in 350° oven for ½ hour uncovered. Cover casserole and bake an additional 15 minutes.

Mrs. A.W. SoRelle, III (Judy Jolley)

BOBOTIE
(African Beef
Casserole)

Serves 8

2 pounds ground beef
1 onion, chopped
2 slices white bread,
  soaked in milk
  and squeezed
2 tablespoons sugar
2 tablespoons vinegar
2 tablespoons butter, melted
1 tablespoon apricot glaze,
  or more

2 eggs, beaten
1 teaspoon salt
2 teaspoons curry powder
½ teaspoon ground ginger
⅔ cup raisins
2 tablespoons lemon juice
2 tablespoons butter
1 cup milk
1 egg

In a large bowl combine beef, onion and bread. Add next ten ingredients. Mix thoroughly. Press mixture into 1½ quart casserole. Dot with butter. Bake in 300° oven for 30 minutes. Combine milk and egg. Pour over meat. Return to oven for an additional 15 minutes or until set. Serve with yellow rice.

Mrs. Witcher Rawlins (Ginger Witcher)

PASTA DOUGH

1½ cups unsifted all-purpose flour
1 egg
1 egg white
1 tablespoon olive oil
1 teaspoon salt
Few drops of water

Form well in flour. Put egg, egg white, oil and salt in center of well. Begin mixing. Knead, adding a few drops of water to make a ball. Knead for 10 minutes until dough is shiny and elastic. Divide into two parts. Wrap the dough in wax paper and let rest 10 minutes before rolling it. Can use pasta machine to roll. It takes a good while to roll paper thin by hand.

Cut into 2x3 inch rectangles (measure with ruler).

Bring 6 to 8 quarts of water and 1 tablespoon of salt to a rolling boil over high heat in a large pot. Drop in the pieces of pasta and stir gently with a wooden spoon for a few moments to be sure they don't stick to one another or the pot. Return the water to a boil and cook pasta over high heat, stirring once in a while, for 5 minutes or until tender but not soft. Drain, cool slightly, then spread pasta pieces side by side on cloth towels to dry.

It is possible to substitute crepes for the pasta if time is of the essence.

CREPES

2 eggs
1 cup milk
1 cup flour, sifted
1 tablespoon butter, melted
Pinch of salt

Beat eggs well, then add milk, flour, butter, and salt. (Can mix all in a blender until smooth). Cover and let stand at least 30 minutes. Heat 7" skillet or crepe pan, butter it with paper towel. Pour in several tablespoons of batter, then quickly tilt to spread batter evenly. When edges lift easily from pan turn and lightly brown other side. Remove to plate or waxed paper and butter pan again before repeating.

FILLING

2 tablespoons olive oil	**1 pound round steak**
¼ cup finely chopped onion	**ground twice**
1 teaspoon finely chopped	**5 tablespoons grated**
garlic	**Parmesan cheese**
1 package (10 ounces) frozen	**2 tablespoons heavy cream**
chopped spinach, thawed,	**2 eggs, lightly beaten**
squeezed completely dry	**½ teaspoon dried oregano**
and chopped again	**Salt**
2 tablespoons butter	**Freshly ground pepper**

Heat olive oil in 10 inch enameled skillet. Add onions and garlic. Sauté over moderate heat stirring often until soft, but not brown. Stir in spinach and cook, stirring constantly for 3-4 minutes or until dry. Spinach will stick lightly to the pan. Transfer to large bowl. Melt 1 tablespoon butter in the same skillet and lightly brown the beef. Add meat to the onion-spinach mixture. Add Parmesan, cream, eggs, and oregano. Mix gently, but thoroughly. Salt and pepper to taste.
168

BALSAMELLA (Sauce)

4 tablespoons butter
4 tablespoons flour
1 cup milk

1 cup heavy cream
1 teaspoon salt
⅛ teaspoon white pepper

Melt butter in a heavy 3 quart sauce pan. Remove pan from heat and stir in flour. Pour in milk and cream all at once, whisking constantly. Return pan to high heat and cook, stirring constantly with whisk. When the sauce comes to a boil and is smooth, reduce the heat. Simmer, still stirring for 2 to 3 minutes longer until it is thick enough to coat the wires of the whisk heavily. Remove from heat and season with salt and white pepper.

TOPPING

3 cans (8 ounces each)
  tomato sauce
4 tablespoons grated
  Parmesan cheese

2 tablespoons butter
  cut in small pieces

Assembling and Baking the Cannelloni

Preheat oven to 375°. Place 1 tablespoon of filling on the bottom third of each pasta rectangle and roll. Pour a film of tomato sauce into two 10x14 inch baking dishes. Lay the cannelloni side by side in one layer on tomato sauce. Pour the balsamella over it and spoon the rest of the tomato sauce on top. Top with 4 tablespoons grated cheese and dot with 2 tablespoons of butter. Bake uncovered for 20 minutes or until cheese is melted and sauce bubbles. Broil for 30 seconds to brown top. May be frozen before baking, but thaw well before baking.

LASAGNA
Serves 12

2-3 pounds ground beef
1 large onion, chopped
1 clove garlic, minced
1 stalk celery, chopped
1 teaspoon Italian
  seasoning
  Salt and pepper
  to taste

3 cans (8 ounces each)
  tomato sauce
1 package (8 ounces) lasagna
  noodles, cooked and rinsed
1 carton (24 ounces)
  cottage cheese
½ pound mozzarella or
  Swiss cheese
½ pound mellow
  Cheddar cheese

Brown meat, onion, garlic, celery, Italian seasoning, salt and pepper in a large skillet. Add tomato sauce. Simmer about 10 minutes over medium heat. Line the bottom of 11x6 inch pan with 1/3 of the noodles. Add 1/3 meat sauce, 1/3 cottage cheese, 1/3 mozzarella and 1/3 Cheddar cheese. Repeat twice. Bake 30-40 minutes in 350° oven. May be frozen.

Mrs. John V. Cottle (Sammye Kinkade)

LASAGNA NAPOLI

Serves 12

- 4 cups (2 large) finely chopped onions
- 5 cloves garlic, minced
- ⅓ cup vegetable oil
- ¼ cup minus 2 tablespoons olive oil
- 2 cans (2.8 ounces each) mushrooms
- 2 cans (1 pound 3 ounces each) Italian tomatoes or 10 fresh tomatoes
- 2 cans (6 ounces each) tomato paste
- 4 teaspoons salt
- 1 tablespoon oregano
- 3 teaspoons basil
- 1 teaspoon pepper
- 1 tablespoon sugar
- 1 tablespoon chili powder
- 4 tablespoons parsley
- 2 pounds lean ground beef
- 2 cans (4½ ounces each) chopped black olives, drained
- 2 eggs
- 2 packages (10 ounces each) frozen chopped spinach, thawed
- 2 pounds cottage or Ricotta cheese
- ½ cup Parmesan cheese
- 1 package (16 ounces) lasagna noodles, cooked according to package directions
- 1 package (3½ ounces) pepperoni, sliced (more if desired)
- 2 pounds mozzarella cheese, grated

In large skillet, lightly brown onion and garlic in vegetable and olive oil. Add mushrooms and liquid. Add next nine ingredients. Cover and simmer for several hours, until thick. Brown meat slowly in a little oil. Add to sauce. Add olives. Beat one egg and add to sauce. In a bowl, combine second egg, spinach, cottage cheese and Parmesan cheese. Layer half of each of the ingredients in a 9x12 inch baking dish in the following order: sauce, noodles, spinach mixture, pepperoni and mozzarella cheese. Repeat layers, reserving the second half of cheese. Cover and bake in a 350° oven for 45 minutes. Top with reserved cheese and return to oven for an additional 15 minutes.

Water may be added to the sauce while cooking if necessary. May be made early and stored in the refrigerator before baking. Also freezes well.

Mrs. David Kritser, III (Sally Simpson)

GREEN ENCHILADAS

Serves 6-8

1 pound ground beef
2 tablespoons oil
1 package soft corn tortillas
½ pound American cheese, grated
1 large onion, chopped
1 can (4 ounces) chopped green chilies

1 can mushroom soup
¾ soup can water
Tabasco, optional
1 teaspoon salt
Pepper to taste

Brown meat thoroughly in oil. Fry tortillas in hot oil and drain on paper towel while meat cooks. In a 9x14 inch baking dish spread alternate layers of ingredients putting salt, pepper and Tabasco on each layer according to taste. First layer tortillas, ½ of cheese, onion and ½ of green chilies. Then add tortillas, meat and chilies, and top with cheese. Dilute soup with water. Mix thoroughly and pour over casserole. Bake in 350° oven for 30 minutes. Onion can be sautéed and Tabasco left out to make casserole milder.

Mrs. Paul Fields (Barry Beck)

ENCHILADA CASSEROLE

Serves 10-12

2½ pounds ground beef
1 green pepper, chopped
1 onion, chopped
2 tablespoons chili powder
2 cans cream of mushroom soup
½ soup can of water

2 cans (4 ounces each) chopped green chilies
1 can (8 ounces) enchilada sauce, hot or mild
¼ teaspoon garlic powder
¼ cup ripe olives, chopped
1 pkg. corn tortillas, (12)
1 lb. Cheddar cheese, grated

Combine meat, pepper, onion and chili powder. Cook in a skillet over medium heat until meat is browned. Drain off excess fat. Remove from heat and add remaining ingredients, reserving cheese and tortillas. In a greased 9x12x3 inch casserole dish place a layer of tortillas, meat and cheese, ending with meat mixture. Garnish with Cheddar cheese. Refrigerate casserole for 24 hours to enhance flavor. When ready to serve, bake in a 350° oven for 45 minutes.

Mrs. Charles Rittenberry (Cynthia Lindley)

This casserole freezes very well. If frozen, let the casserole thaw partially and cook at a slightly lower temperature for a little longer than the recipe specifies.

TOSTADOS

Large crisp tostados or 2 large bags Fritos

CHILI

4 pounds coarsely
  ground beef
3 onions, chopped
2 cans (1 pound each)
  tomatoes
1 can (15 ounces)
  tomato sauce

2 cans (6 ounces each)
  tomato paste
4 tablespoons chili powder
2 tablespoons garlic salt
2 teaspoons ground camino
1 can (4 ounces)
  chopped chilies

Brown beef and drain grease. Add remaining ingredients and simmer two hours.

CONDIMENTS

1 box rice, cooked
1 pound cheese, grated
2 heads lettuce, shredded
1 large bottle Picante sauce
6-8 tomatoes, chopped

1 large can ripe olives,
  chopped
10 ounces pecans, chopped
1 package (8 ounces) coconut
  or freshly grated coconut
1 bunch green onions,
  chopped

On a serving table, place tostados, chili, and condiments in individual serving dishes. Each person makes his own tostado by stacking tostados, chili and the condiments of his choice on a plate.

Mrs. Phillip Campbell (Mary Jane Potter)

This dish is served in the Spanish community of Friona, Texas on Christmas Eve. It is called "La Comida de Fiesta Navidad." The Cookbook Committee served this to Giuliano Bugialli when he was in Amarillo teaching his Italian Cooking School.

ALLISON GUYNES' CHILI

Serves 6

4 pounds stew meat
Cooking oil
2-3 small, whole, hot red chilies (Jap)
1 tablespoon oregano
1 tablespoon crushed cumin seeds

Dash cayenne pepper
Dash Tabasco
2-3 garlic pods, chopped
1 tablespoon chili powder
2 tablespoons masa harina
Freshly ground pepper
1 tablespoon salt

Trim fat from stew meat. Cut meat into bite-sized pieces. Brown meat in oil in heavy iron pot. Add chilies and enough water to cover meat. Simmer for 30 minutes. Add next seven ingredients. Bring to a boil. Reduce heat and simmer another 30 minutes. Remove pan from heat. Stir in masa harina. Simmer an additional 30 minutes. Taste frequently, and add fresh ground pepper, salt, and other seasonings to taste.

QUICK CHILI

Serves 4-6

1 pound ground beef
1 teaspoon salt
¼ cup minced onion
¼ cup minced green pepper
1 package (1 ⅝ ounces) chili seasoning mix

¼ teaspoon crushed oregano
½ cup beer
1 can (1 pound) tomato wedges
1 can (1 pound) red kidney beans
Sour cream
Minced green onion

In a large skillet, brown ground beef. Season with salt. Add onion and green pepper. Cook until vegetables are tender. Add chili seasoning, oregano and beer. Stir in tomatoes and beans. Mix well. Heat to boiling. Reduce heat and simmer, uncovered for 10 minutes. Stir occasionally. Top with sour cream and a sprinkling of green onions.

Mrs. Richard Bittman (Agnes Leachman)

GOURMET CHILI

Serves 8-10

1½ pounds ground beef, salted
1 large onion, chopped
4 strips bacon, fried crisp and diced
2 cans (4 ounces each) mushroom stems and pieces
1 can (1 pound) tomatoes
1 can (8 ounces) tomato juice

1 can (1 pound) pinto beans
1 can (1 pound) red beans
1 can (1 pound) chili beans
1 package Williams Chili Seasoning
¼ cup parsley flakes
¼ cup chives

Brown beef with onion and bacon. Add mushrooms. Add remaining ingredients. Cook slowly for 1½ hours.

Mrs. Greg F. Mitchell (Julie Bowers)

CHILI

Serves 16

- 1 3 ounce bottle Gebhardt's chili powder
- 3 tablespoons flour
- 2 tablespoons salt
- ¾ teaspoon pepper
- 1 rounded tablespoon camino seed, mashed
- 1 tablespoon oregano, optional
- 6 pounds chili meat, coarsely ground
- 3 tablespoons butter
- 2 large onions, chopped
- 3 tablespoons finely chopped garlic
- 8 dry chili peppers, boiled and pressed through a sieve
- 1½ quarts cooked pinto beans

Combine chili powder, flour, salt, pepper, camino seed, oregano and mix with the chili meat until all dry ingredients adhere to it. Melt butter in large pan. Sauté onions and garlic until transparent. Add meat and sauté slowly until brown, about 20 minutes. Add 2 cups hot water and simmer for 3-4 hours. While chili is simmering, add the chili peppers. Add water as needed so that chili is consistency of soup. Serve with cooked pinto beans. Can be frozen.

Mrs. James E. Herring (Margaret Johnson)

CURRIED BEEF WITH PEAS

Serves 4

- 2 tablespoons butter
- 2 medium onions, chopped
- 1½ pounds ground beef
- 1½ teaspoons salt
  Pepper to taste
- 2 teaspoons curry powder
- 1 tablespoon ground coriander
- ¼ teaspoon crushed red pepper flakes
- 1 cup (8 ounces) canned peeled tomatoes
- 1½ cups fresh peas or
- 1 package (10 ounces) frozen peas

Melt butter in skillet, sauté onions until limp. Add meat, salt, pepper, curry powder, coriander and pepper flakes. Cook 10 minutes; add tomatoes and simmer covered for 20 minutes. Add peas, cover and simmer until peas are tender. Serve with rice.

Mrs. Jim Southern (Linda Ann Duke)

ROBERT'S CASSEROLE   Serves 8-10

1 package (8 ounces)
  egg noodles
1 pound ground beef
2 cans (8 ounces each)
  tomato sauce
1 large package cream cheese
1 pint cottage cheese
⅓ cup chopped green onions
  with tops
1 tablespoon shortening
¼ cup sour cream
1 tablespoon chopped
  green pepper

Cook noodles according to package directions. Brown beef. Add tomato sauce and set aside. Combine remaining ingredients. Layer using half of noodles and half of meat. Repeat. Cover with cheese mixture. Bake uncovered in 350° oven for 30 minutes.

Mrs. Robert D. Forrester (Carol Tate)

VEAL PICCATA   Serves 4

8 pieces of veal scaloppine
½ cup flour
1 teaspoon salt
¼ teaspoon freshly
  ground pepper
  Paprika
4 tablespoons butter
1 tablespoon olive oil
3 tablespoons white wine
  Juice of 1 lemon
3 tablespoons capers
  (optional)
3 tablespoons (minced)
  fresh parsley

Pound veal until thin. Combine flour, salt, pepper and paprika in a bag. Add veal and coat well. Heat butter and oil in large skillet until bubbly. Sauté veal 2-3 minutes on each side. Place on warm platter and keep in warm oven. Add wine to skillet scraping bottom to loosen any browned bits. Add lemon juice and cook for 1-2 minutes. Place veal back in skillet. Add capers and parsley, stirring quickly. Immediately remove veal and pour sauce over it.

Mrs. Glen Brosier (Kay Wagner)

Four boned chicken breasts, skinned and halved may be substituted for veal.

LEMON VEAL   Serves 4

1 pound thinly sliced veal,
  floured
2 tablespoons butter
2 tablespoons cooking oil
1 beef bouillon cube
¼ cup dry white wine
1 egg, beaten
¼ cup lemon juice
1 tablespoon parsley
¼ teaspoon salt

Brown veal in butter and oil. Remove from pan and add remaining ingredients to the pan drippings. Pour over veal and serve.

Mrs. Edward Morris (Gladys McGlasson)

VEAL CUTLETS PARMESAN

Serves 4

4 veal cutlets, 4 ounces each
   sliced thin (may use
   tenderized steaks)
   Salt
   Pepper
2 eggs, beaten with 2
   tablespoons cold water
   Bread or cracker crumbs

   Oil
½ pound mozzarella cheese,
   sliced
1 can (8 ounces) tomato sauce
¼ teaspoon oregano
   Parmesan cheese, grated

Pound cutlets with meat tenderizer. Sprinkle with salt and pepper. Dip in flour and pat off excess. Dip in beaten eggs and then in crumbs. Pat crumbs well into cutlets. Chill for an hour or so, if possible. This will help crumbs adhere to cutlets. Pour oil to depth of ¼ inch into electric skillet and heat to 300°. Sauté until light brown on both sides. Place in greased shallow pan. Place cheese over cutlets. Bring tomato sauce and oregano to a boil. Pour over meat. Sprinkle with Parmesan cheese. Bake in a 350° oven for 20-25 minutes, or until Parmesan cheese is browned. This may be made a day or two early or frozen.

Mrs. Hugh E. Hagen (Susan Sanders)

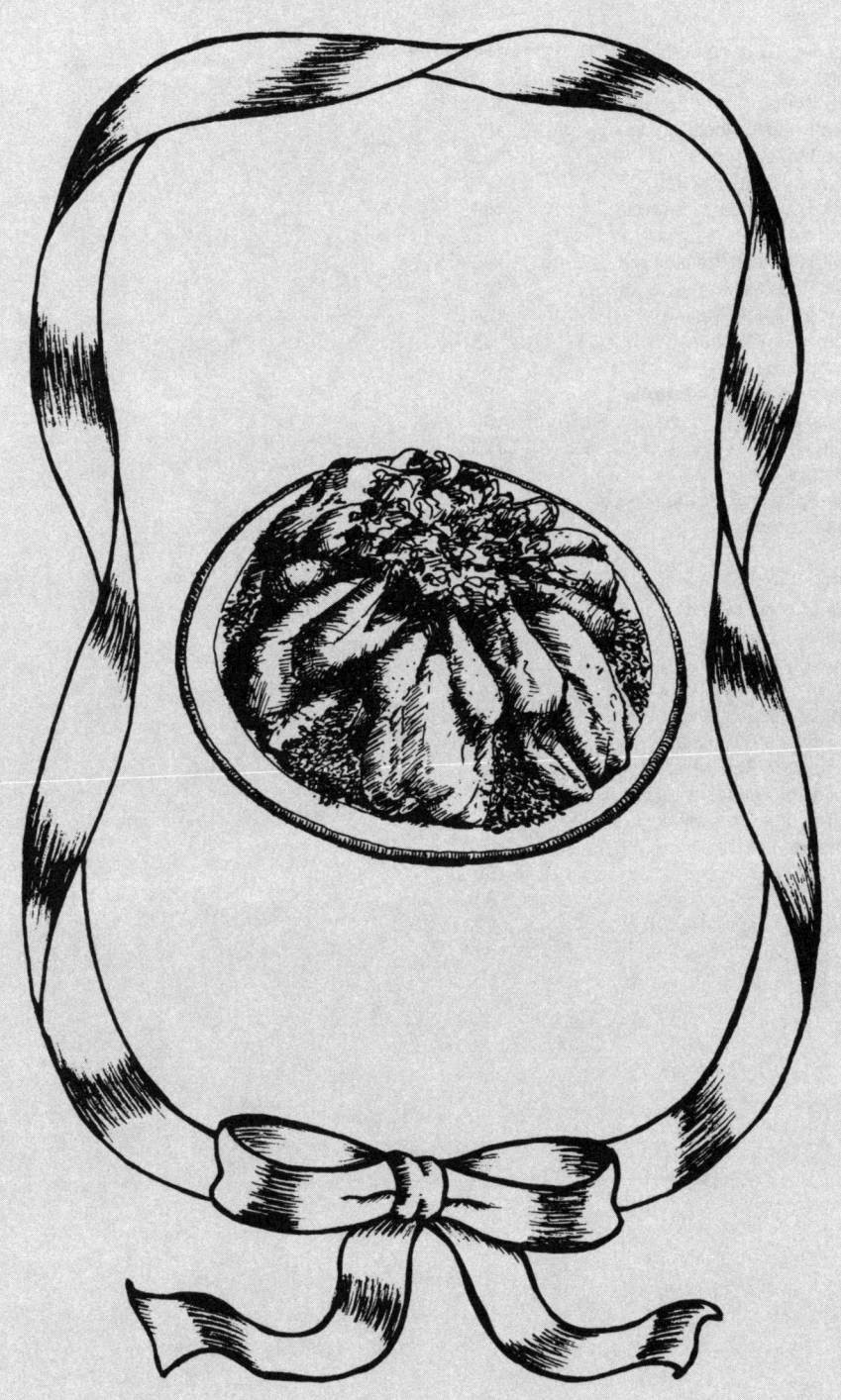

Fish

Game

CRAB LASAGNA

Serves 6-8

- 1 package (8 ounces) Lasagna noodles
- 1 tablespoon oil
- 4 quarts water
- 2 cans cream of shrimp soup
- 14 ounces king crab
- 2 cups cottage cheese
- 8 ounces cream cheese
- 1 egg
- 1 cup chopped onion
- 2 teaspoons basil
- 1 teaspoon salt
- ¼ teaspoon pepper
- 1 cup Cheddar cheese, shredded
- 4 medium tomatoes, peeled and sliced
- 2 teaspoons sugar
- 2 tablespoons Parmesan cheese

Boil noodles in oil and water about 15 minutes. Drain. Combine soup and crab in medium saucepan and heat until bubbly. Combine next seven ingredients. In baking dish, layer ⅓ of the noodles, ½ of the cheese mixture, ⅓ of the Cheddar cheese, ⅓ of the noodles, all of the crab sauce, ⅓ Cheddar cheese, ⅓ noodles, ½ cheese mixture and ⅓ Cheddar cheese. Top with tomatoes and sprinkle with sugar. Cook 15 minutes in 350° oven. Sprinkle with Parmesan cheese. Bake for an additional 45 minutes. Let stand 15 minutes before serving. The flavors have a chance to blend and it's even better if it's made the day before serving.

Mrs. Roy Mason (Diane Whittington)

CRAB MOLD

Serves 10-15

- 1 can undiluted cream of mushroom soup
- 1 envelope unflavored gelatin
- ½ cup cold water
- 1 package (8 ounces) cream cheese
- 1 cup Hellmann's mayonnaise
- ¾ cup diced celery
- 1 teaspoon grated onion
- 1 can (6 ounces) shredded crab
- 1½ teaspoons Worcestershire sauce
- Tabasco sauce, if desired
- Sliced cucumbers

Heat soup. Mix gelatin and water. Add to soup. Combine cream cheese and mayonnaise. Add to soup mixture. Add the next five ingredients. Pour into a one quart mold and refrigerate until firm. Garnish with cucumbers. Freezes well.

Mrs. Greg E. Mitchell (Julie Bowers)

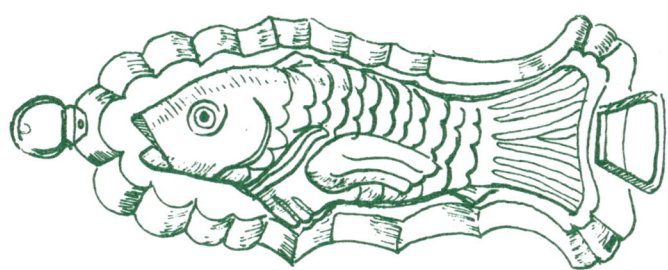

HOT SPICY
CRACKED CRAB

Serves 2-4

1 frozen Dungness crab or
   Alaskan king crab legs in
   shell, thawed, cleaned
   and cracked
½ cup butter
3–4 cloves garlic, crushed

1 can (14 ounces)
   chicken broth
1½ cups dry vermouth
   Juice of 1 lemon
1 teaspoon cracked
   peppercorns
2 tablespoons
   Worcestershire sauce

Combine butter, garlic, chicken broth and 1 cup Vermouth, lemon juice, pepper, and Worcestershire sauce. Simmer 10 minutes. Add crab. Bring to a boil. Gently steam for 10-15 minutes. Add ½ cup Vermouth before serving.

Mrs. Richard H. Forrester (Judy Bolton)

MARY'S
CRABMEAT CASSEROLE

Serves 4

1 pound crabmeat
1⅓ cups mayonnaise
2 cups fresh bread crumbs
1 small onion, minced
1 can (8½ ounces)
   water chestnuts

½ pound mushrooms
1 dash salad herbs
5 hard boiled eggs, sliced
   Salt and pepper
   Crushed cornflakes

Mix first nine ingredients gently. Pour into buttered casserole. Sprinkle with crushed cornflakes. Bake in 350° oven for 1 hour. May be served in individual shells.

Mrs. Robert D. Forrester (Carol Tate)

DEEP-FRIED
HALIBUT CHUNKS

Serves 2-4

1 cup sifted flour
1 teaspoon baking soda
½ teaspoon salt
1 tablespoon sugar

1 egg
¾ cup buttermilk
   Halibut, about 1 pound

Combine first six ingredients and beat well. Cut fish into 1 inch squares. Dip into batter. Fry in oil heated to 380° for about 5 minutes.

Mrs. Hugh E. Hagen (Susan Sanders)

SCALLOPED OYSTERS

Serves 4

½ cup stale bread crumbs
1 cup cracker crumbs
½ cup melted butter
1 pint oysters

Salt and pepper, to taste
4 tablespoons oyster liquor
2 tablespoons cream
Mace or nutmeg (optional)

Mix bread and cracker crumbs. Stir in butter. Spread a thin layer in the bottom of buttered shallow baking dish. Cover with oysters and sprinkle with salt and pepper. Add one-half each: oyster liquor and cream. Repeat. Cover top with remaining crumbs. Bake in 375° oven for 30 minutes. Never use more than 2 layers of oysters. A sprinkle of mace or nutmeg to each layer is good. Sherry may be substituted in place of cream.

Mrs. Herb Greiner (Kay Thomson)

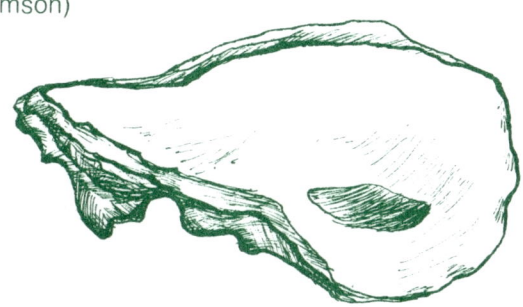

COQUILLES ST. JACQUES (Scallops)

Serves 6

1 pound mushrooms, sliced
2 tablespoons butter
1 pound scallops
  (cut up, if too large)
¾ cup dry vermouth

¼ cup water
1 bay leaf
½ teaspoon salt
⅛ teaspoon white pepper
Bread crumbs

Sauté mushrooms briefly in butter. In another saucepan, place scallops with vermouth, water, bay leaf, salt and pepper and bring to a boil. Simmer 5 minutes. Drain, reserving 1 cup broth.

WHITE SAUCE

3 tablespoons butter
3 tablespoons flour

1 cup reserved broth
1 cup light cream

Melt butter in saucepan. Blend flour into melted butter. Add broth and cream gradually. Cook until slightly thick and smooth. Add mushrooms and scallops. Spoon into 6 seafood shells. Top with buttered bread crumbs and bake in 400° oven for 10 minutes.

Mrs. George Parr (Zua Gae Warner)

SHRIMP
Á LA JACQUES

Serves 10

3 cups thick white sauce
10 egg yolks
2 jiggers of white wine
3 pounds cooked shrimp,
    cut into bite-sized pieces

1½ teaspoons garlic butter
    Salt to taste
2 packages Gouda cheese
    (10 slices)
    Lemon juice and additional
    garlic butter
10 seashells or shell dishes

Make white sauce. Add egg yolks, stirring quickly. Add wine and shrimp. Stir in butter and salt. Put mixture into shells and top with cheese. Brown under broiler. Just before serving add more garlic butter, if desired, and a dash of lemon juice to each. Serve piping hot.

Mrs. Michael Campbell (Maggie Larson)

SHRIMP AND RICE
CASSEROLE

Serves 8-10

1 cup wild rice
1 cup white rice
3 tablespoons butter
1 cup chopped celery
    small onion, chopped
1 cup shrimp

1 cup crab
2 cans mushroom soup
1 cup almonds
    Parsley
    Grated cheese
    Bread crumbs

Cook rice according to directions on package. Sauté celery and onion in butter. Combine with rice, shrimp, crab, soup and nuts in a buttered 2 quart casserole. Sprinkle with parsley, cheese and crumbs. Bake in a 350° oven for 40 minutes.

Mrs. Bill Stevenson, Jr. (Joy Vertreese)

SHRIMP AND EGG NEWBURG

Serves 6

4 tablespoons butter
4 heaping tablespoons flour
2 cups milk
1 teaspoon grated onion
1 teaspoon parsley
¼ teaspoon paprika

¼ teaspoon salt
6 eggs, hard boiled and sliced
2 cans (7 ounces) deveined shrimp
1 tablespoon sherry
1½ cups Cheddar cheese, grated

Make white sauce with first three ingredients. Add onion, parsley, paprika and salt. Cook a few minutes stirring constantly. Add sherry. Slice eggs into 8x11 inch flat casserole dish. Layer shrimp over eggs. Pour white sauce over all and top with cheese. Bake in 350° oven for 20 minutes. Good served over rice.

Mrs. Edward Morris (Gladys McGlasson)

SHRIMP BISQUE

Serves 6

2 cans frozen shrimp soup
Liquid from mushrooms
½ cup coffee cream
½ roll garlic cheese
2 packages frozen shrimp, raw
1 can (3 ounces) mushrooms
½ teaspoon salt

Dash curry powder
1 package (10 ounces) frozen English peas
½ teaspoon Accent
Pepper
Sherry or vermouth to taste

Heat soup, liquid, cream and cheese. Add remaining ingredients. Cook about 5 minutes and allow seasoning to be absorbed by shrimp. If a thicker sauce is desired, omit liquid from mushrooms. Serve on rice.

Canned shrimp soup can be used if frozen is unavailable.

Mrs. Robert Green (Kathryn Pitts)

SHRIMP CREOLE

Serves 4

2 tablespoons bacon drippings
1 large onion, chopped
¾ green pepper, chopped
3 stalks celery, chopped
3 pods garlic, chopped

1 can (28 ounces) tomatoes
Salt and pepper to taste
2 tablespoons sugar
1 cup water
1 pound boiled shrimp
Rice

Melt bacon drippings in hot skillet. Add onion, green pepper, celery and garlic. Sauté until onion is brown. Add tomatoes, salt and pepper. Add sugar and simmer for 15 minutes. Then add water and shrimp. Cook in Dutch oven for 30 minutes. Serve on rice.

Mrs. Jack Hughes (Leona Allen)

SEAFOOD CREOLE TULANE

Serves 6

2 tablespoons butter
2 small onions, chopped
2 or 3 green onions and tops, chopped
1 clove garlic, finely minced
½ green pepper, chopped
½ cup celery, chopped
1½ tablespoons flour
1 can (1 pound 14 ounces) whole tomatoes
1 teaspoon salt

1 teaspoon sugar, white or brown
2 bay leaves
½ teaspoon thyme
¼ teaspoon allspice
1 tablespoon Worcestershire sauce
¼ teaspoon Tabasco sauce
2 pounds fresh shrimp
1 cup fresh crabmeat
2 tablespoons parsley flakes

Melt butter in large skillet. Add onions, green onions, garlic, green peppers and celery. Cook until tender but not brown. Blend in flour. Add tomatoes and seasonings. Simmer 15 minutes. Add seafood and simmer 15 minutes longer. Sprinkle with parsley flakes. Serve hot over cooked rice.

Mrs. Vance Suffield (Martha Bowman)

SHRIMP SOUFFLE

Serves 4-6

2 cups shrimp, boiled and peeled
1½ cups milk, scalded
1 cup soft bread crumbs
¼ cup butter, melted
2 eggs
2 tablespoons pimientos, chopped

1½ tablespoons chopped onion
1½ cups grated American cheese
1 teaspoon salt
½ teaspoon pepper
1 teaspoon paprika
1 teaspoon chopped parsley

Cut shrimp into bite-sized pieces and set aside in a mixing bowl. Pour scalded milk over bread crumbs and butter. Stir in eggs. Pour this mixture over shrimp. Add remaining ingredients and stir well. Pour into a small greased casserole. Bake in 325° oven for 1-1½ hours. May be prepared ahead and put in oven at last minute.

Mrs. Anne Reid (Anne Ansley)

FRIED TROUT

1 can (5.33 ounces)
   evaporated milk
1 teaspoon salt
1 egg

¼ teaspoon pepper
1 cup cracker meal (Nabisco)
¼ cup flour
10 small trout

Mix first four ingredients. In separate bowl, combine cracker meal and flour. Dip fish in milk mixture and roll in meal and flour mixture. Deep fry fish.

Mrs. Thomas A. Bunkley (Myra Anne Stanley)

POACHED TROUT
WITH
PONTCHARTRAIN SAUCE   Serves 4

Trout or Halibut
   (approximately 4
   medium trout)
1½ tablespoons butter, melted
2 tablespoons finely
   chopped celery
2 tablespoons finely chopped
   onion or chives
1 tablespoon parsley flakes

1 teaspoon
   Worcestershire sauce
1 cup cream or
   evaporated milk
2 tablespoons capers
½ teaspoon paprika
2–3 dashes Tabasco
   White seedless grapes

Heat fish on both sides in butter in 300° oven. Combine next eight ingredients to make a sauce. Pour half this sauce over the heated fish. Cover and poach 20-30 minutes until fish flakes. Pour remaining sauce over fish on serving platter. Garnish with grapes.

Mrs. Vance Suffield (Martha Bowman)

TUNA-SPINACH
CASSEROLE   Serves 4-6

1 package (10 ounces) frozen
   spinach or 1 can, drained
1 can (10 ounces)
   tuna fish, drained
2 tablespoons
   Parmesan cheese

2 tablespoons lemon juice
¼ cup diced onion
   Salt and pepper
   Garlic
   Mayonnaise to moisten

Mix all ingredients and put into 4 or 6 greased seafood shells. Sprinkle with more Parmesan cheese. Bake in 325° oven for 30 minutes until hot and bubbly.

Mrs. James A. Besselman (Lynn Curtis)

TUNA SUPREME

Serves 6-8

2 cans (7 ounces each)
   white tuna
1 medium onion, chopped
1 medium green pepper,
   chopped
1 can tomato soup
1 cup half and half

2 cans (4 ounces each)
   mushrooms
2 whole pimientos, chopped
   (optional)
4 tablespoons
   Major Gray's chutney
   Rice

Pour boiling water over tuna and drain thoroughly. Sauté the onion and green pepper in butter. Combine. Add next four ingredients. Cook 45 minutes. Add chutney. Simmer 10 more minutes.

Serve over rice.

Mrs. Gene Edwards (Elaine Johnson)

DOVE

Serves 6-8

16 doves
   Pepper
   Morton's Nature's
   Seasoning
   Flour
½ cup corn oil

½ cup chopped green onion
½ pound whole
   fresh mushrooms
1½ cup sauterne
¼ cup chopped
   fresh parsley

Shake dove in bag with seasonings and flour. Brown in oil in electric skillet. Add mushrooms and onions, and sauté. Add wine, cover, and simmer about 1½ hours until very tender. Baste several times while cooking. Add parsley before serving. More wine may be added to gravy to thin if desired.

Mrs. Don T. Curtis (Suzanne Stokes)

JAY TAYLOR'S CHESAPEAKE BARBEQUED DUCK

Serves 4

½ pound butter
½ cup catsup
1 tablespoon sugar
1½ tablespoons lemon juice
1 tablespoon
   Worcestershire sauce

Ground pepper to taste
1 teaspoon salt
1 clove garlic, pressed
1 small onion, chopped
½ teaspoon Tabasco

Combine all ingredients and simmer, covered for 5 minutes. Split two ducks in halves and flatten with side of cleaver. Place on rack in flat baking pan and bake in 375° oven for 1 hour. Baste every 10 minutes with barbeque sauce. Turn and cook other side 1 hour. Continue basting.

WILD DUCK

Serves 4

4 wild duck breasts
  Salt and pepper

½ cup light Karo
1 tablespoon Kitchen Bouquet

Rub duck breasts with salt and pepper. Mix Karo with Kitchen Bouquet and baste ducks with mixture. Bake in 500° oven for 20-25 minutes.

Mrs. John Whinery (Mary Van Vliet)

GAME BIRDS

Quail, chukar, doves,
pheasant, or combination
of these
Bacon
Onion

Flour
Salt and pepper
Wine
Water

Allow two birds per person, except pheasant. Cut pheasant in 4 pieces and allow 2 pieces per person. Fry bacon in skillet and remove. Saute onion in bacon grease and remove. Flour birds and brown well in same skillet. Cover birds with bacon and onion. Salt and pepper well. Pour water into skillet ¼ inch deep. Cover. Bake one hour in 325° oven. Add wine and cook one more hour. Keep birds moist as they cook, adding water or wine as needed. If birds are young and tender, they need not cook full 2 hours. If cooking dove, use burgundy. Otherwise, use white wine.

Mrs. James Upchurch (Nancy Brown)

BAKED
CORNISH HENS

Serves 6

1 box of Chicken Rice-a-Roni
6 Cornish hens

  Butter
1 can (6 ounces)
  orange juice concentrate

Prepare Rice-a-Roni according to directions on the box. Use mixture to stuff the hens. Place in baking dish. Bake in 350° oven for 1½ hours. Baste with butter every 15 minutes for the first hour. Then baste with undiluted orange juice.

Mrs. David Waitt (Nancy Longtin)

SMOKED GAME HENS   Serves 4

4 **Rock Cornish game hens**
  Salt and pepper to taste
1 **stick butter, melted**

4 **tablespoons**
  Worcestershire sauce
2 **cloves garlic, mashed**

Wash hens. Salt and pepper to taste. Combine butter, Worcestershire sauce and garlic. Pour over hens and marinate 2-3 hours. Cook outdoors in covered smoker 6-7 hours.

Delicious with tossed salad, wild rice and hot bread.

Mrs. George Green (Rosemary McMurtry)

GOLDEN GOOSE FOR TEN ON CHRISTMAS EVE

1 **10-12 pound goose**
  Salt and pepper
½ **lemon**
1 **head cabbage, shredded**
  and chopped
6 **apples, chopped**
1 **lemon, peeled**
1 **cup raisins**
1 **teaspoon thyme**

1 **teaspoon chervil**
1 **teaspoon sage**
1 **teaspoon allspice**
1 **cup parsley leaves**
1 **cup Madeira wine with**
½ **cup lemon juice**
1 **cup white wine**

Salt and pepper goose and rub with some lemon. Prick all over with a fork and roast in 475° oven for one hour. (The fat is reduced by the hour's baking in a hot oven.) Then remove and let cool. Blanch cabbage for one minute. Drain. Add apples, lemon, raisins and toss. Add condiments, wine, salt and pepper. Stuff cooled goose and put back in roasting pan. Cook in 350° oven 20 minutes per pound or until juices are clear yellow and goose is golden.

This is good with wild rice and red burgundy.

Mrs. Stanley Marsh, 3 (Wendy O'Brien)

PHEASANT IN SAUCE

Serves 8

4 pheasants
1 stick butter
¾ cup chopped onion
2 cans (2 ounces each)
   mushrooms, sliced buttons
1 tablespoon flour
½ cup milk

½ cup water
¼ cup parsley
   Pinch of thyme
   Salt and pepper, to taste
½ pint sour cream (optional)
   Paprika

Split breasts. Separate legs and thighs. Brown in butter. Place in a large baking dish. Sauté onion and mushrooms in remaining butter in same skillet. Add flour. Add milk and water to make a thin gravy. Add parsley, thyme, salt and pepper. Pour gravy over pheasant. Bake covered for 1½ hours in a 325° oven. Add sour cream. Return to oven and bake until bubbly. Add paprika for color. Let sour cream reach room temperature before adding to prevent curdling.

Mrs. Paul Fields (Barry Beck)

QUAIL RICHELIEU

Serves 3-4

6 quail
   Salt and pepper
   Pinch of allspice
2 tablespoons lemon juice,
   strained
2 tablespoons onion,
   finely chopped
2 large bay leaves
4 or 5 ground peppercorns
6 grape leaves

   Salt pork
¾ cup carrots, finely chopped
¾ cup celery, finely chopped
¾ cup onion, finely chopped
¾ cup mushrooms,
   finely chopped
1½ cups chicken stock
2 teaspoons butter
1 teaspoon flour

Clean quail and truss legs close to the body. Sprinkle birds with salt and pepper. Add next five ingredients and marinate for 2 hours. Wrap birds in grape leaves and then in large slices of salt pork. Tie with string. Heat roasting pan to 450° oven. Roast birds 5 minutes on each side and back. (Total of 15 minutes). Discard pork. Remove birds to casserole and set aside. Add a little water to the juices in the roasting pan. Cook and stir the water and juices. Parboil vegetables for 2-3 minutes. Drain and cook until tender in chicken stock. Combine butter and flour and add to quail juice and heat well. Pour sauce over birds and simmer for 4 or 5 minutes longer or cook in 350° oven for 20-30 minutes.

Mrs. David Kritser, III (Sally Simpson)

JAY TAYLOR'S
BLUE QUAIL

Serves 4

8 quail
Salt
Flour

1 stick margarine
1½ cans consomme
1¼ cups sherry, divided

Rinse and drain quail for 30 minutes on paper towels. Salt and roll in flour. Brown birds quickly in margarine in a heavy skillet. Start with ¼ stick margarine and add more as needed. As birds are browned, remove to a flat roaster type pan. Pour off some excess grease in skillet and add one can consomme and ¾ cups sherry. When this bubbles, scrape all dregs, stir, and pour over birds. Place, uncovered, in 350° oven for 30-40 minutes, basting every 10 minutes. Remove from oven and add ½ can consomme and ½ cup sherry. Place a sheet of foil over birds, but do not seal. Lower oven to 300° and continue cooking, basting every 10 minutes for 30 more minutes, and serve. Birds may be kept warm if covered in a 200° oven. Place on warm platter and pour sauce over birds and serve.

JAY TAYLOR'S
BOB WHITE QUAIL
OR PHEASANT

Serves 2-4

4 quail or 1 pheasant
Sweet cream
Flour
Salt and pepper

1 can undiluted chicken soup
2 tablespoons Worcestershire
Juice of 1 lemon
1 tablespoon finely
minced onion

Soak birds 30 minutes in sweet cream. Roll in flour, salt and pepper. Pan fry until brown. Place in pan and add remaining ingredients. Simmer 45 minutes under tight cover. Place on platter and cover with sauce.

QUAIL

Serves 8-10

Flour
Seasoning salt
12 quail
Shortening
1 cup apple juice

2 cups water
1 apple
1 onion
1 stick butter
1 cup sherry

Mix flour and seasoning salt. Coat quail with mixture. Brown in an iron skillet with ½ inch melted shortening. Place quail in roasting pan. Add apple juice, water, apple and onion. Cover. Bake in 350° oven for 1½-2 hours. Melt butter. Stir in sherry. Baste quail with this mixture for the last 15 minutes of baking. Serve with the juice.

Mrs. James T. Herring (Margaret Johnson)

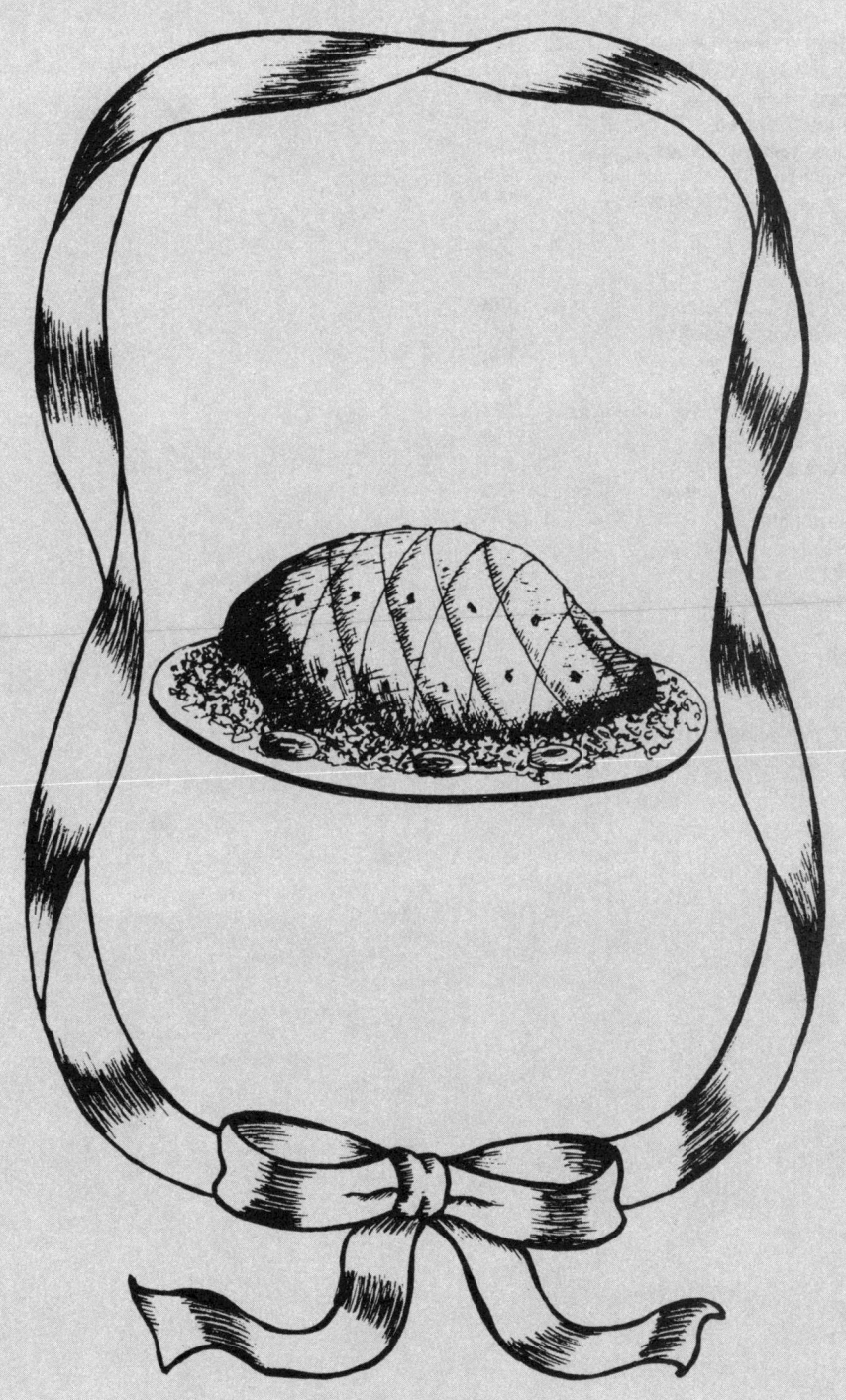

Pork

Lamb

PORK CHOPS

Pork chops
1 jar (10 ounces)
apricot preserves

1 package onion soup
(dehydrated)
1 bottle (8 ounces)
red Russian dressing

Place pork chops in shallow pan. Combine remaining ingredients and pour over pork chops. Bake in 350° oven approximately 1 hour and 15 minutes.

Mrs. Robert Green (Kathryn Pitts)

PORK AND APPLE CASSEROLE   Serves 6

2 pounds lean pork,
cut in 1½ inch cubes
2 large onions, sliced
1 pound cooking apples,
cored and sliced
Salt and pepper

3 teaspoons sage
Sugar
2 cups beef stock
2 tablespoons tomato purée

In greased casserole, layer pork and onion seasoned well with salt, pepper and sage. Add sliced apples and sprinkle with sugar. Repeat layers until all meat is used. Combine stock and purée and pour into casserole. Cover and bake in 350° oven for 2½ hours or until done.

Mrs. James A. Hedgecoke, Jr. (Sallye Dees)

PORK CHOP AND RICE CASSEROLE   Serves 4

4-6 pork chops
Finely ground pepper
Paprika
Hickory-smoked salt
Beau Monde seasoning
1 onion, chopped

1 tablespoon chopped
green pepper
1 cup instant rice or ¾ cup
long grain rice
1 can Swanson's
chicken broth

Trim excess fat from pork chops and use it to grease skillet. Season chops with paprika, hickory-smoked salt, and Beau Monde. Remove pieces of fat and brown chops on both sides. Add remaining ingredients. Cover. Bake in 325° oven for 1 hour.

Mrs. Terry A. Curtis (Melonye Lowe)

PORK CHOP CASEROLE

Serves 6

3 pounds pork chops
  Bacon drippings
1 clove garlic, cut
2 onions, thinly sliced
4 apples, cored and
  thickly sliced
1 jar (32 ounces)
  sauerkraut, well drained

3 tablespoons butter
3 tablespoons flour
2 cups flat beer
3 tablespoons chopped chives
3 tablespoons chopped
  parsley
  Salt and pepper

Brown pork chops in bacon drippings and set aside. Rub flameproof casserole with garlic; heat 2 tablespoons bacon drippings in casserole and add layer of onions. Cover onions with layer of apples. Set casserole over low heat until onions are wilted and apples are hot. Arrange pork chops on top and season to taste with salt and pepper. Cover with sauerkraut, cover and simmer over low heat for 20 minutes.

Make white sauce with butter, flour and flat beer, stirring until it is smooth and thickened. Add parsley and chives and pour over casserole. Bake in 350° oven for 1-1½ hours.

Natures Seasons by Morton Salt may be used instead of salt and pepper.

Mrs. Witcher Rawlins (Ginger Witcher)

PORK CHOPS WITH AMBER RICE

Yields 6

6 pork chops cut
  ¾ inch thick
  Salt and pepper

1⅓ cups instant rice
1 cup orange juice
1 can condensed
  chicken rice soup

Brown pork chops and season with salt and pepper. Place rice in greased 2 quart baking dish. Pour orange juice over rice. Arrange browned pork chops on rice. Pour soup over all. Cover and bake in 350° oven for 45 minutes. Uncover and bake 10 minutes longer.

Mrs. Victor W. Shawgo (Mary Kaye Dolan)

PORK CHOPS WITH MUSHROOM SAUCE

Serves 6

6 rib or loin pork chops
   cut ¾ inch thick
2 tablespoons shortening
1 teaspoon salt
⅛ teaspoon pepper
1 can condensed
   mushroom soup
1½ cups water

1 can (4 ounces) whole
   button mushrooms, drained
1 tablespoon minced onion
¾ cup diced green pepper
1 package (1½ ounces)
   dried onion soup

Brown chops in shortening. Pour off drippings. Season with salt and pepper. Combine remaining ingredients and pour over chops. Cover tightly and cook slowly 45-60 minutes or until done.

Mrs. Bill Gilliland (Sandra Edwards)

PORK CHOPS IN WINE

Serves 6

1 large onion, sliced
3 tablespoons butter
¼ cup butter, softened
½ teaspoon dry mustard
1½ teaspoons salt

⅛ teaspoon pepper
6 pork chops, ½-
   ¾ inches thick
1 cup dry white wine
3 tablespoons
   chopped parsley

Sauté onion in 3 tablespoons of butter in a large skillet. Drain on paper towel and set aside. Mix ¼ cup butter, mustard, salt and pepper into a paste. Spread on both sides of chops and brown. Pour off grease. Add onions and wine. Cover and simmer about 30 minutes-1 hour or until done. Sprinkle with parsley before serving.

Mrs. John Mozola (Jo Rush)

PORK TENDERS

Serves 6

½ cup flour
   Salt
   Pepper
2 pounds pork tenderloin,
   cut into 2 inch strips

1 stick butter
⅛ cup wine vinegar
2 tablespoons Grey Poupon
   mustard
½ pint whipping cream

Mix flour with salt and pepper. Dip meat in flour mixture. Brown meat in butter in an electric skillet and continue cooking at 350° for 30-40 minutes. Remove from skillet and keep warm. Using the same skillet, pour vinegar over drippings. Add mustard and cream, stirring until thick. Serve sauce over meat.

Mrs. Arthur S. Lamb (Pearlene Jenkins)

GERMAN PORK ROAST

Serves 4-6

5-6 pound pork loin roast
  Salt and pepper to taste
2 pounds canned sauerkraut,
  drained
1 large onion, chopped

1 garlic clove, sliced
1 can (6 ounces) frozen
  apple juice concentrate,
  thawed

Season roast with salt and pepper. Place on a rack in a roasting pan and brown in a preheated 500° oven for 10 minutes. Pour off excess fat. In a saucepan, heat sauerkraut and onion. Pour over the roast. Place garlic on top and pour in the apple juice. Reduce oven temperature to 200° and bake roast, covered, for 8-9 hours. Slice in thick slices and serve with sauerkraut.

Mrs. Thomas S. Thatcher (Joann Vaughn)

HAM SLICES

1 ham
4 tablespoons apple
  cider vinegar

1 teaspoon dry mustard
1 cup brown sugar

Slice ham. Add vinegar and dry mustard to brown sugar. Spread over each ham slice. Bake in a 350° oven for 30 minutes.

Mrs. Robert F. Jolley (Soeurette Seay)

HAM LOAF

Serves 6-8

1 pound ground cured ham
½ pound ground lean beef
½ pound ground lean pork
1 jar (4 ounces) pimientos
1 large onion, chopped

1 bell pepper, chopped
½ cup chopped celery
½ cup milk
1 egg
½ teaspoon salt

Mix all the above ingredients and mold into loaf.

SAUCE

⅓ cup vinegar
1½ cups water
2 teaspoons dry mustard

1 cup brown sugar
1 cup catsup

Mix ingredients in a saucepan and bring to a boil. Boil 2-3 minutes. Pour some of it over the ham loaf. Bake the loaf at 325° for 1 hour and 10-15 minutes. Baste the loaf every 20 minutes with the sauce.

Mrs. Richard Reeves (Louise Coe)

ASPARAGUS-HAM CRÊPES

Serves 6

12 crêpes
2 pounds fresh asparagus

12 slices ham, cut thin
12 slices Swiss cheese

Steam asparagus 10-15 minutes. On crêpe, layer 1 slice ham, 1 slice cheese, and 3-4 asparagus spears. Roll up crêpe. Cover with mushroom sauce. Bake in 350° oven for 20-30 minutes.

MUSHROOM SAUCE

3 tablespoons butter
3 cups sliced mushrooms
3 tablespoons flour
¾ cup chicken broth

1 tablespoon chives
1 teaspoon horseradish
¼ cup cream

Melt butter and sauté mushrooms for 3-5 minutes. Stir in flour. Add broth, chives and horseradish. When thick, stir in cream.

Mrs. John Mozola (Jo Rush)

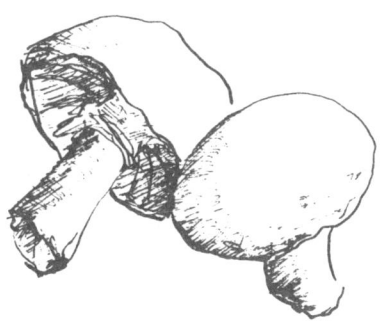

HAM-ASPARAGUS CASSEROLE

Serves 4-6

1 cup chopped ham
1 package (10 ounces) frozen asparagus, cooked and drained
2 tablespoons chopped bell pepper
2 tablespoons chopped onion
2 tablespoons chopped parsley
2 tablespoons lemon juice

2 tablespoons tapioca
1 cup grated Colby cheese
1 can cream of mushroom soup
½ cup evaporated milk
4 hard cooked eggs
½ cup bread crumbs

Combine first eight ingredients. Slice eggs and cover bottom of 1½ quart casserole with half of the sliced eggs. Top with half of the ham-asparagus mixture. Layer remaining eggs and ham-asparagus mixture. Combine soup and milk and pour over casserole. Top with bread crumbs and dot with butter. Bake in 350° oven for 30 minutes.

Mrs. Paul E. Cizon (Laurie Gray)

SAUSAGE APPLE RING
WITH SCRAMBLED EGGS   Serves 8

2 pounds bulk sausage
1½ cups cracker crumbs
2 eggs, slightly beaten
½ cup milk
¼ cup minced onion

1 cup finely chopped apples
Grated cheese
Parsley
Broiled peach halves

Combine all ingredients. Mix thoroughly. To shape, press lightly into a 6 cup ring mold. Turn into a shallow baking pan. Bake in a 350° oven for 1 hour. Drain excess fat.

Fill center with scrambled eggs. Top with grated cheese, if desired. Decorate platter with parsley and broiled peach halves.

Ring may be cooked 30 minutes the day before and refrigerated. Cook the remaining 30 minutes just before serving.

Mrs. George Parr (Zua Gae Warner)

JAY TAYLOR'S
PORK SAUSAGE
SCRAPPLE   Serves 10

½ pound bulk pork sausage
3 tablespoons chopped onion
3 tablespoons chopped celery
1½ cups cold water
1 cup enriched cornmeal

2 tablespoons flour
1 teaspoon salt
⅛ teaspoon poultry seasoning
3 cups boiling water

Pan-fry sausage, onion and celery until sausage is brown and crumbly; drain well. Combine cold water, cornmeal, flour, salt and poultry seasoning; slowly pour into boiling water stirring constantly. Return to boiling. Cover and continue cooking over low heat for 5 minutes, stirring occasionally. Add drained sausage mixture. Mix well. Pour into an 8½x4½x2½ inch loaf pan which has been rinsed with cold water. Cool slightly; cover and chill several hours or overnight. Cut chilled scrapple into ¾ inch slices. Fry on greased griddle or fry pan until golden brown on both sides. Serve with maple syrup or molasses, if desired. Garnish with sautéed apple slices and parsley.

ELIZABETH TIDWELL'S SAUSAGE-FILLED CRÊPES

Yields 16

Crêpes
- 3 eggs, beaten
- 1 cup milk
- 1 tablespoon cooking oil
- 1 cup flour
- ½ teaspoon salt

Combine eggs, milk, and oil. Add flour and salt. Beat until smooth. Pour 2 tablespoons of batter into greased 10 inch skillet; tilt. Cook on one side about 1 minute, invert on toweling. Repeat to make 16 crêpes.

Filling
- 1 pound bulk sausage
- ¼ cup chopped onion
- ½ cup shredded processed cheese
- 1 package (3 ounces) cream cheese
- ¼ teaspoon dried marjoram

Cook sausage and onion. Drain. Add remaining ingredients. Place 2 tablespoons filling down center of each crêpe and roll. Place in 11¾ x 7½ inch baking dish. Bake in 375° oven for 40 minutes. Spoon leftover sausage mixture over crêpes. Bake uncovered 5 minutes.

CABBAGE ROLLS

Serves 4-6

- 6 large cabbage leaves
- 6 tablespoons raw rice
- 1 pound lean sausage (Owens extra mild)
- Salt and pepper to taste
- 2 large onions, chopped
- 1 can (16 ounces) tomatoes, chopped

Soak cabbage leaves in hot water until limber. Wash rice several times in cold water. Shape sausage into 6 patties. Place one patty, 1 tablespoon of rice, salt and pepper in each cabbage leaf. Roll and tie securely with string. Place in flat 2 quart casserole. Combine onions and tomatoes and pour over rolls. Cover and bake in 325° oven for 2 hours.

Mrs. Dean Campbell (Lynn Stuart)

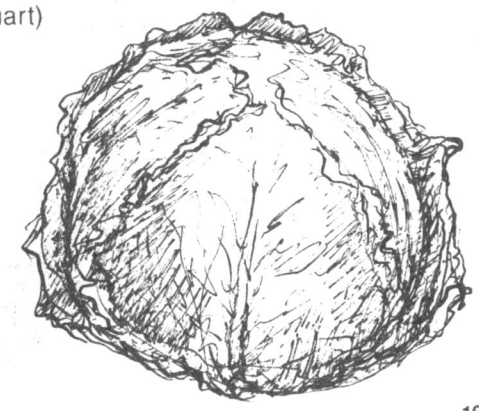

BULGARIAN STUFFED CABBAGE LEAVES

Serves 6-8

1 large cabbage
  Salt and pepper
2 pounds lean ground pork or
  mild pork sausage
  Paprika

1 onion, chopped
¼ cup butter
1 carrot, chopped
½ cup raw rice
  Tomato juice

Soak cabbage in cold water for 30 minutes. Drain; cover with boiling water for 10 minutes. Pull off 24-36 leaves. Scald again if they are stiff. Trim off coarse stem. Shred remaining cabbage and place it in a large buttered casserole in a 1½ inch layer. Season with salt and pepper. Mix pork with salt, pepper and paprika. (Sausage only needs paprika). Sauté onion in butter. Combine carrot, pork and rice. Cook over medium heat until rice is glossy and meat is browned. Add one cup water and stir until absorbed. Put 2-3 tablespoons of pork on each cabbage leaf and roll. Lay rolls folded side down on shredded cabbage. Add tomato juice until cabbage rolls are about two-thirds covered. Cover and weigh down with a plate and cook over low heat for about 1 hour. This recipe can cook longer if your guests are late in arriving and still be delicious.

Mrs. Witcher Rawlins (Ginger Witcher)

SAUSAGE CASSEROLE

Serves 10-12

2 pounds bulk sausage
1 onion, chopped
1 small green pepper,
  chopped
2 cups chopped celery
2 cups uncooked
  long grain rice

3 packages dehydrated
  chicken soup mix
9 cups boiling water
⅓ cup slivered almonds

In a large Dutch oven, brown sausage, drain. Add onion, pepper, celery, and cook until limp. Add rice, soup mix, water, almonds and cook for 45 minutes at medium heat, stirring occasionally. Freezes. Good with spicy hot sausage.

Mrs. Hugh Harmon (Jo Morgan)

LEG OF LAMB

Serves 6-8

1 leg of lamb
1 clove of garlic
Salt
Pepper
1 can tomato soup
3 apples, cored, sliced
and unpeeled

1 cup brown sugar
Juice of 1 lemon
2 medium white onions,
coarsely chopped
¼ teaspoon thyme
1 bay leaf

Rub lamb with garlic, salt and pepper. Place in roasting pan with a little water. Bake in 400° oven for 45 minutes uncovered. Combine remaining ingredients. Pour over lamb. Cook covered in 325° oven for 3 hours. Serve with mashed potatoes. Lamb should be cooked in as small a container as possible.

Mrs. Warren J. Freeman, Jr. (Celine Seay)

MOTHER'S SPECIAL LEG OF LAMB

Serves 8

5 pound leg of lamb
1 teaspoon salt
Dash pepper
2 cups water
⅓ cup Worcestershire sauce
½ cup catsup

⅓ cup water
1 tablespoon fresh
lemon juice
½ teaspoon salt
1 tablespoon sugar
1 cup water

Preheat oven to 450°. Salt and pepper lamb. Place in roaster with 2 cups water. Roast 40 minutes or until meat is brown. (Water will be almost evaporated at this point.)

Combine Worcestershire sauce, catsup, ⅓ cup water, lemon juice, ½ teaspoon salt and sugar. (Half of this mixture is for basting and half for gravy.)

Reduce oven temperature to 325°. Bake lamb for 3 hours brushing surface every 15 minutes with basting sauce. Remove lamb to a platter and keep warm while making gravy.

Spoon all fat from drippings. Add 1 cup water and second half of basting sauce to the drippings. Cook until slightly thickened, scraping sides. Serve over hot sliced lamb.

Mrs. Ed Fancher (Shirley Feierabend)

DOLMA

2 pounds ground lamb
½ cup uncooked rice
2 medium onions, chopped
1 (1 pound 3 ounce)
 can tomatoes
Salt and pepper

Accent
Garlic powder
Grape leaves
1 medium onion, sliced
1 lemon quartered

Mix lamb, rice, onions and ½ can tomatoes (reserve other half). Use seasonings according to taste. If using bottled grape leaves, drain and rinse. If using fresh grape leaves, par boil. Put 2 tablespoons of mixture in each grape leaf. Roll tightly. Pack filled grape leaves tightly in 2½ quart pan or Dutch oven. On top of leaves, put sliced onion and quartered lemon. Pour the other half of tomatoes over all. Add enough water to cover the rolled grape leaves. Bring to a boil. Cover. Simmer 2-2½ hours.

Serve with cooked rice if desired.

Mrs. Peter A. Dallas (Tricia Culp)

Chicken

Turkey

CHICKEN CORDON BLEU

Serves 6

3 large chicken breasts,
  boned, skinned and halved
  OR
6 small chicken breasts
  boned and skinned
  Salt
6 thin slices boiled ham
6 ounces natural Swiss
  cheese, cut in 6 sticks
¼ cup flour
2 tablespoons butter

½ cup water
1 teaspoon chicken flavored
  gravy base
1 can (3 ounces) broiled
  sliced mushrooms
⅓ cup sauterne
2 tablespoons flour
½ cup cold water
  Toasted almond slices

Place chicken pieces, boned side up, on cutting board. Working from center out, pound chicken lightly with a wooden mallet to make cutlets ¼ inch thick. Sprinkle with salt. Place one piece of ham and cheese on each cutlet. Tuck in sides of each and roll, jelly roll style. Press to seal. Skewer or tie securely. Coat rolls with ¼ cup flour; brown in butter. Remove chicken to 11x7 inch baking pan. In same skillet combine ½ cup water, gravy base, mushrooms and wine. Heat, stirring to incorporate any crusty bits from skillet. Pour mixture over chicken. Cover and bake in 350° oven for 1 to 1¼ hours, or until tender. Transfer chicken to warm platter. Blend remaining flour and water. Add to gravy in baking pan. Cook and stir until thickened. Pour a little gravy over chicken; garnish with almonds. Pass remaining gravy.

Mrs. Elayne Shults (Elayne Steele)

EASY CHICKEN CORDON BLEU

Serves 12

12 chicken breasts, boned
12 thin slices ham
12 chunks Swiss cheese

2 cans cream of celery soup
1 cup buttered bread crumbs

Pound breasts until thin. Place slice of ham on each chicken breast. Put chunk of cheese on top and roll each breast placing rough side down in a shallow pan. Stir soup and pour over all. Put buttered crumbs on top. Bake in 325° oven for 1-1½ hours or until sauce bubbles.

Mrs. Robert D. Forrester (Carol Tate)

CRAB-STUFFED CHICKEN

Serves 8

4 large chicken breasts, halved, skinned, and boned
4 tablespoons butter
¼ cup flour
¾ cup milk
¾ cup chicken broth
⅓ cup dry white wine
¼ cup chopped onion
1 can (7½ ounces) crabmeat, drained

1 can (3 ounces) chopped mushrooms, drained
½ cup saltine crackers, coarsely crumbled (10 crackers)
2 tablespoons chopped parsley
½ teaspoon salt and pepper
1 cup (4 ounces) grated Swiss cheese
½ teaspoon paprika

Pound chicken breasts between 2 pieces of waxed paper. In saucepan, melt 3 tablespoons butter; blend in flour. Add milk, chicken broth, and wine all at once. Cook and stir until mixture thickens and bubbles. In another skillet, sauté onion in remaining butter. Stir in crab, mushrooms, crackers, parsley, salt, and pepper. Stir in 2 tablespoons of the sauce. Top each chicken breast with about 2 tablespoons of crab mixture. Fold sides in and roll up. Place seam side down in baking dish. Pour remaining sauce over all. Cover and bake in a 350° oven for 1 hour, or until chicken is tender. Uncover, sprinkle with cheese and paprika. Bake 2 minutes longer or until cheese melts.

Mrs. Roy Northrup (Dena Goldston)

COQ AU VIN

Serves 8

2 chickens, cut up
Salt and pepper
Paprika
Flour
½ pound salt pork, cut in finger size strips
24 whole small onions, peeled

Bouquet Garni

2 sprigs green celery tops
Thyme
6 or 7 sprigs parsley

3 tablespoons brandy
1 bottle red burgundy
2 cloves garlic, mashed
12 whole small mushrooms, remove stems
Cornstarch or arrowroot

Rosemary
Bayleaf

Wipe chicken clean and rub with salt, pepper and paprika. Dredge in flour. In a Dutch oven, brown salt pork. Add small white onions and brown lightly. Add chicken pieces, brown on all sides, turning frequently. Drain. Pour warm brandy over chicken and set it aflame. When the flame burns out, pour in the bottle of burgundy. Add garlic, mushrooms and bouquet garni. Cook 45 minutes or until tender. If sauce is too thin, thicken by adding one tablespoon cornstarch or arrowroot made into a paste with a small amount of the sauce and simmer 10 minutes or until it is clear.

Mrs. Charles Green (Babette Diehl)

COUNTRY CAPTAIN

Serves 8

2 chickens (4 pounds) cut in
  serving pieces or 12 chicken
  breasts and thighs
  Seasoned flour
½ cup shortening
1 tablespoon butter, optional
2–3 onions, finely chopped
1–2 green peppers, chopped
1–2 garlic cloves, minced
¼–4 teaspoons curry powder,
  depending on taste
1½ teaspoons salt

½–1 teaspoon white pepper
½ teaspoon thyme
*2 cans (28 ounces) tomatoes
½ teaspoon to 1 tablespoon
  parsley, chopped
  Hot cooked rice
¼–1 pound almonds, toasted
* ¼–⅔ cup currants or
  raisins (optional)
1 can (4 ounces)
  mushrooms (optional)
  Parsley sprigs

Remove skin from chicken if desired. Dredge in seasoned flour. Fry in shortening, until brown. Remove chicken. Keep warm. Cook onions, green peppers and garlic in remaining fat or butter until tender. Stir in curry, salt, pepper, thyme, tomatoes and parsley. Heat well. Place chicken in large casserole. Pour sauce over chicken. Bake covered in 350° oven for 45 minutes or until tender. Serve in a ring of rice. Top with sauce. Garnish with almonds, currants and parsley sprigs.

*One can of water or 1 can (8 ounces) tomato sauce may be added to tomatoes if desired. Currants or raisins and 1 can (4 ounces) mushrooms may be added 15 minutes before serving.

Mrs. Jacob P. Laeufer (Sue Dye)

BAKED CHICKEN

Serves 8

1 cup juice from lemons, limes
  or sour oranges
1 teaspoon salt
1 teaspoon freshly ground
  black pepper
1½ cups dry white wine

6 cloves garlic, crushed
1 teaspoon basil
6 chicken breasts,
  halved and boned
1 cup butter, melted
3 cups crumbled potato chips

In a large bowl combine first six ingredients. Add chicken and cover. Marinate in refrigerator for 4 hours, turning occasionally. Preheat oven to 400°. Remove chicken from marinade and pat dry. Dip each piece into melted butter. Then roll in crumbled chips. Arrange pieces in a large, flat baking dish. Bake uncovered in 350° oven for 1 hour.

Mrs. Edward Yingling (Barbara Hume)

BONELESS
BREAST OF CHICKEN   Serves 4

4 whole chicken breasts,
   boned
10 large fresh mushrooms or
1 can mushroom stems and
   pieces, drained and chopped
1 tablespoon finely chopped
   shallots or green onion

½ cup butter
   Salt and pepper to taste
   Drippings from chicken
   Chicken stock or milk
4 tablespoons flour
½ cup light cream

Flatten chicken breasts slightly. Sauté mushrooms and shallots in ¼ cup butter over medium heat for 5 minutes stirring constantly. Salt and pepper to taste. Stuff chicken breasts with mushroom mixture and fasten securely with toothpicks. Place in foil lined shallow baking pan. Bake in 375° oven for about 40 minutes. Reduce heat to 350° and bake 10-15 minutes or until done. Baste occasionally if browning too fast. Measure drippings; add enough chicken stock or milk to make one cup. Melt remaining butter and stir in flour. Remove from heat and add chicken dripping mixture and cream. Stir until smooth. Return to heat and cook 3-4 minutes. Serve over chicken while hot.

Mrs. J.C. Arthur (Nan Johnson)

DEVILED
CHICKEN BREASTS   Serves 6

6 chicken breasts,
   split or boned
1 teaspoon salt
½ teaspoon pepper
¼ cup salad oil
3 tablespoons flour
1 can (10¾ ounces)
   undiluted consommé

½ cup water
1 tablespoon
   Worcestershire sauce
1 tablespoon catsup
1 tablespoon mustard
¼ tablespoon paprika

Wash and dry chicken breasts. Season with salt and pepper, and brown in hot oil. Remove from pan. Stir flour into remaining oil. Cook over low heat, stirring until smooth. Gradually add the consommé and water. Mix remaining ingredients and add to consommé mixture. Place browned chicken in sauce. Cover tightly and simmer 45 minutes or until tender. Remove cover and continue cooking for 15 minutes, basting frequently. Serve over rice.

Mrs. T. Boone Pickens, Jr. (Bea Carr)

CHICKEN TAOS
WITH RICE

Serves 6

12 pieces (about 2 pounds)
    choice chicken parts
¼ cup flour
2 teaspoons salt
¼ teaspoon pepper
¼ cup butter
1 cup chopped onions

¼ teaspoon garlic powder
2 tablespoons
    Worcestershire sauce
1 cup chili sauce
1½ cups chicken broth
½ cup dry sherry (optional)
3 cups hot cooked rice

Roll chicken in combined flour, salt and pepper. Brown in butter. Push chicken to side of pan. Add onions and sauté until transparent. Stir in remaining ingredients except rice. Bring to a boil. Cover and reduce heat. Simmer for 35 minutes. Serve chicken and sauce over bed of fluffy rice.

Miss Susan E. Roach

CHICKEN
TCHAKHAKHBELLI

Serves 6

½ cup butter
2 (2 pounds) chickens,
    18 pieces
1 onion sliced
½ cup sherry
½ cup tomato juice

1 teaspoon paprika
1 teaspoon salt
    Pepper to taste
1 cup water

Melt butter in large skillet. Add chicken pieces and braise until light brown. Remove chicken to an 11x13 inch shallow baking dish. Sauté onions in remaining butter in skillet. Combine sherry, tomato juice, paprika, salt, pepper and water. Add to onions and heat. Pour over chicken. Bake uncovered in 400° oven for 30 minutes. Turn chicken and bake 30 minutes. Turn again and bake 15 minutes. Serve with rice pilaf.

Rolled chicken breasts may be used in place of cutting up whole chickens.

Mrs. Tom Cambridge (Norma Taggart)

CHICKEN ENCHILADAS   Serves 6

1 large white onion, chopped
1 tablespoon butter
2 cans cream of chicken soup
1 can (4 ounces) chopped green chilies
¾ can chicken broth
1 chicken fryer, cooked, boned and cut into small pieces
1 package corn tortillas, torn into quarters
1 cup grated American cheese
1 cup grated Cheddar cheese

Grease 12x8 inch Pyrex dish. Sauté onion in butter. Add soup, chilies, broth and chicken. Mix well and heat. Layer tortillas, sauce and cheese. Repeat layers, ending with cheese. Bake in 350° oven for 20 minutes. Freezes well.

Mrs. James B. Austin, III (Ann Franklin)

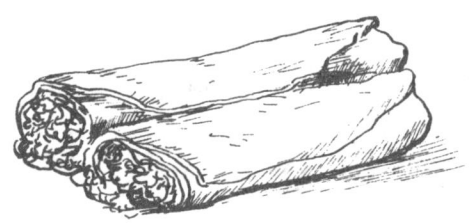

CHICKEN CHOW MEIN   Serves 4-6

¼ cup margarine
1 (3 pound) fryer, cooked and boned
1 cup green onions, chopped with some tops
1 teaspoon salt
½ teaspoon pepper
1 cup celery, chopped
1½–2 cups hot water
1 can bean sprouts, drained
1 can chow mein vegetables, drained
½ cup cold water
3 tablespoons cornstarch
2 teaspoons La Choy Soy Sauce
1 teaspoon sugar
1 tablespoon La Choy Brown Sauce

Melt margarine in pan. Add chicken and sear quickly, *don't* brown. Add onions. Fry 5 minutes. Add celery, salt, pepper, hot water and meat juices. Cover and cook 10 minutes. Add bean sprouts and vegetables. Mix thoroughly and heat to boiling. Add cornstarch to cold water, blend and add to boiling meat mixture. Add to meat mixture: soy sauce, sugar, and brown sauce; cook all together about 30 minutes more.

Mrs. Dick Frazer (Sylvia Lindley)

MOO GOO GAI PAN
(Chicken and Mushrooms) Serves 4

2 whole large chicken breasts, skinned, boned, halved and cooked
1 tablespoon cornstarch
2 tablespoons dry sherry
¾ teaspoon peeled ginger root, minced, or ¼ teaspoon ground ginger
⅛ teaspoon monosodium glutamate
2 teaspoons salt
⅓ cup salad oil

¾ cup walnuts
1 can (15 ounces) Chinese straw mushrooms, drained, or
2 cans (4½ ounces each) whole mushrooms, drained
1 can (8½ ounces) sliced bamboo shoots, drained
¼ pound snow peas or
1 package (7 ounces) snow peas, thawed

About 35 minutes before serving: Slice across width of chicken to make very thin pieces. (This can be done by holding sharp knife in slanting position). Combine chicken, cornstarch, sherry, ginger, monosodium glutamate and 1½ teaspoons salt. Mix well; set aside. Sauté walnuts in hot oil in 12 inch skillet about 3 minutes or until lightly browned. Stir constantly with slotted spoon. Spoon walnuts onto paper towels to drain, leaving oil in skillet. Stir-fry (stirring quickly and frequently) mushrooms, bamboo shoots, snow peas and ½ teaspoon salt in same skillet until snow peas are tender-crisp, about 3-5 minutes. Spoon vegetables into a medium bowl, leaving oil in the skillet. Stir-fry the chicken mixture in remaining oil about 5 minutes or until chicken is tender. Stir in vegetables. Spoon mixture onto warm platter; sprinkle with walnuts.

Mrs. Paul Fields (Barry Beck)

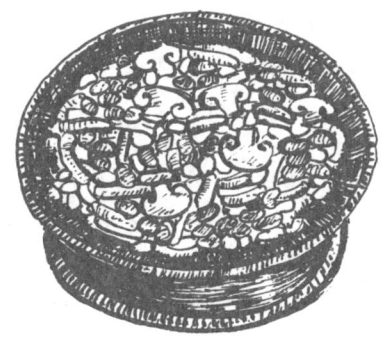

CHICKEN AND VEGETABLE
STIR-FRY

Serves 6-8

1 tablespoon cornstarch
3 tablespoons soy sauce
2 tablespoons dry sherry
1 teaspoon sugar
1 teaspoon ground ginger
½ teaspoon crushed
  red pepper
1 teaspoon salt
3 whole chicken breasts, cut
  into 1 inch chunks

3 medium zucchini squash,
  cut into bite-sized pieces
1 pound mushrooms
1 pound Chinese pea pods or
1 package (6 ounces)
  frozen pea pods
¾ cup oil
  Rice or crispy noodles
½ cup toasted almonds

Combine first seven ingredients in a medium bowl. Marinate chicken in this mixture while preparing vegetables. Wash mushrooms and pea pods in cold water and pat dry. Heat ½ cup oil in 8 quart Dutch oven or wok. Stir-fry zucchini, mushrooms and pea pods until tender but crisp. (About 5 minutes). Add salt. Spoon onto platter. Add ¼ cup oil to Dutch oven or wok, if necessary. Stir-fry chicken mixture over high heat for 10 minutes. Toss chicken and vegetables together. Serve immediately with rice or noodles.

Mrs. Mike Ballou (Debra Mitchell)

CHICKEN
TETRAZZINI

Serves 8-10

2-4 pounds chicken, cooked,
  boned and cubed,
  reserve broth
8 ounces spaghetti
½ pound butter
1 can (4 ounces)
  sliced mushrooms
1 green pepper, chopped

1 small onion, chopped
⅔ cup flour
1 pint half-and-half
½ pound Cheddar cheese,
  grated
½ pound American cheese,
  sliced

Cook spaghetti in broth and drain, reserving broth. Keep broth to thin cheese sauce if necessary. In skillet, sauté mushrooms, pepper and onion in butter until tender, but not brown. Add flour and blend. Add half-and-half stirring constantly until thick. Stir in cheese until it melts. Mix with spaghetti and chicken in 9x14 inch pan or two smaller ones. Bake in 350° oven for 40 minutes. Make ahead and freeze, or use half and freeze half.

Mrs. James H. Simms (Freeda Daugherty)

CHICKEN SPAGHETTI

Serves 8-10

1 (3-5 pound) hen
1 large onion, chopped
1 green pepper, chopped
1 can (1 pound) tomatoes
1 tablespoon chili powder

Salt
Cayenne
1 package (1 pound) spaghetti
1 can (4 ounces) mushrooms
1½ pounds mild
   Cheddar cheese, grated

Cover hen with enough water adding seasonings for a rich stock. Cook until done. Let cool in stock overnight in refrigerator. Next day remove chicken from stock and cut into bite-sized pieces, reserving stock. Return stock to heat, add onion, green pepper, tomatoes & chili powder. Add salt and cayenne pepper to taste. Simmer for several hours. One hour before serving, add spaghetti and simmer slowly. Cook mushrooms in their own juices, drain and add to stock mixture. Add cut up chicken and cheese. Simmer until ready to serve.

Mrs. Byron Singleton, Jr. (Janie Linnen)

CHICKEN TETRAZZINI

Serves 4-6

1 (3 pound) chicken,
   steamed and cubed
1 package (4-5 ounces)
   spaghetti, cooked
4 tablespoons butter
1½ teaspoons salt

6 tablespoons grated
   Parmesan cheese
½ pound mushrooms, sliced
   Pepper and garlic to taste

Steam chicken in water until tender. Remove chicken; reserve stock. While chicken is cooling prepare sauce. Cook spaghetti according to package directions. Drain, and pour into a large bowl. Season with 1 teaspoon salt, 2 tablespoons butter, 2 tablespoons Parmesan cheese and 1 cup of sauce. Set aside. Sauté mushrooms in 2 tablespoons butter, ½ teaspoon salt, pepper and garlic to taste. Combine sautéed mushrooms with spaghetti mixture. Add cubed chicken and remaining sauce. Mix well. Pour into large casserole. Top with Parmesan cheese. Bake in 350° oven for 30 minutes.

SAUCE FOR CHICKEN TETRAZZINI

¼ cup butter
⅓ cup flour
2 cups warm coffee cream

1 cup warm chicken stock
1½ teaspoons salt
2 tablespoons sauterne

Melt butter in saucepan. Blend flour into melted butter. Add cream and chicken stock gradually. Cook until thick and smooth. Add salt and sauterne.

Mrs. Mack Gordon (Dixie Conley)

CAROLE ERICKSON'S
MINIATURE DRUMSTICKS Serves 6

10–12 chicken wings
 1 or 2 eggs, beaten
 ½ cup cornstarch
 seasoned with garlic
 ¼ cup chicken broth
 ¼ cup catsup

 ¼ cup sugar
 ¼ cup vinegar
 1 teaspoon soy sauce
 1 teaspoon salt
 ½ teaspoon Accent

Split wings in two and remove tips. Dip each piece in beaten egg, then in seasoned cornstarch. Brown wings in oil. Combine remaining ingredients. Place browned chicken in baking dish. Pour sauce over chicken and bake in 375° oven for 40 minutes.

Any parts of chicken can be substituted for the wings.

CHICKEN DIVAN Serves 4

 1 package (10 ounces) frozen
 broccoli spears
 4 chicken breasts, boned,
 split, skinned
 1 can condensed cream
 of chicken soup

 ½ cup mayonnaise
 ½ teaspoon lemon juice
 ½ teaspoon curry powder
 ½ cup grated Cheddar or
 American cheese
 ¼ cup soft bread crumbs
 2 tablespoons butter, melted

Cook broccoli in boiling salted water. Drain and arrange in shallow 1½ quart baking dish. Simmer chicken in small amount of water for 35 minutes or until tender. Drain and arrange on broccoli. Mix soup, mayonnaise, lemon juice and curry powder. Pour over chicken and broccoli. Top with combined cheese, bread crumbs and butter. Bake in 350° oven for 25 minutes. Easy, but good.

Serve with Uncle Ben's Wild Rice Mix, and fruit salad, fresh or frozen.

Mrs. Prescott Haralson (Jo Anne Grimm)

PARISIENNE CHICKEN DIVAN

Serves 6

4 chicken breasts, cooked and boned
1 package dehydrated onion soup mix
1 pint sour cream
2 packages (10 ounces each) frozen broccoli, cooked
1 cup heavy cream, whipped
2 tablespoons grated Parmesan cheese

Slice chicken into large pieces. Add the soup mix to sour cream and beat with rotary beater until well blended. Arrange the broccoli in a single layer in a long shallow baking dish. Spoon half of the sauce over broccoli; then cover with chicken slices. Fold the whipped cream into the remaining sauce and pour over the chicken. Bake in 350° oven for 20 minutes or until bubbly. Sprinkle with cheese and brown under broiler.

Mrs. Jacob P. Laeufer (Sue Dye)

CHICKEN IN TARRAGON

Serves 4

1 (2-3 pound) fryer, cut-up
3 tablespoons butter
¼ cup chopped onion
1 clove garlic, minced
2 tablespoons flour
2 tablespoons catsup
1½ cups chicken stock
1 teaspoon salt
½ teaspoon pepper
1½ teaspoons dried tarragon
¾ cup sour cream
2 tablespoons Parmesan cheese

Brown chicken pieces in butter in large, heavy skillet. Remove from skillet. Add onion and garlic and cook until tender. Stir in flour and catsup and add chicken stock slowly bringing to a boil, stirring until thickened. Stir in salt, pepper, and tarragon. Return chicken to skillet. Cover, and simmer gently, about 45 minutes, or until tender. Remove chicken to warm platter. Gradually stir in sour cream. *Do not allow to boil.* Pour over chicken and sprinkle with cheese. This recipe is also good with wild game such as quail, teal, dove or pheasant.

Mrs. John Kelleher (Cindy Leiphart)

BAKED CHICKEN BREASTS WITH SOUR CREAM

Serves 4-5

4-5 chicken breasts (halved)
¼ cup flour
1 tablespoon paprika
1 tablespoon salt
¼ cup shortening

2 cups hot water
1 large onion, sliced
1 carton (8 ounces) sour cream
1 package Uncle Ben's Long Grain and Wild rice, cooked

Mix flour, paprika and salt together. Coat chicken with mixture. Brown chicken in shortening. When browned, add water and onions. Cover and simmer for one hour. Stir in sour cream, remove from heat, cover and let stand for 5-10 minutes. Serve over rice, spooning sour cream mixture on top.

Mrs. William A. Sansing (Betty Ann Troutman)

SIMON AND GARFUNKLE CHICKEN

Serves 6

3 chicken breasts, boned, skinned and halved
1 stick butter, softened
   Salt and pepper to taste
6 small slices Mozzarella cheese
   Flour
1 egg, beaten

1 cup fresh bread crumbs
2 tablespoons chopped parsley
¼ teaspoon sage
¼ teaspoon thyme
¼ teaspoon rosemary
½ cup dry white wine

Flatten chicken between sheets of wax paper. Spread breasts with part of the butter and sprinkle with salt and pepper. Place one slice of cheese on each chicken piece. Roll and tack end with toothpicks. Coat lightly with flour. Dip in egg, then roll in bread crumbs. Arrange in 11¾x7½x1¾ inch casserole. Melt remaining butter. Add seasonings to melted butter and baste chicken with mixture. Bake 30 minutes in 350° oven, basting occasionally. Pour wine over chicken; bake 20 minutes longer, basting with liquid in pan.

Mrs. Don Buckley (Patty Smith)

CHICKEN BREASTS

Serves 6-8

4 whole chicken breasts
Salt and pepper
Paprika
8–12 medium mushrooms,
 sliced
½ to ⅓ cup Madeira,
 or dry sherry or sauterne

½ green pepper, diced
1 can cream of chicken soup
½ to 1 cup sour cream
 Sweet basil
 Parsley
1 jar (2 ounces) pimientos

Bone, skin and cut the breasts in two. Sprinkle with salt, pepper and paprika. Brown in a skillet and place in a greased casserole. Brown the mushrooms and green pepper. Make a sauce with soup, sour cream, salt, pepper and sweet basil. Stir in Madeira. Add mushrooms, green peppers and about ½ of the jar of pimientos. Pour the sauce over chicken breasts and bake covered in a 325° oven for 45-60 minutes.

Mrs. Herbert Dodson (Eva Jane Maxey)

ROLLED CHICKEN BREASTS

Yield 6 Rolls

3 whole chicken breasts,
 boned, skinned and halved
6 slices ham, cut thin (may use
 packaged sliced ham)
6 slices Monterey Jack
 cheese

2 tablespoons
 Parmesan cheese
2 tablespoons parsley flakes
⅓ cup bread crumbs
4 tablespoons butter

Pound chicken between plastic wrap to about 3x5 inches. Place ham slice on top then slice of cheese. Tuck in sides and roll up. Secure with toothpicks. Mix together the cheese, parsley and bread crumbs. Dip chicken rolls in melted butter and then in crumb mixture. Place in shallow pan. Cover and bake in 350° oven for 40-45 minutes. May be frozen. Thaw before baking. Variation: Chicken Saltimbocca — use Mozzarella cheese instead of Monterey Jack. Add dash of sage to each roll. Peel, seed and chop medium tomato and add a little tomato to each roll.

Mrs. Danny Conklin (Carolyn Kerns)

CHICKEN-CHESTNUT CASSEROLE

Serves 5-6

2 cups chicken,
  cooked and boned
2 cups French style
  green beans, drained
2 cups Uncle Ben's Wild Rice
  with seasonings, cooked
1 can cream of celery soup
½ cup mayonnaise
1 can (8½ ounces)
  water chestnuts, sliced
1 can (4 ounces) mushrooms
1 jar (2 ounces) pimientos
2 tablespoons chopped onion,
  sautéed in butter
¼ teaspoon salt
¼ teaspoon pepper
  Almonds, slivered
  and toasted

Mix all ingredients together in a large mixing bowl. Butter a large casserole. Place mixture in casserole and bake in 350° oven for 30 minutes. Sprinkle with broiled, diced almonds. Serve with hot spiced fruit on the side. This can be frozen immediately after cooling.

Mrs. Nelson Lane (Catharine Denise Turner)

CHICKEN CASSEROLE WITH WINE

Serves 4-6

½ pound butter
1 cup flour
1 teaspoon salt
1 teaspoon pepper
4 whole chicken breasts,
  halved
¼ cup brandy
1½ cups Burgundy wine
½ bay leaf
Pinch of thyme
1 teaspoon finely chopped
  parsley
1 clove garlic, minced
3 tablespoons butter
½ pound fresh mushrooms,
  sliced
2 center cut ham slices
  (1 inch thick)
12 pearl onions

Melt ½ pound butter in large skillet. Combine flour, salt and pepper in a bag. Add chicken and shake to coat. Sauté chicken in butter until golden; remove from pan and keep warm. Add brandy to pan drippings and ignite. Cover with lid until flame burns out. Add wine, bay leaf, thyme, parsley and garlic. Stir and keep warm. In saucepan, melt 3 tablespoons butter. Slice mushrooms and sauté in butter for 4 minutes. Cut ham in cubes. Peel and pierce the stem ends of the pearl onions. Arrange the chicken in a 3 quart buttered casserole. Layer ham, mushrooms and onions on top of the chicken. Pour wine sauce over all. Cover and bake in 325° oven for about 1½ hours.

Mrs. James B. Austin, III (Ann Franklin)

HOPKINS COUNTY STEW   Serves 8

2 pound chicken
Salt
1 can (16 ounces) tomatoes
1 package (10 ounces) frozen
whole kernel corn

1 pound potatoes, cubed
1 large onion, chopped
2 tablespoons chili powder
Salt and pepper to taste

Simmer chicken in slightly salted water to cover until tender. Remove chicken from broth; cool, remove meat from bones and cut into pieces. To broth, add tomatoes, corn, potatoes, onion, and chili powder. Add salt and pepper to taste. Simmer 10-15 minutes or until potatoes and onion are tender. Add cut-up chicken; warm thoroughly and serve.

Sally Bivins

CHAFING DISH
CHICKEN   Serves 2-3

2 chicken breasts, boned and
cut into thin strips
Salt and pepper to taste
1 teaspoon dry mustard
1 small onion, diced

3–4 tablespoons butter
½ pint whipping cream
Dash of Scotch
Chopped parsley

Dredge chicken strips in salt, pepper and mustard. Brown onions in melted butter in skillet or chafing dish. Add chicken. Cook, stirring constantly until done, about 10 minutes. Pour in cream. Continue to cook briefly, stirring constantly. Add Scotch and parsley. Serve with rice.

This dish can be embellished by adding chopped mushrooms or green peas.

Mrs. Richard Reeves (Louise Coe)

CHICKEN AND
DUMPLINGS   Serves 4-6

1 large chicken, boiled,
reserve stock
1 cup flour
½ teaspoon salt

1½ teaspoons baking powder
½ cup milk
1 egg, well beaten
2 tablespoons cooking oil

For a seasoned stock add your own herbs, carrots, celery, onion and seasonings.

Bone chicken. Keep broth hot. Sift flour, salt and baking powder together. Add milk, egg and oil. Mix well into a soft dough. Roll dough on a well-floured board. Cut into small pieces and drop into boiling broth. Cover and simmer 15 minutes. Do not overcook. Serve with chicken.

Mrs. Robert Lanier (Susie Hodges)

PARMESAN CHICKEN

Serves 30

4 pounds chicken,
  cut in chunks
1 cup butter, melted
2 tablespoons soy sauce
  (optional)
1 cup Parmesan cheese

4 tablespoons
  chopped parsley
1 tablespoon oregano
4 teaspoons paprika
1 teaspoon salt
1 teaspoon white pepper

Combine butter and soy sauce. Combine remaining ingredients in another bowl. Dip chicken in butter mixture and roll in cheese mixture. Place in shallow pan on foil. Dribble with remaining butter mixture. Bake in 350° oven for 1 hour.

Mrs. James E. Herring (Margaret Johnson)

This recipe was used at a league meeting for Pandora's box lunch. The chunks of chicken were placed on a skewer with fresh pineapple chunks, Chinese Barbecue Pork and Marinated Mushrooms.

Check index for these recipes.

CHICKEN LOAF

Serves 12

9 slices white bread,
  crust removed
4 cups cubed white meat
  of chicken, cooked
½ pound mushrooms, sautéed
  in ½ cup butter
1 can (8½ ounces)
  water chestnuts, sliced
½ cup mayonnaise
9 slices American cheese

4 eggs, well beaten
2 cups milk
1 teaspoon salt
1 can cream of
  mushroom soup
1 can cream of celery soup
1 jar (2 ounces)
  chopped pimientos
2 cups buttered
  bread cubes

Line greased 10½x11½ inch pan with bread. Place chicken on top, then mushrooms with butter. Add the water chestnuts. Spread the mayonnaise over all. Top with cheese. Combine eggs, milk and salt. Pour over chicken. Mix soups thoroughly and spoon over carefully so as to not disturb cheese. Top with pimientos. Cover with foil and refrigerate overnight. Bake uncovered in 350° oven for 1¼-1½ hours. Fifteen minutes before done, cover with bread cubes and finish baking. Do not overcook.

Mrs. S.B. Whittenburg (Frances Grimes)

A WEAVER'S CHICKEN

Serves 6-8

2 fryers, cut up
Salt
Pepper

1 bottle cooking sherry
  (about 24 ounces)
1 can mushroom soup

Wash chicken and lay in a 14x10 inch pan. Salt and pepper to taste. Mix sherry and mushroom soup together, and pour over chicken. Bake in 350° oven. Turn after 1 hour and bake another hour. Bake uncovered.

Line pan with aluminum foil before baking to save a messy pan.

Mrs. Tom Fotheringham (Carolyn Furr)

LEMON-PEPPER CHICKEN

Serves 4-6

2 pounds chicken pieces
½ cup margarine, melted
1 teaspoon butter flavoring

½ teaspoon onion salt
2 teaspoons
  lemon-pepper marinade

Preheat oven to 350°. Place chicken pieces in one layer in 3 quart rectangular pan. Add butter flavoring to margarine. Pour over chicken. Sprinkle with onion salt and lemon-pepper marinade. Bake uncovered for 30 minutes. Baste with pan drippings and bake for 45 minutes more. Serve with rice.

Mrs. Walter Mount (Marjorie Quaile)

BAR-B-Q CHICKEN MINUS BAR-B-Q SAUCE

Serves 6-8

2 fryers, cut up
3–5 strips bacon

Salt and pepper
French dressing

Wash chicken. Place in 10x14 inch pan. Salt and pepper to taste. Lay strips of bacon on top of chicken. Zig zag French dressing across chicken. Bake in 350° oven, uncovered, for 2 hours. Do not turn.

Mrs. Tom Fotheringham (Carolyn Furr)

If you wish to use homemade French dressing, see Index.

221

OVEN-FRIED CHICKEN   Serves 4

1 chicken cut-up
  or chicken breasts
1 teaspoon salt
1 teaspoon pepper

Dash garlic salt
1 package (7½ ounces)
  potato chips, crushed
¼ pound butter, melted

Season chicken with salt, pepper and garlic salt. Dip chicken into butter and roll in crushed potato chips. Place chicken in large Pyrex baking dish, skin side up. Cover, bake in 350° oven 30 minutes, uncover, bake 30 minutes more.

Variation: Use sour cream and onion flavored potato chips.

Mrs. William A. Sansing (Betty Ann Troutman)

GRILLED HONEY CHICKEN   Serves 4

¼ cup soy sauce
¼ cup Worcestershire sauce
¼ cup sherry
¼ cup honey
1 clove garlic, crushed

¼ teaspoon ground ginger
3 tablespoons butter, melted
2 (2 to 2½ pounds each)
  broiler fryers, cut up

Combine first seven ingredients. Cook 5 minutes, stirring constantly. Place chicken in shallow pan and cover with sauce. Marinate 15 minutes. Place chicken, skin side up on grill. Cook 1 hour or until tender. Turn and baste often.

If deboned chicken is used, cooking time will be shorter.

Mrs. John Mozola (Jo Rush)

AUNT SCOTT'S CHICKEN LIVERS   Serves 4

1 pound chicken livers
  Salt and pepper to taste
½ cup butter
8–10 mushrooms, sliced

1 package (6 ounces) wild rice
  or 1 box long grain and
  wild rice combination
1 cup chicken bouillon
  Rice

Prick chicken livers with fork. Salt and pepper livers, dredge in flour, and fry slowly in butter until done. Remove livers from pan, sauté mushrooms in same pan. Remove. Stir chicken bouillon slowly into pan and simmer until thick. Add mushrooms to gravy and heat until warm. Serve on rice.

Mrs. Merrill Winsett (Catherine Monning)

CHICKEN CASSEROLE   Serves 4-6

4 chicken breasts,
  boned and halved
  Salt and pepper
8 slices of bacon
2 jars chipped beef

1 can cream of
  mushroom soup
½ pint sour cream (optional)
  Slivered toasted almonds
  (optional)

Lightly salt and pepper chicken. Wrap each breast with a slice of bacon. Line lightly greased baking pan with crumbled chipped beef, place chicken breasts on top. Combine soup and sour cream. Pour over chicken. Sprinkle with almonds. Bake in 250° oven for 3½-4 hours.

Mrs. S.S. Stephens (Mikala Faville)

CHICKEN ASPARAGUS OLÉ   Serves 8-10

6 whole chicken breasts
1 medium onion, chopped
½ cup butter
1 can (8 ounces)
  mushrooms, drained
1 can cream of
  mushroom soup
1 can cream of chicken soup
1 can (5.33 fluid ounces)
  Pet Milk
½ pound sharp cheese, grated

¼ teaspoon Tabasco
2 teaspoons soy sauce
1 teaspoon salt
1 teaspoon pepper
1 teaspoon Accent
1 jar (2 ounces)
  chopped pimentos, drained
2 cans (10 ounces each) green
  tipped asparagus, drained
½ cup sliced almonds

Boil chicken and debone. Set aside. Sauté onions in butter and add next eleven ingredients. Simmer until cheese is melted. Line bottom of casserole with half the chicken. Cover with half the asparagus. Pour half the sauce over top. Repeat. Top with almonds. Cook in 350° oven until bubbly.

Mrs. Richard Reeves (Louise Coe)

TURKEY STUFFED WITH TAMALES

Turkey
Barbeque sauce or oil

Canned hot tamales, amount
depends on size of turkey

Rub turkey with oil or barbeque sauce. Remove paper and grease from tamales. Mash until the consistency of regular dressing. Stuff turkey with the tamales. Roast as you normally would in the oven or on the grill. Serve with a rice-jalapeño dish and spinach salad.

Mrs. H. Fred Johnson (Olla Carter)

TURKEY INDIENNE   Serves 4

½ cup chopped green pepper
2 tablespoons shortening
2 tablespoons flour
½ teaspoon curry powder
   (optional)
1 can Campbell's
   onion soup

½ cup water
2 cups diced, cooked turkey
1 can (4 ounces) sliced
   mushrooms, drained
½ cup chopped,
   toasted almonds
Hot rice

Sauté pepper in shortening. Blend in flour, curry powder, soup and water. Cook slowly until thick, stirring constantly. Add turkey, mushrooms and almonds. Simmer for 10 minutes. Serve over hot rice.

Mrs. R.G. Rogers (Lynda Rogers)

TURKEY HASH

3 cups diced cooked turkey
1 stick butter
2 tablespoons flour
½ cup whipping cream
½ cup soft bread crumbs
½ cup chopped green pepper

½ cup chopped onion
2 tablespoons
   chopped parsley
½ teaspoon ground sage
½ teaspoon salt
Freshly ground pepper

Melt half stick of butter in large pan. Blend in flour and cream. Stir until thickened. Add turkey and all other ingredients. Keep adding more butter and stirring as needed to brown. Sauté for 25 minutes uncovered. Brown hash under broiler before serving.

Mrs. Ed Yingling (Barbara Hume)

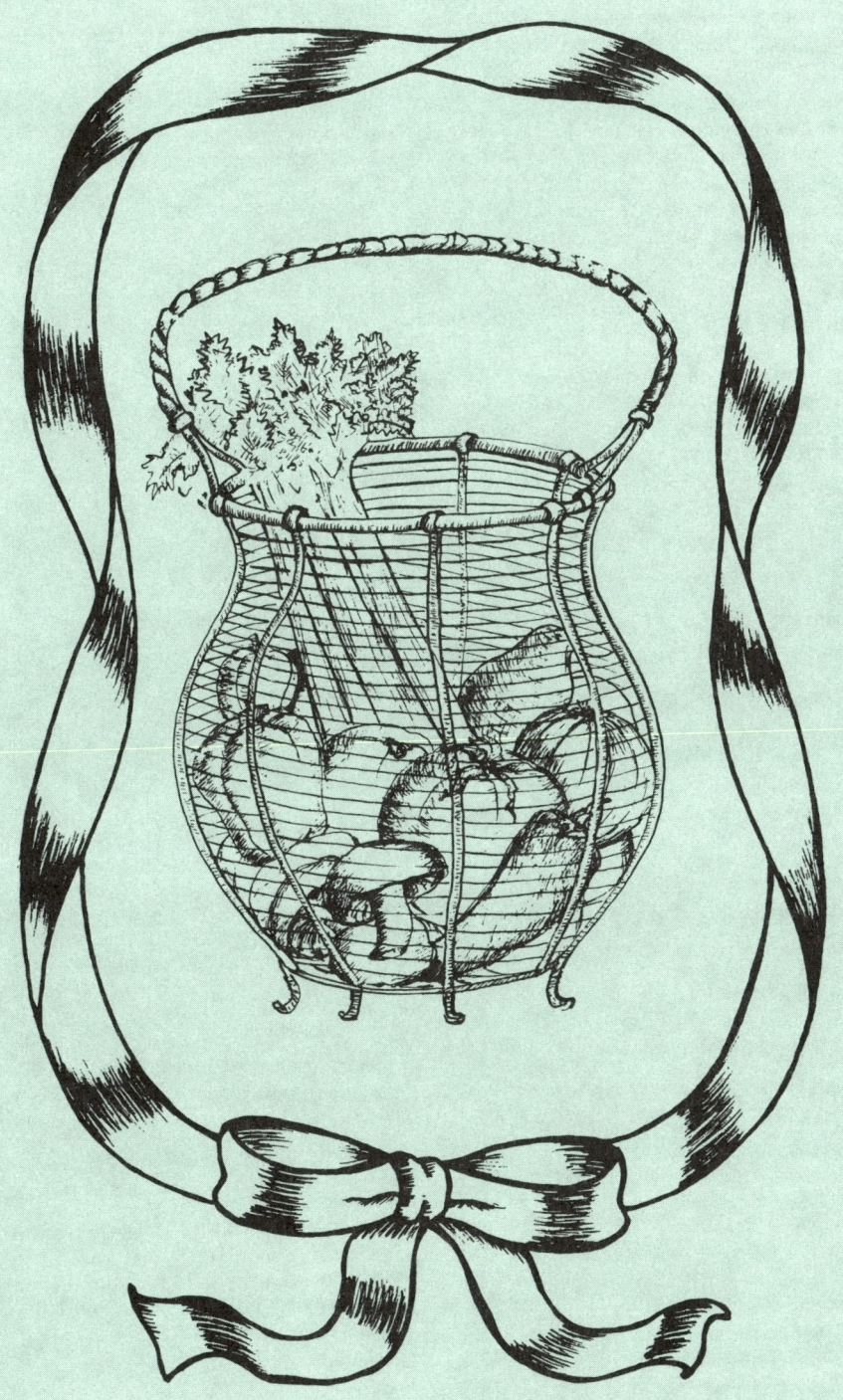

ASPARAGUS EGG DELIGHT

Serves 8

1 tablespoon butter
2 tablespoons flour
½ teaspoon salt
½ cup milk
1 cup cottage cheese, creamed
¼ cup grated sharp Cheddar cheese

1 teaspoon Worcestershire sauce
2 cans asparagus tips
4 hard cooked eggs, halved lengthwise
Salt and pepper
Paprika

Melt butter. Blend in flour and salt. Add milk. Cook until thick, stirring constantly. Remove from heat. Stir in cottage cheese until well blended. Cook over medium heat, stirring constantly until cheese curds disappear. Add Cheddar cheese and Worcestershire, stirring until cheese melts. Arrange asparagus in glass pie pan in a spoke design. Place eggs between asparagus spokes. Pour cheese sauce over all. Sprinkle with paprika. Bake in 400° oven for 25-30 minutes until lightly browned and sauce is bubbly. This can be made early in the day and stored in the refrigerator, covered. Remove from refrigerator 45 minutes before serving and let stand at room temperature. Nice for brunch.

Mrs. Hugh A. Sticksel (Pan Purdy)

CREAMED ASPARAGUS

Serves 6

2 cans asparagus, frozen or fresh as preferred
1 cup light white sauce
1 cup Hellmann's mayonnaise

Lemon juice (approximately one lemon)
Grated Cheddar cheese
Paprika

Place asparagus in 7x12 inch Pyrex dish. Combine all remaining ingredients and pour over asparagus. Bake in 325° oven for about 25 minutes or until asparagus is heated through and cheese is melted. The more cheese used, the better. Try different kinds of cheese for variety.

Mrs. Hugh Harmon (Jo Morgan)

ASPARAGUS, PETIT PEAS AND MUSHROOM CASSEROLE

Serves 8-10

2 cans (15 ounces each) green
asparagus, drained
2 cans (1 pound each) petit
peas, drained
1 can cream of
mushroom soup

¾ cup grated sharp
Cheddar cheese
1 cup soft white bread crumbs
2 tablespoons melted butter

Chill the cans of asparagus for 2-3 hours to prevent them from breaking. About 40 minutes before serving time, open and drain. Arrange half the asparagus in a buttered 6 cup casserole. In a bowl gently mix the peas, soup and cheese. Spoon half the mixture into casserole. Add remaining asparagus and top with remaining peas. Toss crumbs with butter and sprinkle on top of casserole. Bake in 350° oven for 30 minutes or until crumbs are golden brown.

Mrs. William G. Landess (Claudette Leachman)

ASPARAGUS-TOMATO STIR-FRY

Serves 4-6

¼ cup cooking oil
1 pound fresh asparagus,
woody base snipped and
discarded, and cut on bias
into 1½ inch lengths
4 green onions

1½ cups fresh mushrooms
1 tablespoon cold water
1 teaspoon cornstarch
2 teaspoons soy sauce
½ teaspoon salt
2 small tomatoes

Preheat a wok or skillet over medium-high heat. Add ¼ cup cooking oil. Place asparagus and onions into wok and stir-fry for 3 minutes or until tender. Add mushrooms and stir-fry for 1 more minute. Push the vegetables up the side of wok or skillet. Combine water, cornstarch, soy sauce and salt. Pour this mixture into center of pan and let it bubble slightly. Then stir in vegetables, add tomatoes and heat them thoroughly. Serve at once with cooked rice or as a side dish with broiled or grilled steaks. Broccoli may be substituted for asparagus.

Mrs. Mike Ballou (Debra Mitchell)

For a main dish, add thin strips of beef marinated in soy sauce.

228

BAKED ARTICHOKES — Serves 6

2 cans (8½ ounces each)
  artichokes, drained
  and halved
  Lemon pepper
½ cup butter, softened

2 packages (3 ounces each)
  cream cheese, softened
1 jar (.14 ounce) chives,
  freeze dried
1 cup Parmesan cheese

Place artichokes in bottom of buttered casserole (either 6 individual or one medium-size casserole). Sprinkle with lemon pepper. Mix cream cheese, butter and chives. Spread on artichokes. Sprinkle with Parmesan cheese. Bake at 375° for 20 minutes, then broil to brown.

Mrs. Virgil Pate (Mary Graham)

BROCCOLI CASSEROLE — Serves 8-10

2 packages (10 ounces each)
  frozen chopped broccoli,
  cooked
1 chopped onion
1 roll (6 ounces) garlic cheese
1 can (8½ ounces) water
  chestnuts, drained
  and sliced

1 can cream of
  mushroom soup
1 can (4 ounces)
  mushrooms, drained

Combine all ingredients and pour into a 2 quart greased casserole. Bake in 350° oven for 45 minutes.

Variation: Make a sauce of 2 tablespoons butter, 2 tablespoons flour, ¼ teaspoon salt, 1 package (3 ounces) cream cheese, softened, 1 ounce blue cheese, crumbled and 1 cup milk. Cook and stir until mixture boils. Stir in broccoli. Pour into 1½ quart casserole. Top with ⅓ cup crushed Ritz cracker crumbs. Bake for 30 minutes in 350° oven.

Mrs. Walter S. Berry (Mary Knupp)

Variation: Combine 1 can mushroom soup with ½ cup grated American cheese. Gradually add ¼ cup milk, ¼ cup mayonnaise and 1 beaten egg. Pour sauce over broccoli in 10x6x1½ inch baking dish. Top with ¼ cup bread crumbs mixed with 1 tablespoon melted butter. Bake in 350° oven 45 minutes.

Mrs. Don Buckley (Patty Smith)

BROCCOLI CASSEROLE   Serves 6

3 boxes (10 ounces each)
  broccoli spears
1 teaspoon salt
1 tablespoon sugar
1 pound processed cheese,
  cut in strips
1 stick butter

1 tablespoon flour
1 teaspoon salt
½ teaspoon freshly
  ground pepper
Pinch garlic powder
½ pint sour cream
2 cups cornflakes, crushed

Boil defrosted broccoli for two minutes in water, salt and sugar. Layer broccoli in greased 1½ quart casserole. (Two layers.) Top each layer with half the cheese. Make a white sauce with ½ stick melted butter, flour, salt, pepper and garlic powder. Add sour cream. Stir sauce over low heat until thick. Pour over broccoli. Melt ½ stick butter. Stir in cornflakes. Pour over entire casserole and cover. Bake in 400° oven for 35 minutes.

Mrs. D. Dale Gillette (Dare M. Majors)

SESAME BROCCOLI   Serves 4

1 pound fresh broccoli
1 tablespoon salad oil
1 tablespoon vinegar

1 tablespoon soy sauce
4 teaspoons sugar
1 tablespoon toasted
  sesame seeds

Cook broccoli in boiling, salted water until tender. Drain. Combine remaining ingredients and heat to boiling. Pour over broccoli to coat spears. There are about 75 calories per serving.

Mrs. Thomas A. Bunkley, Jr. (Myra Anne Stanley)

BRUSSEL SPROUTS
AND ARTICHOKES   Serves 6

1 package (10 ounces) frozen
  brussel sprouts
1 can (14 ounces) artichoke
  hearts, drained
½ cup water
⅔ cup mayonnaise

½ teaspoon celery salt
¼ cup grated
  Parmesan cheese
¼ cup margarine
2 teaspoons lemon juice
¼ cup sliced almonds
  (optional)

Cook brussel sprouts in ½ cup water, until tender. Drain. Arrange brussel sprouts and artichokes in a greased 1-quart casserole. Combine remaining ingredients and spoon over vegetables. Bake uncovered for 8-10 minutes at 425°.

Mrs. Elayne Shults (Elayne Steele)
230

CABBAGE CASSEROLE

Serves 6-8

1 head cabbage,
  cut into chunks
1 cup sugar
½ pint whipping cream

20 individual soda crackers
¼ stick of butter
Salt
Pepper

Cover cabbage with water, add sugar and bring to a boil. Boil 10 minutes. Drain water and place cabbage in casserole dish. Pour on cream and dot with butter. Cover cabbage with cracker crumbs. Bake in 350° oven for 20 minutes.

Mrs. Robert Ringo (Carolyn Huseman)

KIRA HARRIS' SCALLOPED CABBAGE WITH NUTMEG SAUCE

Serves 6

1 small head cabbage
  (coarsely shredded)
2 tablespoons butter
2 tablespoons flour
1½ cups milk
½ teaspoon salt

Dash of pepper
¼ teaspoon nutmeg
6 tablespoons grated
  Parmesan cheese
1 tablespoon lemon juice

Boil or steam cabbage until tender, but still crisp. Melt butter in saucepan and stir in flour. Remove from heat and gradually blend in milk, stirring until smooth. Add salt, pepper and nutmeg. Cook stirring constantly, until thickened. Add 4 tablespoons cheese and stir until melted. Remove from heat and stir in lemon juice. Place cabbage in greased baking dish and pour sauce over cabbage. Top with remaining cheese and sprinkle with nutmeg. Bake 6-8 minutes in 450° oven until top is golden brown.

CARROT RING

Serves 10

2 cups mashed cooked carrots
1 cup cracker crumbs
1 cup milk
3 cups grated sharp
  Cheddar cheese
⅔–¾ cup soft butter
¼ cup grated onion

1 teaspoon salt
¼ teaspoon pepper
⅛ teaspoon cayenne pepper
3 eggs
2 packages (10 ounces each)
  frozen peas
Parsley

Combine first 9 ingredients. Beat eggs until fluffy. Fold in. Pour into well greased 1½ quart ring mold. Bake in a 350° oven for 40-45 minutes. Turn out on a warm platter. Pour cooked, buttered peas inside the ring and garnish with parsley.

Mrs. Max Sherman (Gene Alice Wienbroer)

GLAZED CARROTS

Serves 6-8

2 pounds carrots, pared
  and sliced
½ teaspoon salt
½ cup honey

4 tablespoons vegetable oil
4 tablespoons sugar
1 teaspoon grated lemon rind
¼ teaspoon ground ginger

Cook carrots in salt water for 10 minutes. Drain. Add honey, oil and sugar. Cook in large skillet, covered, over low heat, until carrots are tender (about 20 minutes). Stir in lemon rind and ginger.

Mrs. David Waitt (Nancy Longtin)

PAPA SAN'S VEGETABLES

Serves 6

2 tablespoons Wesson oil
1 medium onion, cut in
  half and sliced
2 carrots, sliced diagonally
2 stalks celery,
  sliced diagonally

½ green pepper, cut
  in ½ inch pieces
2 tablespoons soy sauce
2 tablespoons catsup
2 tablespoons water

Heat oil. Add vegetables. Cook over medium heat, about 3 minutes. Add soy sauce, catsup and water (if there is too much vegetable juice, omit the water). Cover and cook over low heat for 10 minutes. Vegetables will remain slightly crisp. Very easy to double or triple. Inexpensive and low-calorie.

Mrs. James M. Goforth (Brenda Lee)

BAKED CAULIFLOWER

Serves 4

1 medium cauliflower
2 slices bacon
¼ cup chopped onion
1 can condensed cream of
  chicken soup

⅓ cup milk
½ cup grated cheese
¼ cup chopped peanuts

Cook whole cauliflower in boiling water until tender, about 15 minutes. If desired, cauliflower can be broken into flowerettes and steamed. Cook bacon, crumble it, and set aside. Pour off all but 2 tablespoons bacon drippings. Add onion and cook until tender. Gradually stir in soup and milk. Add cheese and peanuts. Place drained, cooked cauliflower in a 1-quart casserole. Pour sauce over cauliflower. Bake in 350° oven for 15 minutes. Garnish with bacon.

Mrs. Herbert Dodson (Eva Jane Maxey)

BLUSHING CAULIFLOWER

Serves 4

1 cauliflower
1 tablespoon minced onion
2 tablespoons butter
1 can tomato soup, undiluted

1 teaspoon curry powder
¼ teaspoon salt
1 tablespoon cold water
2 or 3 dashes Worcestershire sauce

Remove stems and leaves of cauliflower. Boil until tender, leave whole or break into flowerettes. Sauté onions in butter. Add other ingredients and simmer 10 minutes. Place cauliflower in 2 quart casserole and pour sauce over cauliflower. Heat until bubbly and serve.

Mrs. Taylor Yoakam (Joni Minnema)

CAULIFLOWER CHEESE SOUFFLÉ

Serves 6

3 tablespoons butter
3 tablespoons flour
1 cup milk
½ teaspoon salt

3 eggs, separated
½ cup grated cheese
1 cup cooked, coarsely chopped cauliflower

Melt butter, blend in flour. Gradually add milk and salt. Cook and stir until thickened. Add beaten egg yolks and half of cheese. Stir until cheese is melted. Add cauliflower. Fold in stiffly beaten egg whites. Pour into buttered casserole. Sprinkle top with remaining cheese. Set in pan of hot water. Bake in 350° oven 50-60 minutes.

Mrs. S.S. Stephens (Mikala Faville)

CORN PUDDING

Serves 6

1 can (16 ounces) whole kernel corn, drained
1 can (4 ounces) chopped green chilies, drained
¼ pound Cheddar cheese, grated

1 cup milk
½ teaspoon salt
3 eggs, beaten

Mix ingredients in order. Turn into a greased 1½-quart baking dish. Place in oven, in a shallow pan of hot water. Bake in preheated 350° oven about 1 hour or until set. Serve hot or cold.

Mrs. A.J. Folley (Rowena Jones)

BAKED EGGPLANT

Serves 6

1 medium eggplant
1 teaspoon salt, divided
2 cups bread crumbs
3 tablespoons chopped onion
2 tablespoons
chopped parsley

2 tablespoons
chopped celery
¼ teaspoon pepper
4 tablespoons butter, melted
1 egg, beaten
2 tablespoons cream

Scoop out center of eggplant. Sprinkle with half the salt and let stand 30 minutes. Rinse and set aside. Cover pulp of eggplant with water and cook for 10 minutes. Drain. Add remaining ingredients. Stuff halves of eggplant and bake in 350° oven for 45 minutes.

SCALLOPED EGGPLANT

Serves 6-8

1 large eggplant, diced
⅓ cup milk
1 can (10 ounces)
cream of mushroom soup

1 egg, slightly beaten
½ cup chopped onion
¾ cup packaged
herb-seasoned stuffing

TOPPING

1 cup grated sharp cheese
½ cup packaged stuffing,
finely crushed

2 tablespoons butter,
melted

Cook eggplant in salted water until tender, 6-7 minutes. Drain. Combine milk, soup and egg. Add eggplant, onion and stuffing. Toss lightly. Pour into greased baking dish. Combine topping ingredients. Spread over eggplant mixture. Bake in 350° oven for 20 minutes.

Mrs. B. Ronald Fortner (Jane Pridgeon)

BARBEQUED GREEN BEANS

Serves 6-8

2 packages (10 ounces each)
frozen cut green beans,
partially thawed
1 teaspoon salt
1 teaspoon sugar
Dash of pepper

4 thin lemon slices
½ cup water chestnuts,
sliced
2 tablespoons sliced
green onion
2 tablespoons margarine

Place beans on large square of double thickness aluminum foil. Season with salt, sugar and pepper. Top with lemon slices, sprinkle with water chestnuts and green onion. Dot with margarine. Seal well. Pierce top of foil for steam escape. Grill over slow coals 35-40 minutes or place in 250° oven.

Mrs. James B. Austin, III (Ann Franklin)

Good with grilled honey chicken.

GREEN BEANS WITH SOUR CREAM

Serves 8

2 cans (16 ounces) French style green beans
4 tablespoons butter
4 tablespoons flour
1 teaspoon salt

½ teaspoon pepper
1 tablespoon sugar
½ cup grated onion
2 cups sour cream
1 pound American cheese, grated

Heat green beans, then drain. Place in an 8x8x2 inch casserole. Melt butter, add flour, salt, pepper, sugar, onion and sour cream. Mix well to make sauce. Pour sauce over beans. Sprinkle with grated cheese. Bake in 350° oven for 20-30 minutes then turn oven on broil, to melt cheese.

Mrs. Robert C. Hill (Betty McComb)

FROSTED GREEN BEANS

Serves 10-12

MARINADE

6 tablespoons vinegar
¾ cup salad oil
2 medium onions, minced

Salt and pepper to taste
4 cans whole green beans, drained

Prepare marinade by mixing together the first four ingredients. Pour over drained beans and chill over night.

DRESSING

8 hard cooked eggs, chopped
4 teaspoons vinegar
2 teaspoons prepared mustard

Salt and pepper
8 slices of bacon, cooked and crumbled
6 tablespoons mayonaise

Place chilled green bean mixture in serving bowl, top with bacon and add dressing.

Mrs. Robert W. Bauman (Frances Schneider)

GREEN BEAN CASSEROLE

Serves 8

1 onion, chopped
¼ cup butter
2 cans (16 ounces each)
  French style green beans
¼ cup flour
1½ cups milk
½ pound Velveeta cheese,
  grated

1 can (8 ounces)
  water chestnuts
  Dash Tabasco sauce
2 teaspoons soy sauce
½ teaspoon black pepper
¼ teaspoon Accent
2 cans (2 ounces each)
  mushroom pieces
  Slivered almonds

Sauté onion in butter. Add next ten ingredients and mix well. Pour into greased casserole. Top with almonds. Bake in 350° oven 30-40 minutes.

Mrs. James A. Hedgecoke, Jr. (Sallye Dees)

SAUTÉED GREEN BEANS

Serves 8-10

2 pounds fresh green beans,
  washed and snapped
¼ cup margarine
1 onion, thinly sliced
½ pound mushrooms,
  washed and sliced

1 package (2 ounces)
  sliced almonds, toasted
  Salt and pepper
  Garlic salt
  Paprika

Boil green beans until tender-crisp, about 10 minutes. Drain and set aside. Melt margarine in a large skillet. Sauté onion and mushrooms. Add beans, almonds and seasonings. Toss and heat thoroughly, about 2 minutes.

Mrs. Virgil Pate (Mary Graham)

WANDA GILVIN'S GREEN BEAN BUNDLES

Serves 8

2 cans (16 ounces each)
  vertical packed green beans,
  drain, reserving juices
½ pound bacon, cut in half
  vertically and
  slightly cooked

¼ cup brown sugar
½ teaspoon allspice
  Black pepper to taste

Wrap 10 green beans with one strip of bacon. Secure with toothpick if necessary. Place bundles in shallow pan. Combine 1 cup bean juice with brown sugar, allspice and pepper. Pour over bean bundles and marinate for 1-3 days. Bake in 350° oven for 25 minutes. Dash of Mei Yen Powder may be added to marinade if desired.

MUSHROOM BUSINESS   Serves 8-10

1 pound mushrooms,
   wiped and chopped
4–6 tablespoons butter
6 slices white bread,
   buttered and cut into
   1-inch squares
½ cup chopped onion
½ cup chopped celery
½ cup chopped green pepper
½ cup mayonnaise

¾ teaspoon salt
¼ teaspoon pepper
2 eggs, slightly beaten
1½ cups milk
1 can mushroom soup
   Bread crumbs,
   approximately 2 slices
1 cup Cheddar cheese,
   grated

Sauté mushrooms in butter. Place half of bread squares in a buttered casserole. Combine onion, celery, green pepper and mayonnaise. Season with salt and pepper. Add mushrooms. Pour over bread squares. Place remaining bread squares on top of mixture. Mix eggs and milk and pour over the top. Refrigerate at least 1 hour. One hour before it is to be served, spoon a can of mushroom soup (undiluted) over the top. Cover with bread crumbs. Bake in 300° oven for 1 hour 10 minutes, or in 325° oven for 50-60 minutes. About 10 minutes before it is done, sprinkle with cheese.

Mrs. Richard Reeves (Louise Coe)

SHERRIED
MUSHROOMS   Serves 4-6

3 tablespoons butter
1 pound fresh mushrooms,
   washed, drained
   and stemmed
1 tablespoon flour
1 chicken bouillon cube

¼ cup dry white wine,
   heated
1 teaspoon
   monosodium glutamate
1 bay leaf
   Dash of nutmeg
2 tablespoons sherry

Heat butter. Add mushrooms and flour. Toss mushrooms while sautéing lightly. Dissolve bouillon cube in wine. Pour over mushrooms. Add seasoning and continue cooking, uncovered, for approximately 6 minutes, stirring occasionally. Add sherry and keep warm, until ready to serve.

Mrs. Douglas Easley (Hilda Stevens)

237

SOUR CREAM MUSHROOMS

Serves 4

2 teaspoons dill weed
  or oregano
¼ pound butter
1½ pounds mushrooms, sliced

Garlic salt
White pepper to taste
8 ounces sour cream

Sauté dill weed or oregano in butter. Add mushrooms, garlic salt, pepper, and stir-fry for 3-5 minutes. Add sour cream and cook for 1 minute. Do not boil.

Mrs. John Mozola (Jo Rush)

BAKED ONIONS

Serves 4-6

4, 6 or 8 small white onions
½ stick butter
Salt

Pepper
Paprika
Sour cream

Parboil onions 10 minutes. Transfer to Pyrex dish. Add 1-1½ inches of water. Dot each onion with butter. Salt and pepper to taste. Sprinkle with paprika. Cook in 350° oven 30-45 minutes. Put spoonful of sour cream on each onion, according to taste.

Mrs. George Green (Rosemary McMurtry)

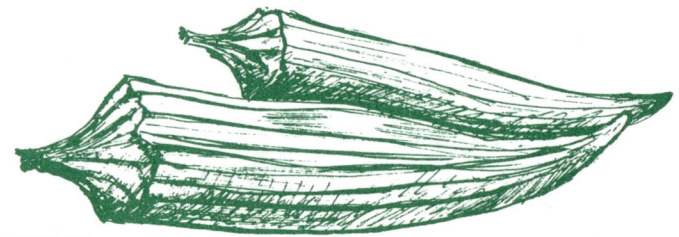

OKRA-ONION CASSEROLE

Serves 4

2 cups sliced okra
1 small onion chopped and
  sautéed in
  2 tablespoons butter
1 cup buttered bread crumbs,
  divided

½ cup shredded
  Cheddar cheese
2 tablespoons melted butter
2 eggs, beaten
½ teaspoon seasoned salt
½ teaspoon pepper

Combine all ingredients except ¼ cup buttered bread crumbs. Spoon into a lightly greased 1½ quart casserole. Bake in 350° oven for 30 minutes. Sprinkle with reserved bread crumbs and bake an additional 5 minutes.

Mrs. H. Boyd Hinton (Maelyn Latham)

GLAZED ONIONS

Serves 4-6

4 pounds white onions,
about 1 inch in diameter,
unpeeled

¼ cup butter
1 cup beef broth
1 tablespoon sugar

Place onions in a pot of boiling water. When water returns to a boil, remove from heat. Let stand for 2 minutes, then drain. Run cold water over the onions. Peel and trim. Melt butter in large saucepan. Add remaining ingredients. Cook over medium heat, 30 minutes or until stock has cooked down and onions are brown and tender. If necessary, more stock may be added or pan may be covered.

Mrs. A.J. Folley (Rowena Jones)

SCALLOPED ONIONS AND GREEN PEPPERS

Serves 6-8

12 medium onions
6 medium bell peppers,
cut in strips
½ cup margarine
(divide in half)

¼ cup flour
2½ cups milk
1 cup grated sharp cheese
2 teaspoons salt
Dash of pepper

Cut an "X" in top of onions and boil in salted water until tender. Drain and cut in half. Sauté pepper strips in ¼ cup margarine, until soft.

Make sauce, by melting ¼ cup margarine in medium saucepan. Stir in flour. Add milk slowly and stir until smooth. When sauce thickens, add grated cheese, salt and pepper. Pour sauce over vegetables and bake in ungreased casserole, for 25 minutes in 350° oven. Freezes well.

Mrs. Jerome Johnson (Wookie Sinclair)

MY AUNT'S FRENCH FRIED ONION RINGS

Serves 10

2 large white onions
2 cups flour

3 teaspoons baking powder
Enough water to make
batter-like flour paste

Peel and slice onions in rings. Combine flour, baking powder and water. Dip separated onion rings in batter. Fry in hot deep fat. Drain on paper towels. Salt while hot.

Mrs. Joe Bob McCartt (Susie Douglas)

MARINATED
PEAS AND BEANS

Serves 4-6

1 large can green peas,
   drained
1 large can French style
   green beans, drained
1 cup Italian dressing

1 jar marinated artichoke
   hearts, chilled
1 jar (2 ounces) sliced
   mushrooms, drained

Combine peas, beans and dressing. Refrigerate a few hours or overnight.
Before serving, add artichokes and mushrooms. Toss gently.

Mrs. William Daniel (Shirley Clark)

CHEESY
SPINACH PUFF

Serves 6

½ cup margarine
3 tablespoons flour
1 package (10 ounces) frozen
   spinach, thawed and drained

3 eggs, beaten
1 carton (12 ounces) small
   curd cottage cheese
½ cup grated American cheese

Melt margarine. Stir in flour. Add spinach, eggs, and cottage cheese.
Pour into a buttered 1 quart souffle dish. Top with American cheese.
Bake in a 350° oven for 45 minutes.

Mrs. Virgil Pate (Mary Graham)

*Can substitute ¾ milk and 1 cup Cheddar cheese for cottage and
American cheese.*

DEBORAH'S
SPINACH CASSEROLE

Serves 6-8

2 packages (10 ounces each)
   chopped frozen spinach
4 tablespoons butter
½ medium onion, chopped
2 tablespoons flour
¼ cup milk

½ teaspoon salt
½ teaspoon celery salt
½ teaspoon garlic salt
½ teaspoon pepper
1 tablespoon
   Worcestershire sauce
1 roll Jalapeño cheese

Cook frozen spinach and drain. Melt butter. Sauté onion. Add flour. Add
milk to make a white sauce. Add other ingredients. Put in a 1½ quart
casserole. Bake in a 350° oven for 30 minutes. This freezes well.

Mrs. William Harlow (Lynn O'Brien)

SPINACH AND ARTICHOKES

Serves 8

2 packages (10 ounces each)
   frozen spinach
2 packages (10 ounces each)
   frozen artichokes or
2 cans (8½ ounces each)
   artichokes
½ pound mushrooms, sliced
6 tablespoons butter

1 tablespoon flour
½ cup milk
⅛ teaspoon garlic powder
½ teaspoon salt
1 cup mayonnaise
1 cup sour cream
¼ cup lemon juice

Cook spinach and artichokes according to package directions. Drain well. Sauté mushrooms in 4 tablespoons butter. Make a cream sauce with 2 tablespoons of butter, flour and milk. Add spinach, garlic powder, salt and mushrooms to sauce. Make a sour cream sauce by slowly heating the mayonnaise, sour cream and lemon juice, until thickened. Place artichokes over bottom of Pyrex pan. Spread spinach mixture over artichokes. Cover with sour cream sauce. Bake in 325° oven for 15 minutes.

This may be made early in the day and refrigerated. Do not add the sour cream sauce until it is baked.

Mrs. Richard F. McKay (Gerry Goleman)

Try topping with bacon bits, hard-cooked eggs, paprika and toasted bread crumbs.

SPINACH CRÊPES

Serves 12-15

Use basic crêpe recipe to make crêpes in advance.

SPINACH FILLING

1 package (10 ounces) frozen,
   chopped spinach
¼ cup butter
3 tablespoons flour
1 cup milk
½ teaspoon salt
⅛ teaspoon ground nutmeg

⅛ teaspoon pepper
1 cup shredded Swiss cheese
1 can (4 ounces) mushrooms,
   stems and pieces, drained
1 teaspoon grated onion
   Parmesan cheese

Cook spinach, drain and set aside. Melt butter in heavy saucepan. Blend flour, stirring for 3-4 minutes. Gradually add milk, cooking and stirring for 6-8 minutes or until thick. Add spinach and remaining ingredients, stirring well. Spoon 2 tablespoons filling onto each crêpe. Roll and put in shallow baking dish. Brush with melted butter and sprinkle with Parmesan cheese. Bake in 375° oven for 15-20 minutes.

Mrs. John Mozola (Jo Rush)

241

SPINACH ROLL

Serves 8

2 packages (10 ounces each) chopped spinach
6 tablespoons butter, melted
Dash nutmeg
3 eggs separated
15 fresh mushrooms, sliced

1 cup chopped onions
3 tablespoons butter
Salt and pepper
Basil
Parsley
Cheddar or Swiss cheese, grated

Cook spinach, drain well, and cool. Melt butter, add nutmeg. Mix spinach, butter, nutmeg and egg yolks. Fold in stiffly beaten egg whites. Spread on greased cookie sheet. Bake 20 minutes in 350° oven. Loosen with spatula and turn onto a sheet of foil. Sauté onions and mushrooms in 3 tablespoons of butter with salt, pepper, basil and parsley. Spread over spinach. Sprinkle with cheese. Using foil to guide, roll spinach into a log or roll, beginning with short side of spinach. Top with more cheese and bake 10-20 minutes more in 350° oven. May be frozen.

Mrs. Jim Whitlock (Sue Smith)

SOUTH AMERICAN VEGETABLE CASSEROLE

Serves 6-8

1 cup chopped spinach, raw or frozen
1 green pepper, chopped
1 cup celery, chopped
1 small onion, minced
1 tablespoon raisins

½ teaspoon sugar
1 teaspoon chili powder
½ teaspoon ground cumin seed
¼ teaspoon salt
½ cup tomato juice

TOPPING

2 tablespoons bread crumbs
½ cup sharp cheese, grated

2 tablespoons butter

Mix first five ingredients together in a casserole. Blend next five ingredients together. Pour over vegetables and mix well. Mix topping ingredients and sprinkle on top of vegetables. Dot with butter. Bake in 375° oven for 20 minutes or until vegetables are cooked.

Mrs. R.G. Morrison, Jr. (Esther Jones)

CALABASITAS

Serves 8

- 4 yellow crook necked squash
- 1 can (6 ounces) green chile salsa (with tomatoes)
- 1 small onion diced, or
- 2 green onions chopped
- 6 crackers, crumbled
- ¼ lb. Longhorn cheese, grated
- Salt and pepper to taste
- Garlic salt to taste
- Butter
- 1¾ cups drained shoepeg corn

Boil squash until tender (about 10 minutes). Do not overcook. Cool. Slice lengthwise, being careful to preserve neck. Scoop out center. Combine with next six ingredients. Fill squash. Dot with butter. Bake in 350° oven until cheese melts, about 30 minutes.

Mrs. Carol Cowan (Carol Craig)

For a quick dish, mix squash with other ingredients, and serve as a casserole.

For microwave cooking, scrub and make slits in squash. Cook for 5 minutes. Cool, while making stuffing. Fill squash. Cook 5-6 minutes more, in microwave. Put in 400° oven for 15 minutes or under broiler for 5 minutes.

STUFFED SQUASH

Serves 8

- 8 medium yellow squash
- 1 package (10 ounces) frozen spinach, cooked and drained
- 1 can mushroom soup
- 2 hard cooked eggs, grated
- Worcestershire sauce
- Tabasco
- Salt and pepper
- ½ cup bread crumbs
- 2 tablespoons butter, melted
- 2 tablespoons Parmesan cheese, grated

Boil squash until just tender. Halve and scoop out centers. To spinach, add soup, eggs and seasonings to taste. Stuff squash with spinach. Mix together bread crumbs, butter and Parmesan cheese. Top stuffed squash with bread crumb mixture. Bake in 350° oven for 20 minutes. Can be frozen.

Mrs. Virgil Pate (Mary Graham)

LOUISIANA SQUASH CASSEROLE

Serves 8

- 2 pounds yellow squash, thinly sliced
- ½ teaspoon salt
- 1 onion sliced
- 2 carrots, sliced
- 1½ sticks oleo, melted
- 1 box Pepperidge Farm Seasoned Crumbs
- 1 cup sour cream
- 1 can cream of chicken soup
- 2 ounces chopped pimiento Paprika

Cook squash in water with salt, onion and carrots until tender. Set aside. Pour oleo over crumbs and set aside. Combine sour cream, soup and pimiento. In 12x8x2 inch buttered casserole, put half of crumb mixture, then vegetables, then soup mixture. Top with remaining crumbs. Sprinkle with paprika. Bake covered in 350° oven for 35-45 minutes, uncovering for the last 10 minutes.

Mrs. Joe Pritchard (Marianne Gerding)

For a twist add 1 bell pepper, chopped and sautéed and Cavender's seasoning, if desired.

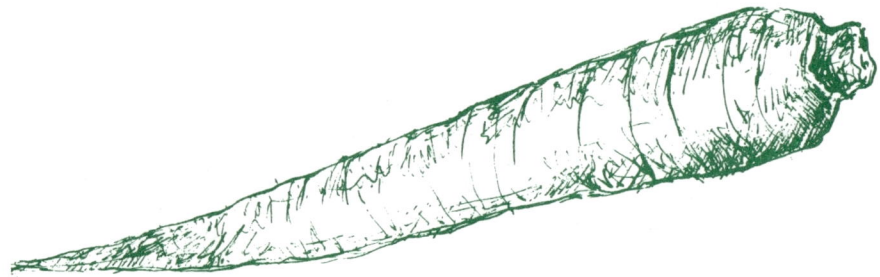

SQUASH 'N PEAS

Serves 6-8

- 5-6 medium summer squash, sliced
- ½ cup frozen green peas, uncooked
- ¼-⅓ cup sour cream
- Cracker crumbs or Pepperidge Farm stuffing mix
- 4 teaspoons margarine Salt and pepper Paprika

Cook squash in small amount of salted, boiling water. Simmer 15-20 minutes. Drain well. Add frozen peas, sour cream, salt and pepper. Mix together and put into buttered, 1 quart casserole. Top with crumbs, dot with margarine and sprinkle with paprika. Bake in 350° oven for 30 minutes.

Clam, onion or other sour cream dips may be used in place of plain sour cream.

Mrs. Ron Hale (Judy Prescott)

SQUASH WITH SOUR CREAM
AND DILL SEED
Serves 6-8

6–8 yellow or zucchini squash,
    sliced
½ medium size onion, chopped
¼ cup butter or margarine

½ pint sour cream
1 tablespoon dill seed or
    fresh basil
Salt and pepper to taste

Slice and cook squash until tender but not soft, in lightly salted water. Drain thoroughly. Sauté onions in butter. Gently stir onions and sour cream into squash. Add salt and pepper to taste. Sprinkle with dill seeds.

Mrs. Jerome Johnson (Wookie Sinclair)

SOUR CREAM SQUASH
Serves 6-8

8 yellow squash, sliced and
    cooked until tender
    in salted water
½ cup bacon, fried
    and crumbled
1 large onion, chopped

1 tablespoon butter
1 carton (8 ounces)
    sour cream
1 roll Kraft garlic cheese
Salt and pepper to taste

Drain squash. Saute onion in butter. Add to squash. Fold in sour cream. Add garlic cheese. Stir bacon through casserole. Bake in 350° oven for 20-30 minutes or until cheese has melted.

Mrs. David Kritser, III (Sally Simpson)

GREEN PUMPKIN WITH
GREEN CHILIES
Serves 6-8

4 cups cubed green pumpkin
    or zucchini
1 cup fresh corn, cut
    from cob
2 green chilies (seeds
    removed), chopped
1 large tomato, chopped

2 small onions, chopped
½ clove garlic, chopped
½ teaspoon chopped
    fresh mint
1½ teaspoons salt
Milk

Heat enough bacon drippings to cover the bottom of a large pan. Add all ingredients except milk. Cover and cook slowly, about 10 minutes. Stir occasionally to prevent burning. Cover with milk and simmer uncovered about 1 hour.

Mrs. Josephine K. Wyatt (Josephine Kuykendall)

A favorite northern New Mexico recipe.

BAKED HERBED
TOMATOES PARMESAN   Serves 6

6 medium size tomatoes
  Onion salt
  Fines Herbs by Spice Island
1 cup Hellmann's mayonnaise

4 tablespoons
  Parmesan cheese
2 tablespoons chopped
  green onions

Cut a slice off the stem end of each tomato. Sprinkle tomatoes with onion salt and Fines Herbes. Bake in 350° oven for 20-25 minutes. Mix mayonnaise, Parmesan cheese and onion. When tomatoes are baked, remove from oven and increase temperature to 500°. Place a spoonful of the mayonnaise mixture on each tomato. Return to oven and cook until the mayonnaise is browned, about 5 minutes.

Mayonnaise mixture can be spread on melba toast, baked and served as an appetizer.

Mrs. Robert W. Bauman (Frances Schneider)

Mrs. T.L. Roach, Jr. (Rosemary Allen)

MARINATED
TOMATOES   Serves 4

4 large tomatoes, peeled,
  and thickly sliced
2 tablespoons chopped onion
½ cup sliced stuffed olives
½ cup salad oil

¼ cup wine vinegar
½ teaspoon salt
½ teaspoon pepper
1 teaspoon dry basil
¼ teaspoon thyme
1 clove garlic, mashed

Arrange tomatoes in a shallow 9x9 inch dish. Sprinkle onions and olives over tomatoes. Combine remaining ingredients and mix well. Pour over tomatoes, onions and olives. Chill 4-6 hours.

Mrs. George Snell (Bonnie Brown)

TOMATO CASSEROLE

Serves 4-6

2 **cups bread crumbs, fresh or 1¾ cups Italian style**
1 **teaspoon sugar**
1 **teaspoon salt**
⅓ **teaspoon dry mustard**
½ **teaspoon paprika**
4 **cups sliced, fresh tomatoes**
2 **cups grated Cheddar cheese**
¼ **cup butter, melted**

Grease shallow 10 inch casserole and sprinkle with ⅓ of crumbs. Mix together sugar, salt, mustard and paprika. Arrange ⅓ tomatoes in casserole. Sprinkle ⅓ dry mixture and ⅓ cheese over tomatoes. Repeat layers. Sprinkle melted butter over bread crumb layer. End with cheese. Bake covered in 375° oven for 30 minutes. Bake 10 additional minutes uncovered.

Mrs. William T. Griffin (Nita Johnson)

TOMATOES STUFFED WITH VEGETABLES

Serves 6

6 **large tomatoes**
3 **large ears of corn**
¾ **cup water**
¼ **cup butter**
   Salt and pepper to taste
2 **cups zucchini, thinly sliced**
1 **clove garlic, crushed**
½ **teaspoon dill weed or basil**
¼ **cup butter**
1 **tablespoon flour**
½ **cup tomato pulp, seeded**

Cut thin slice off top of each tomato. Cut around pulp, leaving enough ''wall'' to stand firm, remove pulp and reserve. Turn tomatoes upside down to drain. Slice kernels off ears of corn, scrape remaining pulp from cob. Combine in skillet with water and butter. Cook, stir occasionally, until corn is tender and water evaporates. Add salt and pepper. Sauté zucchini, garlic and dill weed or basil in butter until zucchini is tender but crisp. Add corn mixture, flour and tomato pulp. Cook over low heat until mixture thickens. Adjust seasonings. Fill tomatoes with mixture, place in single layer in casserole and bake 12-15 minutes in 350° oven, until heated through.

Sally Bivins

TOMATO PUDDING

Serves 6

2 cups fresh bread crumbs
½ cup melted butter
20 ounces tomato purée
½ cup boiling water

½ teaspoon salt
1 teaspoon dried basil
¾ cup brown sugar

Place bread crumbs in a 10x6x1¾ inch Pyrex baking dish. Pour butter over crumbs. In a saucepan, add remaining ingredients. Heat, stirring to a boil. Pour mixture over bread crumbs. Cover dish tightly and bake in 350° oven for 30 minutes. Do not remove cover until ready to serve. This is especially good with turkey at Christmas or Thanksgiving.

Mrs. John Kelleher (Cindy Leiphart)

FRESH VEGETABLE CASSEROLE

Serves 4-6

2 large onions, sliced
2 tablespoons butter, melted
3 carrots, sliced
1 medium-sized green pepper, sliced into rings
½ pound fresh green beans

2 large tomatoes, sliced
¼ cup chopped parsley
1¾ teaspoons salt
¼ teaspoon seasoned salt
½ teaspoon fresh ground pepper

Sauté onions in butter until golden; separate into rings. Place onions, carrots, green pepper, beans, tomatoes and parsley in a greased 2 quart shallow casserole; mix lightly. Add seasonings. Cover and bake in 350° oven for 1 hour.

Mrs. Larry Paulk (Judy Feferman)

GREEN VEGETABLE CASSEROLE

Serves 6-8

1 package (10 ounces) frozen limas
1 package (10 ounces) frozen green peas
1 can (1 pound) green beans

1 large bell pepper
½ pint whipping cream, whipped
½ cup mayonnaise
Parmesan cheese

Cook limas according to package directions. Drain. Thaw green peas. Do not cook. Drain green beans. Cut bell pepper into lengthwise slices. Parboil. In a 1½ quart buttered casserole, layer the limas, ⅓ of the bell pepper, green beans, ⅓ of the bell pepper, green peas, and the rest of the bell pepper. This may be done the day before. Just before cooking, whip the cream. Fold in the mayonnaise. Pour this mixture over the vegetables. Cover the top of the casserole with Parmesan cheese. Bake in a 350° oven for 30 minutes or until the casserole is golden brown and bubbly.

Mrs. Rex Vermillion (Elizabeth Ann Welborn)

VEGETABLE MELANGE AU GRATIN

Serves 6-8

1½ cups sliced carrots
½ cup chopped onion
1 package (10 ounces)
   frozen chopped spinach
2 tablespoons butter

2 tablespoons flour
1 cup milk
¼ teaspoon salt
1 cup shredded
   Cheddar cheese
1 cup buttered bread crumbs

Cook carrots and onions in salted water until tender. Drain. Cook spinach according to package directions and drain well. Melt butter in pan over low heat; stir in flour. Slowly add milk, stirring until thick and smooth. Add salt and cheese, continue cooking until cheese melts. Alternate layers of drained vegetables and cheese sauce in 1 quart casserole. Top with buttered bread crumbs. Bake in 350° oven for 20-30 minutes.

Mrs. Tom Cambridge (Norma Taggart)

This is a good dish to prepare ahead of time.

VEGETABLE CASSEROLE

Serves 12

1 can (16 ounces)
   asparagus, drained
1 can (16 ounces)
   green peas, drained
1 can (8½ ounces)
   water chestnuts,
   drained and sliced

1 can mushroom soup
½ pound grated
   American cheese
1½ cups crushed
   Club Crackers
1 stick margarine

Layer in order in a 9x13 inch pan the asparagus, peas, chestnuts, soup, cheese and crackers. Melt margarine and pour over crackers. Cover and bake in 350° oven for 25-30 minutes.

Mrs. William A. Sansing (Betty Ann Troutman)

MAGGIE CURTIS' HOPPING JOHN

Serves 4-6

4 cups cooked rice
2 cans (1 pound 4 ounces
   each) blackeyed peas
   or fresh

Chopped tomatoes, to taste
Chopped onions, to taste
Oil and vinegar
   salad dressing

Place rice on a dish. Top with peas. Add salad dressing to tomatoes and onions. Put on top of peas. Pour more salad dressing over all.

Mrs. Stephen Curtis (Jerre Lewis)

CAJUN
RED BEANS

Serves 8-10

- 1 pound dried red beans, soaked
- ½ pound salt pork or ham bone
- 1 tablespoon salt
- 2 quarts water
- 1½ cups chopped Bermuda onion
- 1 bunch green onions, chopped
- 1 cup chopped green bell pepper
- 2-3 large cloves garlic, crushed
- ½ teaspoon red pepper
- 1 teaspoon fresh cracked pepper
- ½ teaspoon oregano
- ½ teaspoon thyme
- 3 dashes Tabasco
- 1 tablespoon Worcestershire sauce
- 1 can (15 ounces) tomato sauce
- 2 pounds sausage (Oscar Meyer), optional
- Monosodium glutamate

Cook beans and pork in salted water for 45 minutes. Add vegetables, seasonings, and tomato sauce. Simmer 1 hour.

Shape sausage into balls and lightly brown. Add to beans and cook 45 minutes. Cool. Skim off fat. Reheat and simmer 45 minutes. Add monosodium glutamate, salt and pepper to taste.

This is good over rice and served with cornbread. It is also good as a vegetable served with beef.

Mrs. Guyon Saunders (Mary Frances Collins)

HOMILADA

Serves 4-6

- 2 tablespoons bacon drippings
- 2 tablespoons flour
- 4 tablespoons chili powder (or to taste)
- 1 can (1 pound) tomatoes
- 2 cups hominy liquid and/or water
- 1 teaspoon salt
- ½ teaspoon cumin
- ¼ teaspoon oregano
- 2 cans (14½ ounces each) white hominy, drained
- 1 large onion, chopped
- Butter
- 6 ounces cheese, shredded

Make a roux of bacon drippings, flour and chili powder. Add tomatoes, liquid, salt, cumin and oregano. Cook to make a smooth sauce. It will not be thick. Sauté hominy and onions in butter in separate skillets. In a greased 6 cup baking dish layer half hominy, half onion, half tomato mixture and half cheese. Repeat the four layers. Bake in 350° oven for 25 minutes.

Sally Bivins

HOMINY CASSEROLE

Serves 8-10

4 tablespoons butter
1 can (20 ounces) hominy, drained
1 can (4 ounces) chopped green chilies
1 cup sour cream
½ pound Cheddar or Longhorn cheese, grated
Minced onion, optional

Melt butter in a 2 quart casserole. Add remaining ingredients. Reserve some cheese for top of casserole. Bake in 350° oven for 20-30 minutes.

Mrs. Douglas Easley (Hilda Steven)

CASSEROLE POTATOES

Serves 12

6 medium potatoes
6 tablespoons margarine
2 cups grated Cheddar cheese
3 green onions, chopped
1½ cups sour cream
1 teaspoon salt
¼ teaspoon pepper

Boil potatoes in jackets; chill. Peel and grate. Set aside. Melt 4 tablespoons butter. Slowly add cheese, stirring until almost melted. Remove from heat. Add onion, sour cream, salt and pepper. Fold in potatoes. Pour into buttered 2 quart casserole. Add remaining margarine. Bake covered in 300° oven for 30 minutes or until bubbly. Potatoes could be whipped or sliced for a different texture.

6 slices of cooked, crumbled bacon can be used as a garnish.

Mrs. Walter S. Berry (Mary Knupp)

FRENCH FRIED SCALLOPED POTATOES

Serves 6-8

½ cup butter
½ cup chopped green pepper
½ cup chopped celery
¼ cup flour
1 teaspoon salt
⅛ teaspoon pepper
1 can mushroom soup
2 cups milk
¼ cup chopped pimiento
½ cup grated carrot
½ pound American cheese, grated
2 packages (9 ounces each) frozen French fried potatoes

Melt butter in large saucepan. Add green pepper and celery. Cook until tender. Blend in flour, salt and pepper. Add mushroom soup and milk. Cook, stirring constantly, until slightly thickened. Add pimiento, carrot and ½ of the cheese. Place potatoes in 11¾x7½x1¾ inch casserole. Pour sauce over top. Bake uncovered in 400° oven for 25 minutes. Add remaining cheese and bake 5 minutes.

Mrs. Don Buckley (Patty Smith)

CHEESE GRITS

Serves 12

6 cups water
   Salt to taste
1½ cups grits
1½ sticks butter

1 pound Cheddar cheese,
   grated
3 eggs, beaten
16 drops Tabasco

Bring water to a boil. Add salt and grits. Stir over low heat. Add cheese and butter. Stir until blended. Remove from heat. Add eggs and Tabasco. Pour into a 2½-3 quart greased casserole. Bake uncovered in 350° oven for 1 hour. Sprinkle top with a little cheese before serving.

Mrs. Dick Frazer (Sylvia Lindley)

For a bit of a flare, use 2 rolls of garlic cheese instead of Cheddar.

ARROZ CON JOCOQUI

Serves 6-8

¾ pound Monterey Jack
   cheese
3 cups sour cream, salted
2 cans (4 ounces each) Ortega
   mild green chilies, seeded
   and chopped

3 cups cooked rice
   Salt and pepper
½ cup grated
   Cheddar cheese

Cut Monterey Jack cheese in strips. Thoroughly mix sour cream and chilies. Butter a 2 quart casserole. Season rice with salt and pepper to taste. Layer rice, sour cream mixture and cheese strips, in that order, ending with rice on top. Bake in 350° oven for approximately 30 minutes. During the last few minutes of baking, sprinkle grated Cheddar cheese over rice and allow it to melt.

May be assembled early in day.

Mrs. B.R. Barfield (Carolyn Grissom)

GREEN RICE

Serves 6-8

2 cups cooked rice (instant
   rice may be used)
1 can (13 ounces)
   Carnation milk
1 small onion, minced
1 clove garlic, minced

1 cup fresh parsley or
½ cup dried parsley
½ pound sharp Cracker Barrel
   cheese, grated
⅓ cup salad oil
   Salt and pepper (savory
   salt if desired)

Mix all ingredients well. Pour into a 1¾ quart casserole and bake in 325° oven for 45 minutes or until set.

Mrs. Don Buckley (Patty Smith)

FRIED TERIYAKI RICE

Serves 4-5

¼ cup smoked ham
    (slivers or strips)
⅛ cup chopped celery
¼ cup bacon fat or butter
¼ cup water chestnuts
¼ cup sliced green onion

1 can (2 ounces) mushrooms
2 tablespoons soy sauce
½ teaspoon salt
½ teaspoon
    monosodium glutamate
3 cups cooked rice
1 egg, beaten

Fry ham and celery in butter in large skillet. Add water chestnuts and fry three more minutes, stirring constantly. Add next six ingredients. Just before serving, heat and add beaten egg, stirring gently.

This can be made early in the day and refrigerated in the skillet. Add a little water before heating.

Mrs. Hugh A. Sticksel (Pan Purdy)

This is good with Japanese Kabob's.

JALAPEÑO RICE

Serves 6-8

1 cup rice
¼ cup butter
½ cup chopped onion
½ cup chopped
    green pepper
1 Jalapeño pepper, chopped

2 small cans (4 ounces each)
    diced green chilies
1 cup sour cream
1 cup grated Longhorn
    cheese
1 cup grated Mozzarella

Cook rice according to package directions. Sauté onion, green pepper and Jalapeño pepper in butter and add to cooked rice. Add chilies, sour cream and cheeses. Pour into a casserole dish. Bake in 350° oven for 30 minutes.

Mrs. Mack Gordon (Dixie Conley)

RICE JARDIN

Serves 6

¾ cup chopped onion
1 pound zucchini, thinly sliced
3 tablespoons butter
1 can (8 ounces)
    whole kernel corn,
    drained

1 cup canned tomatoes,
    chopped
3 cups cooked rice
1½ teaspoons salt
¼ teaspoon each pepper,
    ground coriander, oregano

Sauté onions and zucchini in butter until tender. Add remaining ingredients. Cover and simmer 15 minutes. Can be made in smaller quantities.

Mrs. Anne Reid (Anne Ansley)

RICE MUSHROOM RING

Serves 6-8

1 cup rice or wild rice
2½ cups boiling water
1½ teaspoons salt
1½ pounds fresh mushrooms

2-4 chopped green onions
4 tablespoons of butter
Salt and pepper to taste
1 tablespoon dried parsley

Wash rice. Put in heavy pot with lid (iron pot is best). Add boiling water and salt. Cover and bake in 450° oven until barely dry (about 25 minutes). While rice is cooking, chop mushrooms and onions then sauté in butter. Mix rice, onions and mushrooms. Add salt, pepper and parsley. Press firmly into buttered 1 quart ring mold. Put mold in a pan of boiling water and bake in 350° oven for 30 minutes. Unmold ring and fill center with your favorite colorful vegetable. Garnish with fresh parsley.

Mrs. Dan Moreland (Catherine Pierce)

SAUSAGE AND WILD RICE CASSEROLE

Serves 6-8

½–¾ pounds sausage
½ pound fresh mushrooms, sliced, or
1 can (8 ounces) mushrooms, drained and sliced
1 medium onion, chopped
1 box Uncle Ben's Long Grain and Wild Rice mix

1 teaspoon pepper
1 tablespoon butter
2-3 tablespoons flour
¼ cup heavy cream
1 can (13¾ ounces) chicken broth
½ teaspoon salt

Cook sausage. Drain, reserving drippings. Sauté the mushrooms and onions in drippings. Break sausage into small pieces and add to mushrooms and onions. Cook the packet of rice in 2½ cups of water and butter. Bring to boil, cover pan and cook over low heat for 10 minutes. Drain rice. In saucepan, mix flour with cream until smooth. Add chicken broth and cook until thick. Add the seasoning packet (from the rice box), salt, pepper, rice and sausage mixture. Mix well. Bake uncovered in 350° oven for 25-30 minutes.

Mrs. James D. Man (Cordelia Harris)

Cakes

Cheesecake

Torte

Frostings and Fillings

CUSTARD FILLING FOR ANGEL FOOD CAKE

1 pint or ¾ pint of
  sweet milk
6 egg yolks well beaten
1 cup sugar
1 package unflavored gelatin
¼ cup cold water
¾ pint whipping cream,
  whipped

1 cup crushed pineapple,
  drained
1 cup Maraschino cherries
1 cup nuts
1 cup small marshmallows
1 Angel Food cake

Mix milk, eggs and sugar and cook until it coats spoon, stirring all the time while cooking. (Do not overcook.) Dissolve gelatin in cold water and mix with custard. Let cool. When cold, add whipped cream, pineapple, cherries, nuts and marshmallows.

Cut across the middle of cake. Dig out some of the center of bottom half and stuff with custard. Put top on cake and fill center with custard.

TOPPING

¾ pint whipping cream,
  whipped

Sugar to taste
1 teaspoon vanilla

Ice cake with topping.

Mrs. David Beck (Dot Dean)

APPLE-NUT SQUARES

2 cups sugar
¾ cup salad oil
3 eggs
1 teaspoon soda
3 cups flour

3 cups peeled
  chopped apples
2 teaspoons vanilla
1 cup chopped nuts

Combine all ingredients, mixing well. Spread evenly in greased 13x9x2 inch pan. Bake in a 325° oven for 1 hour. Spread topping. Cool and cut in squares.

TOPPING

½ cup butter
1 cup firmly packed
  brown sugar

¼ cup evaporated milk

Combine all ingredients in small pan. Bring to boil and cook 2 minutes. Spread on cake while warm. Freezes beautifully.

Mrs. Rolla Cartwright (Margaret Kerr)

APRICOT BRANDY POUND CAKE

1 cup butter (no substitute)
3 cups sugar
6 eggs
3 cups all-purpose flour, measured after sifting
¼ teaspoon soda
½ teaspoon salt
1 cup sour cream
½ teaspoon rum flavoring
1 teaspoon orange extract
1 teaspoon almond extract
½ teaspoon lemon extract
1 teaspoon vanilla extract
½ cup apricot brandy

Grease and flour large bundt pan. In large bowl, cream butter and sugar thoroughly. Add eggs, one at a time, beating well after each addition. Sift together flour, soda and salt three times. Combine sour cream, flavorings and brandy. Add dry ingredients alternately with sour cream mixture, beginning and ending with the dry. Pour into prepared pan. Bake in 325° oven for 1 hour and 10 minutes or until cake tests done. May be prepared ahead of time. Freezes well.

Mrs. Joe Bob McCartt (Susie Douglas)

BLACK FOREST CHERRY CAKE

WHIPPED CREAM CAKE

1½ cups whipped cream, chilled
3 eggs
1½ teaspoons vanilla
2 cups flour

1½ cups sugar
2 teaspoons baking powder
½ teaspoon salt

In chilled bowl, beat cream until stiff. In separate bowl, beat eggs until thick and lemon colored. Fold eggs and vanilla into whipped cream. Stir together dry ingredients; fold gently into cream-egg mixture until blended. Pour into two 9 inch round layer pans greased and floured. Bake in 350° oven for 30-35 minutes. Cool.

CHERRY FILLING

4 tablespoons cornstarch
4 tablespoons sugar
2 cans (16 ounces each) pitted dark, sweet cherries, drained (reserve syrup)

2 tablespoons brandy flavoring
1½ cups whipping cream
¼ cup confectioner's sugar
½ (4 ounce bar) sweet cooking chocolate, grated

Stir together cornstarch and sugar in small saucepan. Add enough water to reserved syrup to measure 1 cup; stir into sugar-cornstarch mixture. Cook, stirring constantly, until mixture thickens and boils. Boil and stir 1 minute. Cool to lukewarm. Stir in brandy flavoring. Dip 45 cherries into thickened syrup; set cherries aside. Cut remaining cherries into quarters and stir into thickened syrup. Chill thoroughly. In chilled bowl, beat 1½ cups chilled whipping cream and ¼ cup confectioners sugar until very stiff.

ASSEMBLE CAKE

Place one layer upside down on serving plate. With decorator's tube or spoon, form thin rim of the sweetened, whipped cream around outer edge of layer. Fill center with cherry filling. Place other layer top side up on filling. Gently spread whipped cream on side and top of cake. Gently press grated chocolate by teaspoonsful onto side of the cake. If desired, place some of the whipped cream in decorator's tube with star tip. Pipe border of cream around edge of cake. Beginning from center of cake, outline individual portions in a spoke-fashion design. Place desired number of reserved dipped cherries in each outline portion. Cake must be kept refrigerated and is better if it has been chilled several hours before serving. Cake layers can be made the day before assembling.

Mrs. Richard F. McKay (Gerry Goleman)

BLACK FOREST TORTE

CAKE

8 egg whites
½ teaspoon salt
2 cups sugar
3 cups ground,
    unpeeled almonds

1 cup toasted coconut
2 teaspoons vanilla
1½ cups ground,
    unpeeled almonds

Beat egg whites with salt until foamy. Gradually add the sugar, beating until stiff peaks form. Fold in the almonds, coconut and vanilla. Butter three 10-inch round cake pans. Line the bottoms with wax paper and butter again. Cover bottom of each pan with ground almond crumbs (½ cup each). Spread batter over crumbs. Bake in 325° oven for 40 minutes. Remove from pan while hot. Cool.

FILLING

1 quart heavy cream,
    whipped stiff
2 cups powdered sugar

3 tablespoons
    unflavored gelatin
Shaved chocolate

Beat cream until very stiff. Add powdered sugar. Dissolve gelatin in ½ cup hot water and add very quickly to the whipped cream mixture.

Place 1 cake layer on plate and top with 1-inch of whipped cream mixture. Repeat with next layers. Cover top and sides with the whipped cream. Sprinkle shaved chocolate over top. Refrigerate or freeze.

Mrs. Walton Baum (DeDe Watson)

SOUR CREAM TORTE

2 sticks (½ pound) butter,
    at room temperature
3 cups sugar
6 eggs, separated

½ teaspoon vanilla
3 cups flour
¼ teaspoon soda
¼ pint sour cream

Blend butter and sugar until fluffy. Add egg yolks and vanilla. Sift flour and soda into creamed mixture. Beat egg whites until stiff. Fold in whites and sour cream. Pour into a greased and floured 10 inch bundt or angel food cake pan. Bake in 350° oven for 1 hour until golden brown.

GLAZE

¾ cup sugar
¼ cup water

1 teaspoon lemon flavoring
1 tablespoon butter

Combine all ingredients and boil 1 minute. Cool. Pour over the warm cake. This freezes well.

Mrs. John V. Cottle (Sammye Kinkade)

TROPICAL CARROT CAKE

2 cups flour
2 teaspoons baking powder
1 teaspoon soda
1 teaspoon cinnamon
½ teaspoon salt
½ teaspoon nutmeg
½ teaspoon allspice
4 eggs

2 cups sugar
1¼ cups oil
2 cups finely shredded raw carrots (about 6 medium)
1 can (8 oz.) crushed pineapple, drained (about ¾ cup)
1 cup chopped walnuts
½ cup flaked coconut

Stir together flour, baking powder, soda, cinnamon, salt, nutmeg and all-spice; set aside. In a large bowl beat eggs slightly. Beat in sugar until mixture is thick and lemon-colored. With rubber spatula, gradually stir in oil. Add flour mixture, carrots, pineapple, walnuts and coconut; stir until well-mixed. Place in three 9-inch greased and floured cake pans. Bake at 350° for 40 minutes (55 to 60 minutes for sheet cake). Let cool in pan 10 minutes. Frost with Tropical Butter Frosting or Cream Cheese Frosting.

TROPICAL BUTTER FROSTING

¼ cup butter
1 box (1 pound) confectioners sugar
¼ cup crushed pineapple, drained
2 tablespoons sour cream

¾ cup flaked coconut
2 teaspoons grated orange peel
1 teaspoon vanilla
¼ teaspoon salt

Stir butter until soft. Add sugar with pineapple and sour cream until fluffy and smooth. Stir in remaining ingredients.

Mrs. Charles Cathcart (Pat Hill)

CHEESECAKE (in food processor)

1½ cups cracker, cookie or zwieback crumbs
½ cup butter, melted
3 packages (8 ounces each) cream cheese, softened
1 cup sugar

3 eggs
½ teaspoon orange extract, or almond extract or
1 teaspoon vanilla or juice of one lemon

Combine crumbs and butter in processor using steel blade. Press into bottom and ½ inch up on sides of a 9-inch springform pan.

With steel blade process cheese until smooth (on-off). Scrape sides. Add remaining ingredients and process until well blended, 20 seconds, Pour into crust. Bake in a preheated 450° oven for 15 minutes or until lightly brown. Let cool in pan. Garnish with chopped orange peel or lemon peel, toasted almonds, fruit, depending on flavoring used.

Mrs. Ray C. Johnson, Jr. (Joan McCormick)

MOM'S "FAMILY SECRET" CHEESECAKE

1 pound vanilla wafers (crushed to fine crumbs)
1 stick margarine
1 cup sugar
3 teaspoons cornstarch
3 packages (8 ounces each) cream cheese
4 eggs
1 pint sour cream
½ cup sugar
1 teaspoon vanilla

Preheat oven to 375°. Mix crumbs and butter. Pat into springform pan or 9 inch round cake pan. Be sure to keep thickness of crust even. Bake for 10 minutes. Cool 10-15 minutes. Mix sugar and cornstarch. Add cream cheese and eggs. Beat for 20 minutes at almost high speed. Pour into crust. Bake for 30 minutes and cool for 45 minutes. Hand mix remaining ingredients and pour on top of filling. Cook 10 minutes. When cool, refrigerate several hours. Each slice may be topped with blueberry pie filling. Very rich. Freezes well.
The timing is most important. When it says 20 minutes it means 20 minutes, not 15 or 30.

Mrs. Max E. Banks (Toni Lynn Pierce)

CREAM CHEESE CAKE

SHELL

22 graham crackers, rolled
½ cup sugar
½ cup melted butter

Roll crumbs very fine. Add sugar and butter. Save ½ cup crumbs, using remainder to line a 9 inch pie pan, patting firmly with back of spoon. Bake 5 minutes in 375° oven. Chill.

FILLING

4 packages (3 ounces each) Philadelphia cream cheese, softened
½ cup sugar
3 large eggs
Grated rind of one lemon
1 or 2 tablespoons lemon juice
1 pint sour cream, at room temperature
Cinnamon and sugar, mixed

Cream together cheese and sugar. Beat until fluffy. Add eggs, one at a time, stirring each one in only long enough to blend well. Fold in lemon juice and grated rind. Pour into shell. Bake in 350° oven for 30 minutes. Remove from oven and *quickly* spread top with sour cream. Sprinkle with cinnamon sugar. Finally, sprinkle remaining ½ cup buttered crumbs over top. Return pie to oven for 5 minutes. Remove. Chill several hours before serving.

Mrs. Elayne Shults (Elayne Steele)

MINNIE LEE'S CHEESECAKE

GRAHAM CRACKER CRUST

1½ cups graham
    cracker crumbs
¼–½ cup sugar
½ cup butter, melted

Combine all ingredients and mix thoroughly. Reserve ½ cup. Press remaining mixture into a buttered 9-inch pie plate. Cover both bottom and sides. Chill 20 minutes before adding the filling. Sprinkle the filled shell with the reserved crumbs.

FILLING

6 packages (3 ounces each)
    cream cheese, softened
¾ cup sugar
3 eggs, well beaten
1 teaspoon vanilla
Pinch of salt
3 tablespoons lemon juice

Cream the cheese. Add sugar a little at a time. Add eggs and mix well. Add vanilla, salt and lemon juice. Mix thoroughly. Pour into crust and top with crumbs. Bake in 350° oven for 20 minutes. Set to cool, then place in the refrigerator for several hours. May serve with strawberry topping.

STRAWBERRY TOPPING

1 pint strawberries
    (fresh or frozen)

Cut strawberries in half and arrange on top of cheesecake. Or serve frozen berries in a dish with the cheesecake. When using a topping, omit the second layer of crumbs.

Mrs. Stanley Mandel (Patti Jo Solnick)

THE PRESIDENT'S CHEESECAKE
(In Microwave)   Serves 16-20

2 cups graham
    cracker crumbs
½ cup sugar
½ cup butter, melted
½ teaspoon cinnamon
3 packages (8 ounces each)
    cream cheese, softened
5 eggs
1 cup sugar
½ teaspoon vanilla
2½ cups sour cream
1½ teaspoons vanilla
⅓ cup sugar
1 can cherry pie filling

Combine crumbs, sugar, butter and cinnamon. Press into the bottom of a 13x9 inch pan. Cook in microwave 2 minutes. Beat cream cheese until smooth. Stir in eggs, one at a time. Mix in sugar and vanilla. Pour over crust and return to microwave for 15 minutes, turning every 4 minutes. Combine sour cream, sugar and vanilla. Pour on top of cheese and spread evenly. Return again to microwave 1 minute and 15 seconds. Chill. Spread cherry pie filling on top and chill. Can be frozen.

Mrs. W.C. Turner, Jr. (Nancy Carmichall)

CHOCOLATE CHIFFON CAKE

2 egg whites, reserve yolks
1½ cups sugar
1¾ cups cake flour
½ teaspoon soda
¾ teaspoon salt

⅓ cup Wesson oil
1 cup buttermilk
2 egg yolks
2 squares unsweetened
chocolate, melted over water

Grease and flour two 8 inch cake pans. Beat egg whites until frothy. Gradually add ½ cup sugar. Beat until stiff. Set aside. In a large mixing bowl, sift flour, soda, salt and 1 cup sugar together. Add oil and half of buttermilk. Beat 1 minute. Add remaining buttermilk, egg yolks and chocolate and beat 1 minute. Fold in egg white mixture. Bake in 375° oven for 25-30 minutes.

CHOCOLATE FUDGE ICING

2 cups sugar
¼ cup corn syrup
½ cup cream or milk
½ cup margarine

2 squares unsweetened
chocolate, cut fine
Pinch of salt
Vanilla

Combine all ingredients and cook over low heat. Do not bring to a boil until all the sugar is melted and cannot be felt on the spoon. Bring to full boil and cook 1 minute. Remove from heat and beat until lukewarm.

Mrs. Danny Conklin (Carolyn Kerns)

CHOCOLATE PUDDING CAKE

CRUST

1 cup flour
1 stick butter

1 cup chopped nuts

Blend flour, butter and nuts together and spread in 8x12 inch or 9x11 inch pan. Bake in 350° oven for 20 minutes.

FILLING (1st Layer)

1 package (8 ounces)
cream cheese, softened

1 carton Cool Whip
1 cup powdered sugar

Cream together sugar, cream cheese and Cool Whip. Spread on cooled crust.

FILLING (2nd Layer)

1 package (3½ ounces)
instant chocolate pudding
2½ cups milk

1 package (3½ ounces)
instant vanilla pudding
1 teaspoon vanilla

Combine puddings and milk. Add vanilla and spread on top of cream filling. Top with Cool Whip and shaved chocolate.

Mrs. William T. Griffin (Nita Johnson)

WESSON OIL CHOCOLATE CAKE

2 cups sugar
2 cups flour
½ cup cocoa
2 teaspoons soda
¼ teaspoon salt

2 eggs
1 cup buttermilk
1 cup Wesson oil
1 cup boiling water
1 teaspoon vanilla

Mix first eight ingredients. Beat well. Add vanilla and water. Mix. Bake in greased and floured bundt pan in a 350° oven for 35-40 minutes. Top with fudge frosting.

FUDGE FROSTING

2 cups sugar
¼ cup white Karo
½ cup milk
½ stick butter

1 package (6 ounces) chocolate chips
½ teaspoon vanilla

Combine all ingredients. Bring to a boil and cook for 2 minutes. Add chocolate chips and vanilla. Stir until smooth. Drizzle over cake.

Mrs. Phillip Brent (Nancy Fellers)

GINGERBREAD

Serves 20

½ cup sugar
½ cup shortening
1 egg
1 cup New Orleans style molasses
2½ cups flour

1 teaspoon soda
1 teaspoon cinnamon
1 teaspoon ginger
½ teaspoon salt
1 cup hot water

Cream sugar and shortening. Add egg and molasses. Sift together flour, soda, cinnamon, ginger and salt. Add dry ingredients to creamed mixture. Add hot water. Mix with slotted spoon. Pour into 9x13 inch pan. Bake in 350° oven for 30-40 minutes.

LEMON SAUCE

Yield 1⅓ Cups

½ cup butter
1 cup sugar
½ cup water
1 egg, well beaten

3 tablespoons lemon juice (1 lemon)
Grated rind

Combine butter, sugar, water and egg in a medium saucepan. Add lemon juice and rind. Cook over medium heat, stirring constantly until mixture comes to a boil. Pour over gingerbread.

Mrs. John K. Boyce, Jr. (Sidney Stinnett)

ICE CREAM CAKE

4 cups chocolate
wafer crumbs
1 cup butter, melted
2 pints vanilla ice cream,
slightly softened
2 pints pistachio
ice cream,
slightly softened

2 pints chocolate
ice cream,
slightly softened
Coconut, fresh or
flaked

Combine crumbs and butter. Reserve ⅔ cup of mixture. Firmly press remaining crumbs into a 9 inch spring-form pan, covering bottom and sides. Freeze 15 minutes, or until firm. Remove from freezer and spread vanilla ice cream in an even layer. Sprinkle with half of reserved crumbs. Return to freezer until ice cream is firm. Remove from freezer and spread pistachio ice cream in an even layer. Sprinkle with remaining crumbs. Freeze until firm. Add final layer of chocolate ice cream. Cover top of pan with foil and return to freezer. About 10 minutes before serving, invert cake onto chilled serving plate. Garnish with coconut. To serve, cut into wedges with knife dipped in cold water. Can be made up to 2 weeks before serving. Crumbs can be made in an electric blender.

Mrs. Stephen Curtis (Jerre Lewis)

MISSISSIPPI MUD

CAKE

2 sticks margarine
2 cups sugar
4 eggs
2 tablespoons cocoa
1 teaspoon vanilla

1½ cups flour
1⅓ cups coconut
1½ cups chopped pecans
1 jar (16 ounces)
marshmallow creme

Cream margarine until fluffy. Add sugar. Beat in eggs, one at a time. Beat in cocoa, vanilla and flour. Stir in coconut and nuts. Pour into greased 9x13 inch pan. Bake in 350° oven for 35 minutes or until done. Remove and immediately spread with marshmallow creme. Let cool, then frost.

FROSTING

1 box (1 pound)
powdered sugar
1 stick margarine
6 tablespoons
evaporated milk

⅓ cup cocoa
1 teaspoon vanilla

Combine all ingredients and beat until smooth.

Mrs. E.T. Manning (Sally Manning)

Mrs. Leon Swift (Georgia Hawks)

Mrs. Tommy York (Linda Neal)

OATMEAL CAKE

1½ cup boiling water
1 cup quick oats, uncooked
½ cup margarine
1 cup brown sugar
1 cup granulated sugar

2 eggs
1½ cups flour
1 teaspon soda
½ teaspoon cinnamon
½ teaspoon salt

Pour water over oats. Let stand. Cream margarine, brown sugar and granulated sugar. Add eggs. Combine flour, soda, cinnamon and salt. Add to sugar mixture. Add oats and blend. Pour into greased 9x13x2 inch pan. Bake in 350° oven for 30-40 minutes.

TOPPING

1 stick margarine
1 cup brown sugar
3 tablespoons milk

1 cup Angel Flake coconut
1 cup chopped pecans

Combine margarine, brown sugar and milk. Boil 1 minute. Add coconut and pecans. Spread on hot cake and broil until lightly browned.

Mrs. Barry Stone (Linda D'Arcy)

PUMPKIN ROLL   Serves 20

3 eggs
1 cup sugar
⅔ cup pumpkin
1 teaspoon lemon juice
¾ cup flour
2 teaspoons cinnamon
1 teaspoon baking powder

½ teaspoon salt
1 teaspoon ginger
1 teaspoon nutmeg
1¼ cups powdered sugar
1 package (8 ounces) cream cheese
¼ cup butter, softened
½ teaspoon vanilla

At high speed on mixer, beat eggs for 5 minutes. Gradually add sugar and beat well. Stir in pumpkin and lemon juice. Combine flour, cinnamon, baking powder, salt, ginger and nutmeg. Add to pumpkin mixture and blend well. Spoon batter into a well greased and floured 15x10x1 inch jelly roll pan. Spread to corners. Bake in a 375° oven for 15 minutes. Turn cake out onto a towel sprinkled with ¼ cup powdered sugar. Beginning at narrow end, roll up cake and towel together. Cool 1 hour. Combine 1 cup powdered sugar, cream cheese, butter and vanilla. Beat until smooth and creamy. Unroll cake and spread with filling. Roll cake up again and chill seam side down. Will freeze. Cut with an electric knife.

Mrs. Ben Bruckner, Jr. (Peggy Flowers)

SWEET POTATO CAKE

1½ cups salad oil
2 cups sugar
4 eggs, separated
4 tablespoons hot water
2½ cups cake flour
3 teaspoons baking powder
¼ teaspoon salt
1 teaspoon ground cinnamon
1 teaspoon ground nutmeg
1½ cups grated raw
   sweet potato (about
   2 medium potatoes)
1 cup chopped pecans
1 teaspoon vanilla

Combine oil and sugar in a large mixing bowl; beat until smooth. Add egg yolks; beat well. Stir in water. Combine dry ingredients; blend into sugar mixture. Stir in potatoes, pecans and vanilla, blending thoroughly. Beat egg whites until stiff; fold into batter. Spoon batter into three greased 8 inch cake pans. Bake in a 350° oven for 25-30 minutes. Remove from pans; cool on wire racks. Spread coconut filling between layers and on top of cake.

COCONUT FILLING

1 can (13 ounces)
   evaporated milk
1 cup sugar
½ cup butter
3 tablespoons
   all purpose flour
1 teaspoon vanilla
1⅓ cups flaked coconut

Combine milk, sugar, butter, flour and vanilla in a saucepan. Cook, stirring constantly over medium heat until thickened, about 12 minutes. Remove from heat; stir in coconut. Beat until thickened and cooled.

Mrs. Joe T. Davidson (Janet Allen)

PUMPKIN CAKE

1½ cups salad oil
2 cups flour
2 cups sugar
1½ cups pumpkin
4 eggs
2 teaspoon soda
3 teaspoons cinnamon
1 teaspoon vanilla

Mix all ingredients together and bake in greased and floured tube or bundt pan in 350° oven for 1¼ hours. Test with toothpick.

ICING

2½ cups powdered sugar
1 package (8 ounces)
   cream cheese, softened
¼ cup butter, softened
2 teaspoon vanilla
1 cup chopped pecans

Combine sugar, cheese, butter and vanilla and beat until smooth. Stir in nuts. Spread over cake.

Mrs. Joe B. Wells (Brenda Breece)

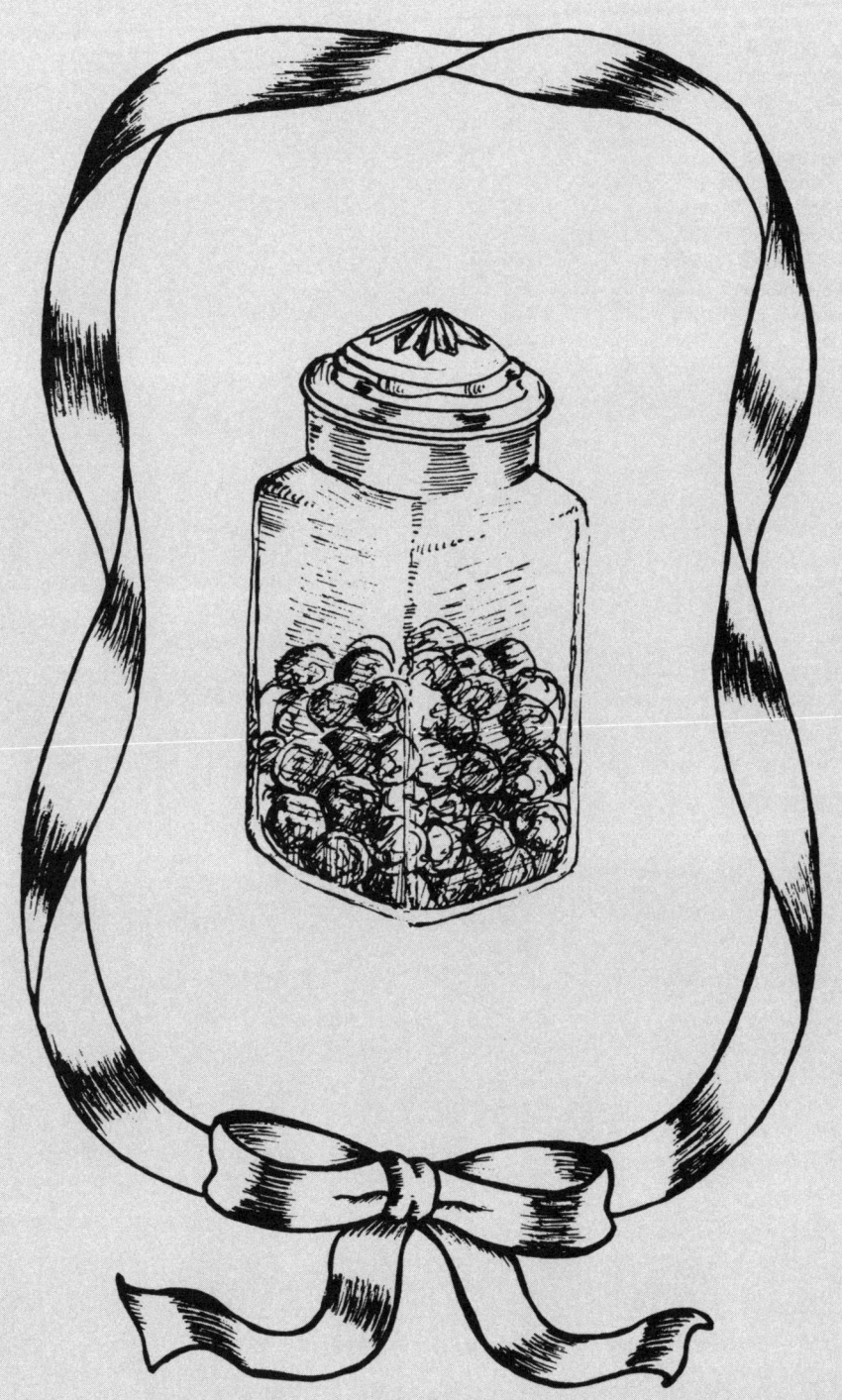

ALMOND BUTTER TOFFEE

Yields 2½ Pounds

1 pound butter, chilled
3 cups sugar
¼ teaspoon cream of tartar

2 cups slivered almonds
1 package (12 ounces)
   semi-sweet chocolate bits

In heavy aluminum pan combine butter and sugar. Place over high heat. Break up butter and stir vigorously at all times during cooking. As mixture starts to bubble along sides of pan, add cream of tartar. Stir vigorously and add almonds when mixture bubbles all over. Keep stirring until mixture turns to color of penuche — a tan color. Pour onto a lightly greased cookie sheet with sides. Drop chocolate bits on toffee; as they melt spread and sprinkle with a few grated nuts. Let cool and break into pieces.

Mrs. James C. Ballard (Barbara Lloyd)

DOROTHY SPEARS' BUTTERFINGER BALLS

2 cups creamy peanut butter
1 stick butter, melted

1 box (16 ounces)
   powdered sugar
3 cups rice krispies

Mix together the peanut butter, butter, powdered sugar and rice krispies. Roll into teaspoon-sized balls and chill.

CHOCOLATE COATING

⅓ stick paraffin
1½ (8 ounces each)
   Hershey bars

1 package (6 ounces)
   chocolate chips

In a double boiler, melt paraffin, chocolate chips and Hershey bars. Dip the balls in the chocolate mixture. Set on wax paper to cool.

Mrs. Barnett Man (Velva Barnett)

CARAMELS

Yields 80 Pieces

2 cups sugar
1 cup white Karo syrup
2 sticks butter
(no substitution)

2 cups heavy cream
Dash salt
1 teaspoon vanilla
1 cup chopped walnuts

Cook sugar, Karo, butter, 1 cup cream and salt until mixture turns to a caramel color. This takes a long time and needs to be stirred constantly. Add remaining cup of cream. Stir and cook to a firm ball stage (238°). Test by dropping small drop into a bowl of cool water. Add vanilla. Stir and pour over nuts which have been spread on entire bottom of 11x17 inch buttered pan or cookie sheet. Refrigerate to cool and set. Slice into bite-sized pieces and wrap in Saran wrap.

Mrs. Don Babcock (Caron Sramek)

ENGLISH TOFFEE

2 cups chopped nuts
1 cup sugar
2 sticks butter

8 (1.5 ounces each)
Hershey candy bars

Grease cookie sheet with butter and sprinkle with nuts. Cook sugar and butter in saucepan until caramel colored, stirring constantly. Pour immediately over nuts. Place candy bars on top and let melt. Smooth out with a spatula. Let cool and break into pieces.

Mrs. Tom Cambridge (Norma Taggart)

BIG MARGARET'S FUDGE

Yields 6 Pounds

1 pint whipping cream
1 cup milk
Pinch salt
7 cups sugar
2⅓ cups white Karo
7 squares unsweetened Baker's chocolate

4 ounces Philadelphia cream cheese
2 tablespoons vanilla
3 tablespoons bourbon
1½ pounds pecans

Heat cream, milk and salt until it simmers. Add sugar and Karo. Stir only until it boils. Let simmer about 3 hours until it reaches firm soft ball stage (236°). Remove from heat. Add chocolate, cream cheese, vanilla and bourbon. In cold water (in the sink) beat with mixer, then by hand until it stands in mounds. Add pecans. Pour into 4 mounds. Freeze if desired.

This same recipe without the chocolate makes white fudge.

Mrs. James E. Herring (Margaret Johnson)

MARBLE FUDGE

Yields 7 Pounds

6 cups sugar
3 cups whipping cream
1 cup milk
Pinch of salt
2 cups white Karo

2 pounds pecans
6 (1 ounce each) squares unsweetened chocolate
3 tablespoons Schillings vanilla

Combine first five ingredients in a six quart aluminum pan. Cook over very low heat until sugar is melted, then boil slowly until syrup forms good soft ball in cold water (238° on candy thermometer). Mixture will turn a light caramel color.

Remove from heat and set in cold water. Beat with mixer or by hand until almost creamy, then add vanilla and beat. Pour half of mixture over chocolate, which has been melted. As mixture begins to get creamy and hard, add pecans.

Pour into five to six mounds with two layers of light and two layers of dark mixture; making each layer smaller than the one before it. The mixture should be hard enough so the white and dark will not run together or spread out too fast.

Let fudge set and harden for several hours, then wrap tightly in foil and cut it as it is to be eaten. The fudge gets creamier and better as it ripens.

Mrs. W.F. Seibold (Mildred Butte)

MICROWAVE FUDGE

Yields 60 Pieces

1 pound powdered sugar
½ cup cocoa
¼ cup milk

1 stick butter
1 tablespoon vanilla
½ cup chopped nuts

Blend sugar and cocoa in a mixing bowl. Add milk and butter. Cook in a microwave oven for 2 minutes. Remove bowl from oven and stir just enough to mix ingredients. Add vanilla and nuts. Stir until blended. Pour into a greased container. Place in freezer for 20 minutes or refrigerator for 1 hour. Cut and serve.

Mrs. Tom Whittenburg (Gil Covington)

BLANCHE'S BRITTLE

2 **cups sugar**	1 **teaspoon vanilla**
1 **cup light Karo**	2 **tablespoons butter**
¾ **cup water**	2 **heaping teaspoons soda**
2 **cups raw, shelled peanuts**	

Combine sugar, syrup and water in a deep saucepan over medium heat. Bring to a boil. When candy thermometer reaches 230°, reduce heat and add peanuts. Cook, stirring occasionally, about 20 minutes or until candy reaches hard crack stage, 300-310°. Remove from heat, add butter, vanilla and soda. As foaming subsides, pour candy onto a large, well buttered, lightly salted piece of heavy-duty foil. As soon as candy can be handled, pull and stretch it out as thin as possible, forming delicate pieces of brittle. Continue until all candy has been pulled. Let cool and store in airtight container for up to two weeks.

Mrs. Ed Notestine (Elaine Folley)

MICROWAVE PEANUT BRITTLE

1 **cup raw peanuts**	1 **tablespoon butter**
1 **cup sugar**	1 **teaspoon soda**
½ **cup white corn syrup**	1 **teaspoon vanilla**
⅛ **teaspoon salt**	

Combine peanuts, sugar, syrup and salt in a 2-quart glass bowl. Place the bowl in a microwave oven and cook 7-10 minutes. Stir well after 4 minutes. Add butter and blend well. Return to the microwave and cook 2 minutes. Add soda and vanilla. Gently stir until light and foamy. Pour onto a 15½x10½x1 inch buttered cookie sheet. Lightly salt the top of candy. Let cool completely (20-30 minutes). Break into pieces and store in an airtight container.

Cooking time may vary with different microwaves. When pouring onto cookie sheet use a buttered spoon to spread candy. It isn't necessary to spread candy from side to side. It will be a free form.

Mrs. Charles Rittenberry (Cynthia Lindley)

Mrs. Max Sherman (Gene Alice Wienbroer)

BROWN SUGARED NUTS

1 cup brown sugar
½ cup sugar
½ cup evaporated milk

1 teaspoon vanilla
2½ cups nuts

Combine sugars and milk in medium saucepan. Cook over low heat, stirring until soft ball stage. Remove from heat. Add vanilla and nuts. Mix until nuts are coated. Turn onto waxed paper and separate nuts. May be dropped by spoonsful onto wax paper for pralines.

Mrs. Victor W. Shawgo (Mary Kaye Dolan)

PENUCHE
Yields 36-40 Pieces

2 cups dark brown sugar, packed
1 cup white sugar
1 cup whipping cream
2 tablespoons light corn syrup

¼ teaspoon salt
2 tablespoons butter
1 teaspoon vanilla
2 cups pecans, broken

Combine brown sugar, white sugar, cream, corn syrup, and salt in heavy saucepan. Cook over medium heat to soft ball stage, (228° on candy thermometer). Do *not* stir after mixture comes to boil. When soft ball stage is reached, remove from heat. Add 2 tablespoons butter (do *not* stir). Let stand until lukewarm (115° on thermometer). Add vanilla. Beat a few minutes. Add pecans and beat until creamy. Turn out quickly onto waxed paper for praline like pieces, this requires two people, as candy hardens fast; or pour into 8 or 9 inch square pan and cut into squares.

Mrs. B.R. Barfield (Carolyn Grissom)

CREAMY PRALINES
Makes 2½ Dozen

2 cups sugar
1 teaspoon baking soda
1 cup buttermilk

2 teaspoons vanilla
2 cups pecan halves

In 5 quart saucepan cook sugar, soda and buttermilk over medium heat until a small amount forms a soft ball in cold water (234° on candy thermometer). Remove from heat and add vanilla and nuts. Begin beating immediately. Beat until mixture thickens slightly. Drop from teaspoon onto waxed paper. Cool. If mixture becomes too thick, stir in a few drops of warm water.

Mrs. William A. Anthony (Katie Billman)

⅓ cup butter may be added to other ingredients.

PRALINES

Yields 24

1½ cups brown sugar
1½ cups granulated sugar
 3 tablespoons dark corn syrup

1 cup milk
1 teaspoon vanilla
1½ cups pecans

Combine sugars, syrup and milk in heavy saucepan. Heat and stir until sugar dissolves and mixture starts to boil. Cook to soft ball stage, stirring occasionally. Cool 10 minutes. Add vanilla and **beat** for 2 minutes. Add pecans. Beat until mixture loses its gloss. Drop by teaspoons on waxed paper. (If candy becomes too hard in pan, add milk by the tablespoon.)

Mrs. Dick Frazer (Sylvia Lindley)

MARGARET BOYCE'S PRALINES

1 stick butter
1 box (1 pound) light brown sugar
2 cups white sugar
½ pint sour cream

½ pint whipping cream
Dash of salt
2 teaspoons vanilla
1 pound pecan halves

Melt butter gently in heavy aluminum saucepan. Add brown sugar and stir over low heat until dissolved and well-blended. Add white sugar, blend well, add sour cream and whipping cream. Add salt. Cook on low heat stirring constantly to avoid scorching on bottom. When well blended, increase to medium heat and cook to soft ball stage (235° on candy thermometer). Remove from heat and allow to cool for ten minutes. Add vanilla and pecans. Beat until creamy. Drop by teaspoonsful on waxed paper. The amount may be increased if larger pralines are desired. Remove from waxed paper when firm, placing hand beneath paper and lifting candy. May be stored indefinitely in a tightly covered container or in freezer.

Mrs. John Ballard (Sadie Claude Curtis)

Bars and Squares

Drop

Rolled

Shaped

APPLE COOKIES

Yields 5 Dozen

½ cup shortening
1½ cups brown sugar
½ teaspoon salt
1 teaspoon nutmeg
1 teaspoon cinnamon
½ teaspoon cloves
1 teaspoon soda

1 egg
1 cup buttermilk
1 cup chopped raisins
1 cup unpeeled,
  chopped apples
2 cups flour
½ cup chopped nuts

Mix ingredients in order listed. Drop onto greased cookie sheet by teaspoon. Bake in 375° oven for 11-14 minutes. Ice while warm.

ICING:

1½ cups powdered sugar
½ teaspoon vanilla

Dash of salt
Milk or cream

Mix sugar, vanilla and salt. Add milk until mixture is of desired consistency.

Mrs. B.L. Morgan, Jr. (Doris Coffee)

APRICOT COOKIES

Yields 3 Dozen

½ cup butter, softened
½ cup sugar
2 eggs, separated
1¼ cups flour

1 cup apricot preserves
⅓ cup sugar
1 cup chopped pecans

Blend together butter, ½ cup sugar and egg yolks. Work in flour (I use pastry cutter). Lightly flour hands and pat mixture into well greased **9x13x2 inch baking dish.** Bake in 350° oven for 15 minutes. Remove from oven and spread evenly with preserves. Beat egg whites until foamy. Gradually add ⅓ cup sugar. Continue beating until peaks are formed. Fold in nuts and spread mixture over preserves. Bake in 350° oven for additional 25 minutes. Cool and cut into squares.

Mrs. James D. Man (Cordelia Harris)

BROWNIES

Yields 2 Dozen

¾ cup butter
1½ cups sugar
3 eggs
1½ teaspoons vanilla

2 squares semi-sweet
  chocolate, melted
¾ cup flour
1 cup coarsely
  chopped pecans

Cream butter and sugar. Add eggs, vanilla and chocolate. Beat. Stir in flour and nuts by hand. Pour into a greased and floured 10½ x 7 inch pan. Bake in 375° oven for 25 minutes. They will be gooey and soft. Let sit several minutes before cutting into squares.

Mrs. Don T. Curtis (Suzanne Stokes)

FROSTED BROWNIES

Yields 2-3 Dozen

4 squares unsweetened chocolate
1 cup butter
4 eggs
2 cups sugar

1 teaspoon vanilla
1 cup flour
¼ teaspoon salt
1½–2 cups chopped pecans

Melt chocolate with butter. Cool and set aside. Beat eggs until frothy. Add sugar, vanilla, flour and salt. Mix well. Add chocolate mixture and pecans. Spread mixture in lightly greased 9x13 inch pan. Bake in 350° oven for 30-35 minutes. Frost when cool.

FROSTING

4 tablespoons butter
2 cups sifted powdered sugar
2 tablespoons milk

½ teaspoon vanilla
1 square unsweetened chocolate
1 tablespoon butter

Cream together first four ingredients. Spread on top of brownies and refrigerate. Melt together chocolate and butter. Drizzle on top of chilled brownies. Cut into squares.

Mrs. Charles K. Hendrick (Phyllis Petty)

NIKKI'S BROWNIES

Yields 2 Dozen

⅓ cup evaporated milk
1 package (10 ounces) light caramels
1 box German Chocolate cake mix

⅓ cup plus 1 tablespoon evaporated milk
¾ cup butter, melted
1 cup chopped pecans
1 package (6 ounces) chocolate chips

Melt milk and caramels together. Set aside. Combine the cake mix, milk, butter and pecans. Spread half of this mixture in a greased and floured 13x9 inch pan. Bake in 350° oven for 6 minutes. Sprinkle with chocolate chips and spread the caramel mixture on top. Crumble the remaining cake mixture on top. (It will be lumpy). Bake in 350° oven for 20-30 minutes, or until the mixture just begins to pull away from the sides of the pan. Cool and cut into squares.

Mrs. W.C. Turner (Nancy Carmichall)

BUTTERFINGERS

Yields 3½ Dozen

⅞ cup butter
5 tablespoons sugar
1 teaspoon vanilla
2 cups flour

2 tablespoons water
1 cup chopped nuts
½ cup sugar
3–4 tablespoons cinnamon

Cream butter and 5 tablespoons sugar. Add vanilla, flour, water and nuts, beating after each addition. Shape in oblong cookies about the size of a finger. Bake in 350° oven for 20-25 minutes. Let cool. Combine ½ cup sugar and cinnamon. Roll cooled cookies in sugar cinnamon mixture.

Freezes well.

Mrs. John L. Milton (Sissy Thornhill)

TEXAS BUTTERSCOTCH SQUARES

Yields 2 Dozen

1 pound brown sugar
⅔ cup shortening
3 eggs
1½ teaspoons vanilla
2¾ cups flour

2 teaspoons baking powder
½ teaspoon salt
1 package (12 ounces) butterscotch chips

Cream together the brown sugar, shortening, eggs and vanilla. Add flour, baking powder, salt and mix well. Spread on greased cookie sheet with sides and bake in 300° oven for 20-25 minutes or until slightly brown (can be tested with a toothpick). After done and while still hot, sprinkle butterscotch chips evenly over bars. As they melt spread with knife as an icing. Cool. Cut into bars before icing has completely cooled.

Variations:

1) Substitute chocolate or peanut butter chips for butterscotch chips or use a combination.
2) Stir in one package Heath Bits o' Brickle before spreading batter onto cookie sheet. Save some to spread on top with icing.

Miss Susan E. Roach

CHEESE CAKE COOKIES

1 cup flour	1 egg
½ cup packed brown sugar	2 tablespoons milk
6 tablespoons butter, softened	¼ teaspoon finely grated lemon peel
1 package (8 ounces) cream cheese, softened	2 tablespoons lemon juice
¼ cup sugar	½ teaspoon vanilla
	2 tablespoons chopped nuts

In a large mixing bowl, combine flour and brown sugar. Cut in butter until mixture forms fine crumbs. Reserve 1 cup crumb mixture for topping. Press remainder over bottom of an ungreased 8x8x2 inch baking pan. Bake in 350° oven for 12-15 minutes or until light brown.

In mixing bowl, cream the cheese and sugar. Add egg, milk, lemon peel, lemon juice and vanilla. Beat well. Spread batter over the crust. Combine the nuts and the reserved crumb mixture and sprinkle over the top. Bake in 350° oven for 20-25 minutes. Cool and cut into squares.

Mrs. Herbert Dodson (Eva Jane Maxey)

CHINESE CHEWS   Serves 12

1 stick butter, melted	2 tablespoons powdered sugar
1 cup flour	

Mix together and press into a greased and floured 8 inch cake pan. Mash down to thin layer like pie crust. Bake in preheated 325° oven for 15 minutes.

2 eggs, beaten	½ cup coconut
2 tablespoons flour	1 teaspoon vanilla
1½ cups brown sugar	½ cup chopped nuts

Mix all ingredients well and pour over cooked shell. Bake in 325° oven for 30 minutes.

Mrs. Roy Northrup (Dena Goldston)

DATE NUT CRISPS

Yields 4 Dozen

1½ cups brown sugar
 1 cup butter
 2 eggs
 2 cups sifted flour
 1 teaspoon soda

½ package dates,
  finely chopped
1 cup oatmeal
1 teaspoon vanilla
1 cup chopped pecans

Cream sugar and butter. Add eggs one at a time. Beat well after each addition. Add remaining ingredients. Mix well. Drop by spoonsful on well-greased cookie sheet. Bake in 350° oven for 15-20 minutes

Mrs. John Ballard (Sadie Claude Curtis)

DESSERT BURGERS

Yields 1 Dozen Large or 2 Dozen Small Cookies

COOKIES

 2 cups flour
½ cup cocoa
1½ teaspoons baking soda
¼ teaspoon salt
½ cup margarine

1 cup sugar
1 egg
½ teaspoon vanilla
1 cup milk

Sift together flour, cocoa, soda and salt. Set aside. Cream margarine and sugar. Add the egg and vanilla. Stir well. Alternately beat in flour mixture and milk until smooth. Drop by tablespoonsful onto ungreased baking sheet to form 24 rounds. Bake in 425° oven for 7 minutes or until finger leaves no imprint in middle. Remove from sheets and cool on wire racks.

FILLING

½ cup margarine, softened
2¼ cups confectioners sugar

½ teaspoon vanilla
2 egg whites

Cream margarine until light. Gradually beat in 1 cup of confectioners sugar. Add vanilla. Set aside. Beat the egg whites until foamy. Then beat in 1¼ cups confectioners sugar until blended. Thoroughly combine both mixtures. Spread on flat sides of 12 rounds. Top with remaining rounds. *Store in refrigerator.*

These devil's food cake-cookies are great for pick-up desserts at parties or for packed lunches. You can increase the yield by making the cookies smaller.

Mrs. Stan Morris, Jr. (Kathleen Boyd)

FORGOTTEN COOKIES

Yields 2 Dozen

2 egg whites
Pinch of salt
1 teaspoon vanilla
⅔ cup sugar

1 package (6 ounces)
chocolate chips
1 cup chopped nuts

Preheat oven to 350°. Beat egg whites, salt and vanilla until soft peaks form. Add sugar gradually, and continue beating until it stands in stiff peaks. Add chocolate chips and nuts. Drop by teaspoon on greased cookie sheet. Place cookies in hot oven and *turn oven off*. Leave in oven 4 or 5 hours or preferably overnight. A very nice party cookie!

Mrs. George Parr (Zua Gae Warner)

GINGERBREAD MEN

Yields 2-3 Dozen

1 cup shortening
1 cup sugar
½ teaspoon salt
1 egg
1 cup molasses
2 tablespoons vinegar

5 cups flour
1 teaspoon ground cloves
1 teaspoon cinnamon
1 tablespoon ginger
1½ teaspoon soda
Raisins

Thoroughly cream shortening, sugar and salt. Stir in the egg, molasses and vinegar. Beat well. Sift together flour, cloves, cinnamon, ginger and soda. Add to batter. Chill for several hours. Roll out on floured surface to ⅛ inch thickness. Cut into gingerbread men. Cut raisins into small pieces to use for eyes, nose, and buttons. Decorate before baking. Bake on greased cookie sheets in a 375° oven for 5 minutes.

Mrs. David Kennedy (Kay Lewis)

GOOD COOKIES

Yields 8 Dozen

1 cup Wesson oil
1 cup butter
1 cup brown sugar
1 cup sugar
1 egg, beaten
1 cup corn flakes
1 cup oatmeal

½ cup coarsely
chopped pecans
½ teaspoon salt
1 teaspoon vanilla
1 teaspon soda
3½ cups flour

Mix all ingredients together. Form into small balls and flatten with a glass dipped in sugar. Bake in 375° oven for 8-10 minutes or until golden. You can refrigerate dough for several days.

Mrs. Sue Alice Stokes (Sue Alice Simpson)

284

MYSTERY COOKIES

Yields 4 Dozen

1 cup butter
2 cups finely chopped pecans
4 teaspoons sugar

2 cups flour
1 teaspoon vanilla
Powdered sugar

Cream butter. Add nuts, sugar, flour and vanilla. Roll into small balls, one inch in diameter. Bake on greased cookie sheet in a 350° oven for 25-35 minutes. Roll in powdered sugar while warm.

Mrs. William F. Countiss (Mary Dee Ledyard)

OATMEAL LACE COOKIES

Yields 5 Dozen

½ cup butter
1½ cups oatmeal
  Pinch of salt
¾ cup sugar
1 tablespoon flour

1 teaspoon baking powder
1 teaspoon vanilla
1 egg
1 cup chopped nuts

Melt butter and pour over oats. Mix with fork. Add all other ingredients. Cover cookie sheet with foil. Drop by small teaspoon, allow space for spreading wafer thin. Bake in a 350° oven for 10 minutes. Cool before removing.

Mrs. Dick Frazer (Sylvia Lindley)

OLD-FASHION OATMEAL COOKIES

Yields 5 Dozen

¾ cup shortening
1 cup brown sugar, packed
½ cup granulated sugar
1 egg
¼ cup water

1 teaspoon vanilla
1 cup sifted flour
1 teaspoon salt
½ teaspoon baking soda
3 cups oatmeal

Beat shortening, sugars, egg, water and vanilla until creamy. Sift together flour, soda and salt. Add to creamed mixture, blending well. Stir in oatmeal. Drop by teaspoonsful onto greased cookie sheets. Bake in 350° oven for 12-15 minutes.

Optional: 1 cup chopped pecans, raisins, chocolate or butterscotch chips may be added with oats.

Mrs. Neely Legacy (Susan Neely)

PALET DE DAMES (LADIES WAFERS)

Yields 1½-2 Dozen

5 tablespoons butter
⅓ cup sugar
¼ cup currants or
1 cup of sliced almonds

½ cup plus 1 tablespoon flour
1 egg
¼ teaspoon rum, or kirsch, or brandy

Cream butter and sugar. Add remaining ingredients. Drop by teaspoonsful two inches apart on buttered baking sheet. Bake in 375° oven until edges only are light brown.

Mrs. Lee T. Bivins (Betty Teel)

PEANUT BLOSSOMS

Yields 40 Cookies

½ cup butter
½ cup peanut butter
½ cup sugar
½ cup brown sugar, packed
1 egg, unbeaten

1 teaspoon vanilla
1¾ cups sifted flour
1 teaspoon soda
½ teaspoon salt
1 bag Hershey Kisses (optional)

Cream together in mixing bowl the butter, peanut butter, sugar and brown sugar. Use wooden spoon and cream thoroughly. Add egg and vanilla to the creamed mixture and beat well. Sift together the flour, soda and salt. Add dry ingredients to the creamed mixture and mix thoroughly. Shape dough into balls about the size of walnuts and roll in granulated sugar. Place on ungreased cookie sheet 2 inches apart. Bake in preheated oven at 375° for 8 minutes. If desired, remove cookies and place chocolate kiss on top, pressing so that cookie cracks around edge. Return to oven, bake for 2-5 more minutes or until golden brown.

Be careful not to overcook — they are better chewy.

Mrs. Ketler Jennings (Karen Ketler)

HUBERTA ERIKSON'S PEANUT BUTTER COOKIES

Yields 12 Dozen

2½ cups margarine
2½ cups peanut butter
2½ cups white sugar
2½ cups brown sugar
4 eggs

5¼ cups flour
3¾ teaspoons baking soda
2½ teaspoons baking powder
1¼ teaspoons salt

Cream margarine and peanut butter. Add both sugars and cream. Add eggs, beating well. Add flour, soda, baking powder and salt. Mix well. Roll into balls the size of walnuts. Place on pan and mash with a fork to make crisscross design. Bake in 375° oven for 10-12 minutes.

286

PECAN BALLS

Yields 20 Balls

1 cup pecans
½ cup butter, softened
2 tablespoons sugar
1 teaspoon vanilla

1 cup sifted
all purpose flour
Pinch of salt
Powdered sugar

Grind the pecans and mix with softened butter, sugar, vanilla, flour and salt. Blend these ingredients together with your hands until it holds together. Pinch off dough the size of walnuts and roll into balls. Bake the pecan balls on an ungreased cookie sheet in 375° oven for 20 minutes. Coat the balls with powdered sugar. The pecan balls can be frozen in tightly sealed container after they are completely cooled.

Mrs. J. Lee Johnson, III (Betty Knight)

PECAN BARS

Yields About 24 Bars

1 cup flour
½ cup oatmeal
½ cup brown sugar
½ cup butter
3 eggs
¾ cup white corn syrup

½ cup brown sugar
1 tablespoon flour
¼ teaspoon salt
1 teaspoon vanilla
1 cup broken pecans

Combine first three ingredients. Cut in butter. Press mixture into buttered 9-inch square pan. Bake in 350° oven for 15 minutes. (This will be only partially baked.) Beat eggs slightly and add the rest of the ingredients, blending well. Pour over crust and bake about 30 additional minutes. Cool and cut into bars.

Mrs. B.L. Morgan, Jr. (Doris Coffee)

BLANCHE WILSON'S SUGAR COOKIES

Yields 8-12 Dozen

2 cups + 3 tablespoons sugar
½ teaspoon salt (1 teaspoon
  if Crisco is used)
1 rounded cup Crisco or butter
½ teaspoon soda in
1 tablespoon water

4 eggs
½ teaspoon lemon rind
2 teaspoons vanilla
  (Mexican suggested)
4 cups flour
  Additional flour & sugar

Mix sugar, salt, Crisco or butter and soda-water. Add eggs 1 at a time. Add remaining ingredients except additional flour & sugar. Dough must be chilled or frozen. When rolling dough dust surface with 1 part sugar & 1 part flour. Bake in 350° oven for 8-10 minutes on greased cookie sheet.

Mrs. A.W. So Relle, III (Judy Jolley)

GERMAN SUGAR COOKIES

Yields 12 Dozen

1 cup sugar
1 cup powdered sugar
1 cup cooking oil
1 cup butter
2 eggs

1 teaspoon vanilla
4 cups flour
1 teaspoon cream of tartar
1 teaspoon baking soda

Beat together sugars, oil and butter. Add eggs and vanilla. Mix in flour, cream of tartar and baking soda. Chill at least 6 hours. Roll into marble sized balls, and place on lightly greased cookie sheet. Flatten with bottom of glass dipped in sugar. Sprinkle a bit more sugar on top. Bake in 350° oven for 8-10 minutes.

Mrs. Larry Doyle (Doris Plaesants)

MOCK SAND TARTS

Yields 3 Dozen

½ cup sugar
1 cup butter
1½ cups flour

1 cup crushed potato chips
1 teaspoon vanilla

Cream sugar and butter. Add remaining ingredients. Drop onto ungreased cookie sheet. Bake in 325° oven for 12-15 minutes. Sprinkle with powdered sugar while warm. Store in a tin container.

These can be frozen.

Mrs. Alton Reeder (Martha Moore)

CHRISTMAS FRUIT COOKIES

Yields 14-15 Dozen

1 cup butter
1½ cups sugar
2 eggs
2½ cups flour
1 teaspoon soda
1 teaspoon salt
1 teaspoon cinnamon
24 ounces dates, chopped

½ pound candied cherries, cut up
½ pound candied pineapple cut up
½ pound slivered almonds
2 cups chopped pecans
¼ cup brandy

Cream butter and sugar. Add eggs. Beat until smooth and creamy. Sift dry ingredients and add to butter-sugar mixture. Add cut up fruit, nuts and brandy to batter. Dough will be stiff, so mix with hands. Drop by teaspoon on greased cookie sheets. Bake in 350° oven for 7-10 minutes.

Mrs. Tom Cambridge (Norma Taggart)

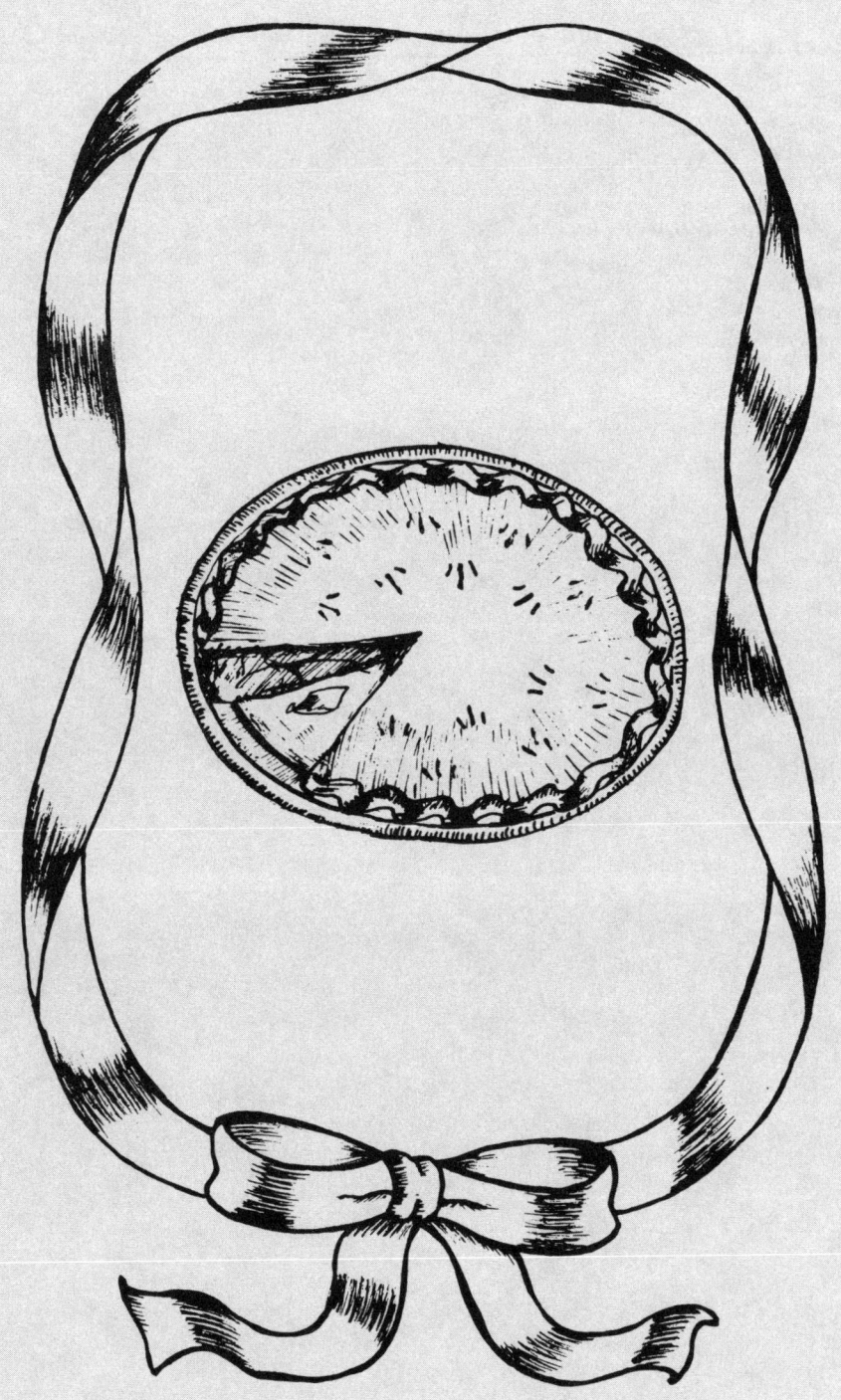

Frozen

PIE CRUST

One Double Crust

2 cups flour
1 cup shortening

½ cup cold water
Dash of salt

Cut shortening into flour until it resembles coarse meal. Add water and mix with a fork. Divide into two parts. Knead on floured board to rolling consistency, adding as much flour as needed. This recipe is easy and foolproof.

Mrs. Keith Taylor (Theo Zweig)

BAKED ALASKA PIE

9– inch pie shell, baked

FILLING

2 packages (10 ounces each)
  frozen raspberries
1½ cups sugar

Dash cream of tartar
½ gallon vanilla ice cream,
  softened

Press partially thawed, mushy raspberries through a sieve into a saucepan. Stir in sugar and cream of tartar. Bring quickly to boiling point, stirring constantly. Pour into a small bowl and chill. Spread a layer of softened ice cream in pie shell, being careful not to break crust. Drizzle with chilled raspberry sauce. Repeat layers of ice cream and raspberry sauce, ending with ice cream in a mound on top. Freeze overnight.

MERINGUE

4 egg whites
  Dash cream of tartar

1 teaspoon vanilla
½ cup sugar

Beat egg whites with cream of tartar and vanilla until foamy. Gradually sprinkle in sugar, beating until meringue stands in firm peaks. Spread over ice cream, working quickly. Freeze until ready to bake. Bake in 425° oven for 5 minutes. Serve immediately. Refreeze leftovers then reheat as directed.

Mrs. Don Babcock (Caron Sramek)

BUTTERMILK CHESS PIE

¼ cup butter
1½ cups sugar
3 eggs, slightly beaten
1 tablespoon flour

⅔ cup buttermilk
½ teaspoon lemon extract
9 inch pie shell, unbaked

Cut butter into sugar. Add remaining ingredients, mixing well. Pour into unbaked pie shell. Bake in 350° oven for 45 minutes, or until custard is set. Pie will have dark crust on top. Cool before serving.

Mrs. A.W. SoRelle, III (Judy Jolley)

CHOCOLATE PIE

1 cup sugar
3 tablespoons cocoa
8 tablespoons flour
2 tablespoons melted butter
1½ cups milk

3 eggs, separated
1 teaspoon vanilla
6 tablespoons sugar
¼ teaspoon cream of tartar
9 inch pie shell, baked

Mix sugar, cocoa and flour in saucepan. Add butter. Stir in milk. Cook over low heat, stirring constantly until thick. (Allow to boil 1-2 minutes.) Remove from heat and add egg yolks one at a time, beating after each addition. Add vanilla. Cool before putting into pie shell. Beat egg whites until frothy. Add cream of tartar. Continue beating, slowly adding sugar. Beat until stiff. Spread meringue on top and bake in 350° oven until golden brown. More chocolate may be added to taste. Store in refrigerator. Cool before eating.

Mrs. Jim Walker (Patsy Roberts)

GRANDMOTHER'S FUDGE PIE

½ cup margarine
1 square
   unsweetened chocolate
1 cup sugar
¼ cup flour

½ cup light Karo
3 eggs, beaten
½ cup pecans
9 inch pie shell, unbaked

Melt margarine and chocolate. Mix sugar and flour. Add to chocolate mixture. Add remaining ingredients, pecans last. Pour into pie shell. Bake in 350° oven for 1 hour or until crust is done. May be frozen.

Mrs. Joe Bob McCartt (Susie Douglas)

CORNMEAL PIE

1¾ cups sugar
1 teaspoon flour
2 tablespoons cornmeal
3 eggs

½ cup butter
1 teaspoon vanilla
¼ cup milk
9 inch pie shell, unbaked

Mix together first seven ingredients. Pour into pie shell. Bake in 350° oven for 30 minutes or until golden brown.

Mrs. Arthur J. Lamb (Pearlene Jenkins)

FROZEN LEMON PIE

CRUST

1½ cups crushed
   graham crackers

5 tablespoons
   melted margarine

Mix crumbs and margarine. Press into 10 inch pie pan. Bake in 350°
oven for 10 minutes. Cool.

FILLING

½ cup sugar
⅛ teaspoon salt
1 teaspoon cornstarch
¼ cup lemon juice
   Grated lemon rind

3 egg yolks
3 egg whites, beaten stiff with
1 tablespoon sugar
1 cup whipping cream,
   beaten stiff

Mix sugar, salt, cornstarch, lemon juice and lemon rind. Cook over low
heat or in double boiler until filling begins to thicken. Cool. Slowly add egg
yolks and cook another minute or two. Cool and fold in egg whites, then
whipped cream. Pour into pie shell. Sprinkle top with graham cracker
crumbs. Freeze. Thaw slightly before serving.

Mrs. Hugh E. Hagen (Susan Sanders)

LEMON CHESS PIE

2 cups sugar
1 tablespoon cornmeal
2 tablespoons flour
½ cup milk
¼ cup lemon juice

1 teaspoon lemon extract
¼ cup butter, melted
3 eggs, well beaten
9 inch pie shell, unbaked

Beat together first six ingredients. Then add butter and eggs and mix
well. Pour into unbaked pie shell. Bake in 300° oven for 10 minutes then
at 350° for 40 minutes or until mixture is set.

Will freeze when cooled completely.

Mrs. Carlton Clemens (Pamela Ketler)

GRANNY'S PECAN PIE

1 cup light corn syrup
1 cup brown sugar
⅓ cup margarine
3 large eggs
⅓ teaspoon vanilla

Pinch of salt
1 tablespoon flour
1 cup pecans
9 inch pie shell, unbaked

Combine corn syrup, brown sugar and margarine in a saucepan. Bring to a boil. Remove from heat and let cool. Cream together the eggs, vanilla, salt and flour. Slowly add boiled mixture to creamed mixture and mix 2-3 minutes. Line pie shell with pecans. Pour mixture over pecans. Bake in 350° oven for 40 minutes or until center is firm.

Mrs. James A. Hedgecoke, Jr. (Sallye Dees)

MILE HIGH LEMON PIE

1 can (15 ounces) sweetened condensed milk
1 can (6 ounces) frozen lemonade

1 tub (9 ounces) Cool Whip
1 prepared graham cracker crust

Combine milk, lemonade and Cool Whip. Pour into crust. Chill and serve.

May decorate top with lemon slices.

Mrs. David Waitt (Nancy Longtin)

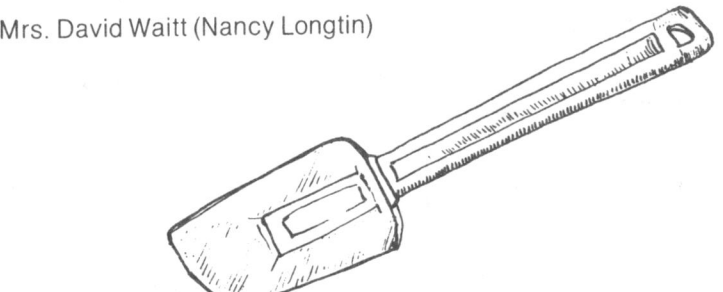

MOTHER'S FRENCH PIE

6 eggs
2 scant cups sugar
3 tablespoons butter, melted

Juice of 2 lemons, strained
¼ teaspoon salt
9 inch pie shell, unbaked

Beat eggs with a fork until light. Add remaining ingredients and pour into pie shell. Bake in 425° oven for 15 minutes and then at 325° for 45 minutes or until knife comes out clean.

Mrs. Anne Ansley Reid (Anne Ansley)

MACAROON PIE

1¼ cups sugar
¼ teaspoon salt
2 eggs, well beaten
½ cup milk
¼ cup flour

¼ cup shortening or
   butter, melted
1 cup shredded or
   flaked coconut
½ teaspoon vanilla

Mix all ingredients. Pour into an empty 10 inch pie pan. Bake at 425° for 10 minutes. Lower to 350° and bake for 30-40 minutes.

Mrs. William Daniel (Shirley Clark)

AMELIA MUD PIE

SHELL

21 Oreo cookies, crushed

6 tablespoons
   melted butter

Mix together, then press in pie pan and freeze.

FILLING

1 quart chocolate ice cream
2 tablespoons instant coffee
2 tablespoons Sanka

4 tablespoons whipped cream
2 tablespoons brandy
2 tablespoons Kahlua

Whip ice cream with Sanka, coffee, brandy, Kahlua and add whipped cream. Place in shell, freeze until very hard.

TOPPING

Fudge topping by Kraft. Dip knife into hot water, spread, work quickly.

Mrs. Glen Brosier (Kay Wagner)

MUD PIE

½ stick margarine
½ package (15 ounce)
   Oreo cookies, crushed
2 quarts chocolate
   ice cream, softened
1 tablespoon
   Grand Marnier Liqueur

2 tablespoons strong coffee
½ container (13.5 ounce)
   Cool Whip
1 jar (10 ounces) fudge
   ice cream topping
   Cool Whip or whipped cream
   Maraschino cherries

Melt margarine in a 2 quart, oblong Pyrex casserole. Mix in Oreos and press down for crust. Cool. In a large bowl combine ice cream, liqueur, coffee and Cool Whip. Pour over crust. Freeze. Add a layer of fudge sauce and return to freezer. Serve wih Cool Whip or whipped cream and top with cherries.
Needs to be made at least one day ahead of time.

Mrs. Jim Southern (Linda Ann Duke)

CREAM OF PECAN PIE

CRUST

1¼ cups graham cracker crumbs	2 tablespoons sugar
	6 tablespoons melted butter

Mix crumbs, sugar and butter. Press on bottom and sides of a 9 inch pie plate. Place in freezer for 15 minutes or in refrigerator for 1 hour. (Can be baked at 375° for 8 minutes for a nuttier taste.)

FILLING

5 eggs	1 tablespoon butter
1¼ cups light brown sugar, packed	1 cup coarsely chopped pecans (toasted if desired)
1 cup heavy cream	1 teaspoon vanilla

GARNISH

Sweetened whipped cream (optional)	Chopped pecans to taste (optional)

In a medium saucepan, beat eggs slightly. Stir in brown sugar, cream and butter until smooth. Stir constantly over low heat until mixture thickens and just begins to boil. *Do not boil.* Remove from heat. Stir in pecans and vanilla. Cool 10 minutes. Pour into crust. Chill 3 hours or until firm. Garnish with whipped cream and pecans if desired.

Mrs. Stan Morris, Jr. (Kathleen Boyd)

GEORGIA HAWKS' PUMPKIN PIE

1 cup pumpkin	½ teaspoon salt
1 cup milk	½ teaspoon cinnamon
½ cup cream	¼ teaspoon each: nutmeg, cloves, ginger, allspice
¾ cup sugar	
1 tablespoon flour	1 teaspoon vanilla
3 eggs, slightly beaten	10 inch pie shell, unbaked

Combine pumpkin, sugar, salt, flour and spices. Add eggs, milk, cream and vanilla. Mix well. Pour into pie shell. Bake in 375° oven for 50 minutes or until a knife inserted halfway between center and outer edge comes out clean. Cool and serve with whipped cream or topping. If some custard is left after filling pastry shell, it may be baked in individual custard cups and placed in a pan of hot water in a 325° oven for about 45 minutes or until custard is set. To test, insert a silver knife as suggested above.

LOW-CAL
SUMMER PIE

30 vanilla wafers, crushed
¼ cup margarine, melted
1 cup boiling water
1 package (3 ounces) orange
  flavored gelatin

3 tablespoons frozen orange
  juice concentrate
½ cup cold water
1 cup plain yogurt
  Coconut flakes

To prepare crust combine crumbs and margarine. Press onto bottom and sides of a 9 inch pie pan. Bake in 350° oven for 5 minutes.

Pour boiling water over gelatin. Stir until dissolved. Add orange juice and cold water. Chill until mixture starts to set. Whip until fluffy. Add yogurt. Pour into crust. Chill until set. Sprinkle with coconut flakes on top.

Mrs. Thomas A. Bunkley, Jr. (Myra Anne Stanley)

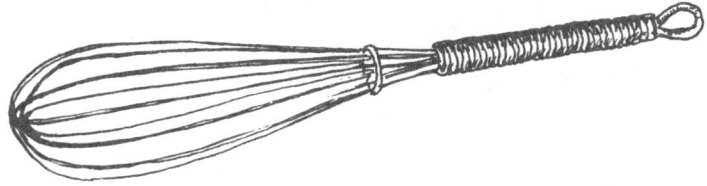

PECAN PIE

3 eggs
1 cup sugar
1 cup Karo
1 tablespoon butter
1 cup whole pecans

1 teaspoon vanilla
  Pinch of salt
8 or 9 inch pie shell,
  unbaked

Beat eggs. Add sugar and Karo. Mix well. Then add remaining ingredients. Pour into unbaked pie shell. Bake in slow oven, 300°-325°, about 1 hour or until brown. This pie freezes well.

Mrs. Jim Walker (Patsy Roberts)

BUTTERMILK PIE

½ cup butter
1⅔ cups sugar
3 eggs, beaten

1 teaspoon vanilla
½ cup buttermilk
8 inch pie shell, unbaked

Melt butter. Add sugar and blend. Stir in eggs and vanilla. Fold in buttermilk. Pour into unbaked pie shell. Bake in 350° oven for 45 minutes or until a knife inserted in the center comes out clean.

Mrs. George Green (Rosemary McMurtry)

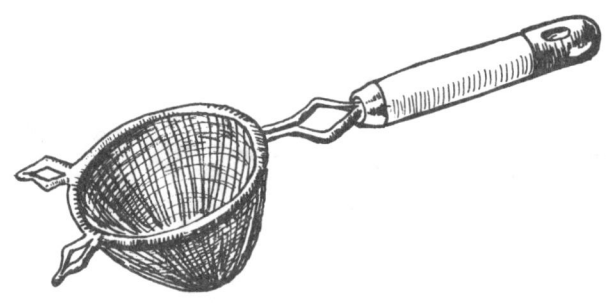

IMPOSSIBLE PIE

½ cup Bisquick
½ cup sugar
4 eggs
2 cups milk

1 can (3½ ounces) coconut
1 teaspoon vanilla
3 tablespoons butter

Place all ingredients in blender. Blend until thoroughly mixed. Pour in buttered 9 inch pie plate. Bake in 400° oven for 30 minutes.

Mrs. James A. Hedgecoke, Jr. (Sallye Dees)

APRICOT PASTRIES

8 ounces cream cheese
½ pound margarine, cold

2 cups flour
1 pound jar apricot jam

Mix margarine, cream cheese, and flour with hands until blended and firm. Roll out ½ of dough on a sheet of waxed paper to fit cookie sheet. Lift carefully and lay in cookie sheet, pulling waxed paper off. Spread with apricot jam. Roll out second half and lay on top of jam. Pinch sides together to seal well. Prick top layer and pat with water. Sprinkle with sugar. Bake in 350° oven for 35-40 minutes. Bake the day before and refrigerate. This freezes well.

Mrs. Robert L. Bass (Allee Curtis)

EASY CHOCOLATE
MOUSSE   Serves 6

1 package (6 ounces)
  semi-sweet chocolate chips
¼ cup water
½ cup packed brown sugar
4 eggs, separated

1 teaspoon vanilla
1 cup heavy cream
2 tablespoons brown sugar
Sliced almonds

Combine chocolate, water and sugar in top of double boiler and cook until chocolate is melted. Beat until smooth. Cool. Beat egg yolks with vanilla. Stir into chocolate mixture. Beat egg whites until stiff. Fold into chocolate mixture. Spoon into 6 individual serving dishes. Chill. Whip cream and 2 tablespoons brown sugar until stiff. Top chocolate mixture with brown sugar cream and sprinkle with almonds.

Mrs. Stan Morris, Jr. (Kathleen Boyd)

ALMOND TORTONI   Serves 8

1 cup whipping cream
½ cup sugar, divided
⅛ teaspoon salt
½ teaspoon vanilla
½ teaspoon lemon extract

1 teaspon powdered
  instant coffee
1 egg white
½ cup chopped
  toasted almonds

Whip cream until fairly stiff, adding ¼ cup sugar, salt, vanilla, lemon extract and coffee. Beat egg white until frothy. Gradually add ¼ cup sugar, beating until stiff. Fold whipped cream mixture and half of the almonds into the egg white mixture. Spoon into paper muffin cups that have been placed in muffin tins. Garnish with remaining almonds. Freeze.

Mrs. Mack Gordon (Dixie Conley)

FOUR LAYER DESSERT

Serves 12-16

1 stick butter,
   room temperature
1 cup flour
1 cup chopped pecans
1 package (8 ounces) cream
   cheese, room temperature
1 cup powdered sugar
1 container (9 ounces)
   Cool Whip

5 cups cold milk
1 package (5 ounces) instant
   vanilla pudding
1 package (5 ounces) instant
   chocolate pudding
   Chocolate shavings

Mix butter, flour and pecans and press into an ungreased 9x13x2 inch pan. Bake in 350° oven for 20 minutes. Cool. Beat cream cheese. Add powdered sugar and 1½ cups Cool Whip. Spread over crust. Mix milk and puddings. Pour over second layer and let set about 5 minutes. Spread remaining Cool Whip over pudding layer. Shave chocolate over top.

Mrs. John V. Cottle (Sammye Kinkade)

GRANNY'S DESSERT

Serves 20

½ pound butter, softened
½ box powdered sugar
6 eggs, separated
2 drops almond extract

1 cup chopped pecans
1 dozen frozen
   lady fingers
1 dozen macaroons

Cream butter and sugar. Add egg yolks one at a time. Add extract. Beat egg whites until stiff and fold into mixture. Mix in nuts. Line sides and bottom of rectangular Pyrex dish with lady fingers that have been cut in half lengthwise (cut side inside). Pour mixture into lined pan. Crumble macaroons over mixture pressing in firmly with palm of hand. Cover with foil. Refrigerate 48 hours before serving.

MACAROONS

8 ounces shredded coconut
1 teaspoon almond extract
⅛ teaspoon salt

⅔ cup Eagle Brand sweetened
   condensed milk
2 egg whites, stiffly beaten

Combine first four ingredients. Fold in stiffly beaten egg whites. Drop from teaspoon onto well greased cookie sheet about 2 inches apart. Bake in a 350° oven for 8-10 minutes.

Mrs. Warren J. Freeman, Jr. (Celine Seay)

KAHLUA PARFAITS

Serves 6-8

1 teaspoon instant coffee
½ cup Kahlua
1 package (10 ounces) small
   marshmallows

24 chocolate wafers
   (approximately),
   crushed fine
1 cup sour cream

Combine coffee, Kahlua and marshmallows in the top of a double boiler. Stir until marshmallows are melted and smooth. Refrigerate until cold. Once mixture is cool, stir in sour cream. To serve, layer in parfait or wine glasses, the crumbs and the cream mixture, starting and ending with crumbs. Refrigerate until firm.

Mrs. S.S. Stephens (Mikala Faville)

CREME DE MENTHE ICE

Serves 8-10

2 cups sugar
4 cups water
¾ cup lemon juice

½ cup green
   creme de menthe
Dash of salt

Boil sugar and water 5 minutes. Let cool. Add lemon juice, creme de menthe and salt. Pour into a loaf pan and freeze. This freezes icy like sherbet and keeps indefinitely.

Mrs. Carlton Clemens (Pamela Ketler)

FROZEN LEMON CREAM

Serves 6

1 cup milk
1 cup heavy cream
1 cup sugar

Grated lemon rind
Juice of 2 lemons

Stir milk, cream and sugar, until the sugar is dissolved. Pour into an ice tray and freeze until mushy. Add lemon rind and lemon juice and beat mixture well. Return to freezer for 2 hours. Beat mixture again thoroughly. Return to freezer and freeze until solid.

Mrs. Ronald E. Walker (Mary Stevens)

LEMON ICE CREAM

Yields ½ Gallon

6 cups half and half
3 cups sugar

3 tablespoons grated lemon rind
1 cup fresh lemon juice

Mix all ingredients together. Freeze in electric freezer.

Mrs. Horace Wilson (Kathrine Kirk)

LEMON SHERBET

Yields 1 Gallon

3 cups sugar
1 cup lemon juice, about 5 lemons

Grated rind of one lemon
1 cup whipping cream
About 3 quarts milk

Mix sugar, juice, rind and whipping cream and pour into ice cream freezer can. Add milk until freezer is nearly full. Freeze according to ice cream freezer instructions.

The more rind used the tastier the finished product. One can use half and half or whipping cream to make it richer if desired.

Mrs. Edward Scott (Elizabeth Fields)

PEPPERMINT OR VANILLA ICE CREAM

Yields 1 Gallon

3 cups sugar (2 cups if making peppermint)
6 eggs
1 pint half & half
1 can (13 ounces) evaporated milk
1½ teaspoons vanilla

1 cup finely crushed or powdered hard peppermint candy
½ pint heavy cream, whipped medium
Milk

Beat sugar and eggs until foamy. Beat in half and half, evaporated milk, vanilla and crushed candy. Pour into ice cream cylinder. Fold in whipped cream. Put in dasher. Fill to, within an inch of top, of cylinder with milk. Freeze.

Mrs. Hugh A. Sticksel (Pan Purdy)

PEPPERMINT ICE CREAM

Yields 6 Quarts

2 cans Eagle Brand milk
¾ cup sugar
4 eggs
1 can (13 ounces) evaporated milk
1 teaspoon peppermint flavoring

10-12 ounces crushed peppermint candies
25 pounds crushed ice
2 pounds rock salt

Mix first five ingredients in a large bowl, stirring well to dissolve sugar. Add candies; stir and pour into 6 quart freezer can. Fill to ⅔ full with milk. Place dasher in freezer can and turn a few times to combine ingredients. If time allows, chill ingredients in freezer can at least 4 hours or overnight before freezing. This will give smoother texture and will freeze faster.

Mrs. Don Babcock (Caron Sramek)

ICE MILK DESSERT

Serves 10

2 cups Rice Chex
⅔ cup brown sugar
⅓ cup butter, melted
⅓ cup coconut flakes

⅓ cup coarsely chopped pecans
½-¾ gallon vanilla ice milk, softened

Mix first five ingredients together. Spread ½ this mixture in a Pyrex dish. Cover with ice milk. Cover with remaining cereal mixture. Freeze. Remove from freezer just before serving.

Mrs. Robert Green (Kathryn Pitts)

RASPBERRY PARFAIT

Serves 8

1 quart raspberries (frozen)
¾ cup water
1 cup sugar

3 egg whites
¼ teaspoon salt
1 pint heavy cream, beaten until stiff

Thaw and crush raspberries. Boil water and sugar to the thread stage (230°-234°). Beat egg whites and salt until stiff. Pour the syrup over whites in a slow stream. Beat constantly until cooled. Fold in berries, then whipped cream. Pour into individual parfait glasses (¾ cup per serving) and freeze. Top with additional whipped cream when serving.

Mrs. T.L. Roach (Rosemary Allen)

FROZEN MOUSSE GRAND MARNIER

Serves 4-6

2 egg whites
Pinch of salt
6 tablespoons sugar

1 cup heavy cream
¼ cup Grand Marnier

Beat egg whites with salt until softly peaked. Gradually add 4 tablespoons sugar and beat till stiff and shiny. In another bowl, whip cream until stiff and add 2 tablespoons sugar. Blend Grand Marnier into cream and fold in egg whites. Freeze in 1 quart mold. Serve with sauce.

SAUCE

1 package (10 ounces) frozen berries

Grand Marnier to taste

Partially defrost any kind of berries and puree in blender. Strain and add Grand Marnier.

Mrs. George W. Morris (Biddy Eckhart)

TORTONI SQUARES

Serves 12

3 cups vanilla wafers, crushed
1 stick (¼ cup) butter, melted
¼ teaspoon almond extract
½ gallon vanilla ice cream rectangular package

Almonds, slivered or chopped pecans
Chocolate fudge topping (2 jars—12 ounces each:
1 jar of Swiss chocolate
1 jar of chocolate topping)

Add almond extract to butter; pour over vanilla wafer crumbs. Mix thoroughly. Reserve ½ cup. Pat remaining mixture into a 9x13x2 inch pan. Slice ice cream ½ inch thick. Put a layer of ice cream on wafer crumbs. Cover ice cream with chocolate mixture. Top with almonds. Repeat layers beginning with ice cream, then chocolate, almonds, finally sprinkling remaining crumbs on top. Cover and place in freezer.

Mrs. Edward Scott (Elizabeth Fields)

RAISIN AND RICE PUDDING

Serves 6-8

2 tablespoons butter
1 cup milk
3 eggs
½ teaspoon salt
1 teaspoon vanilla

1 tablespoon flour
1 cup sugar
¾ cup raisins
1 full cup cooked rice
Nutmeg

Heat butter and milk, but not to boil. Beat eggs. Add salt and vanilla. Sift flour and sugar together and add to eggs. Pour butter and milk slowly into mixture. Add raisins and rice. Sprinkle nutmeg on top, if desired. Pour in a 1 quart baking dish. Place baking dish in pan of hot water and bake in 350° oven for 1 hour or until center is firm. If top browns too soon, cover with foil.

Mrs. Roy Mason (Diane Whittington)

SOPA INDIAN PUDDING

Serves 6

1 cup sugar
2 cups water
1 teaspoon cinnamon
6 slices bread, toasted

Butter
1½ cups grated Longhorn cheese
1 cup raisins or currants

Brown sugar over very slow heat until caramelized. Add water, letting sugar melt well. Add cinnamon as sugar water is bubbling. Thoroughly butter toasted bread. Cut bread into one inch squares. In a buttered casserole, make layers of bread, raisins and cheese. Repeat layers. Pour hot cinnamon sugar syrup over the layers and bake covered in 350° oven for 15 minutes.

Mrs. Richard Reeves (Louise Coe)

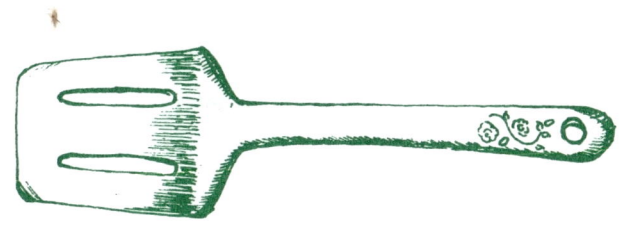

ENGLISH TRIFLE

Serves 8

ENGLISH CUSTARD

- 4 egg yolks
- ½ cup sugar
- 1 cup milk
- 1 cup cream
- ½ teaspoon vanilla

Beat egg yolks and sugar. Add milk, cream and vanilla. Cook over hot water until thick, stirring constantly. Cool. Makes 2 cups.

TRIFLE

- 1 dozen lady fingers
- 1 small loaf angel food cake, torn into pieces
- 2 tablespoons sherry
- 1 package (10 ounces) frozen mixed fruit, thawed
- 2 cups English custard
- 1 cup heavy cream, whipped

Arrange half the lady fingers and cake in a shallow bowl. Sprinkle with half the sherry. Add the fruit and custard. Cover with the remaining lady fingers, cake, sherry and custard. Top with whipped cream. Chill several hours.

Mrs. John Farrell (Ernestine Coe)

APPLE DUMPLING SAUCE

Yields 3 Cups

- Apple Dumplings — homemade or frozen Chef Pierre
- 1½ cups sugar
- 1½ tablespoons flour
- Dash salt
- 1½ cups hot water
- 1½ tablespoons margarine
- ¾ teaspoon lemon juice
- Cinnamon
- Red food coloring (optional)

Partially bake dumplings according to package directions. Combine remainder of ingredients and boil 2 minutes, stirring constantly. Pour half of sauce over half-baked dumplings. Return to oven and finish baking until light brown. Serve with remaining warm sauce. Garnish with ice cream or whipped cream.

Mrs. W.C. Turner, Jr. (Nancy Carmichall)

FLORRY'S HOT FUDGE SAUCE

Serves 8-10

2 squares (1 ounce each)
  unsweetened chocolate
1 can (14 ounces)
  Eagle Brand milk

1 teaspoon vanilla
½ teaspoon salt
¼ cup water (more or less)

Melt chocolate in double boiler. Add milk and mix well. Allow mixture to heat. Add vanilla and salt and enough water to make desired consistency. May be made in microwave oven, cooking for 15 minutes. This is really good poured over vanilla ice cream balls that have been rolled in salted and toasted, chopped pecans!

Mrs. Tom Patterson (Moylan Kritser)

SPICED FRUIT SAUCE

Serves 12-20

1 stick butter
1 cup brown sugar
2 teaspoons curry powder
1 can (20 ounces) pears
1 can (20 ounces) peaches

1 can (20 ounces) apricots
1 can (20 ounces)
  pineapple chunks
1 jar (6 ounces)
  maraschino cherries

Melt butter. Stir in brown sugar and curry powder. Combine syrup and fruits with juices, in 3 quart casserole. Bake in 325° oven for 1 hour.

Suggestions: Serve over ice cream or pound cake. Fill pastry shells and top with whipped cream. Spoon over a slice of ham and cheese. Fruits may be varied.

Mrs. Dan Moreland (Catherine Pierce)

FRENCH SILK CRÊPES　Serves 15-20

DESSERT CRÊPES

4 eggs
1 cup flour
2 tablespoons sugar

1 cup milk
¼ cup water
1 tablespoon melted butter

Combine all ingredients and beat until smooth. Refrigerate at least 1 hour before cooking.

FILLING

½ cup butter, softened
¾ cup confectioners sugar
2 ounces unsweetened
　chocolate, melted
　and cooled

1 teaspoon vanilla
2 eggs

Cream butter. Add sugar and blend until light. Add chocolate, vanilla and one egg. Beat at medium speed for 3 minutes. Add second egg. Beat 3 additional minutes. Chill 2 hours. Spoon onto crêpes. Spiral fold.

TOPPING

1 tablespoon sugar
1 teaspoon vanilla

½ pint whipping cream
Shaved chocolate

Add sugar and vanilla to cream and whip until stiff. Pour over crêpes and sprinkle with shaved chocolate.

Mrs. Mike Ballou (Debra Mitchell)

CHOCOLATE FRENCH CREAMS　Serves 20

4 squares (1 ounce each)
　bitter chocolate, melted
½ pound butter, softened
2 cups sifted powdered sugar
4 eggs

2 teaspoons vanilla
¾ cup finely chopped pecans
　toasted about 15 minutes
　in a little salt
Vanilla wafers, crushed

Cool chocolate. Add butter and sugar. Beat. Add eggs 1 at a time. Beat well after each. Add vanilla. Fold in the pecans. Place vanilla wafer crumbs in the bottom of paper muffin cups. Fill with chocolate mixture. Sprinkle a few crumbs on top. Store in freezer. To serve, peel off muffin cups. Serve frozen. If preferred, fills 40 nut cups.

Mrs. Gene Edwards (Elaine Johnson)

MAMA'S
BLUEBERRY DESSERT

Serves 12-16

18 graham crackers, crushed
½ cup sifted powdered sugar
½ cup melted margarine
1 cup sugar
2 eggs, well beaten

8 ounces, cream cheese, softened
Juice of ½ lemon
1 can (21 ounces) blueberry pie mix

Mix first 3 ingredients and pat into 9x13 inch Pyrex dish. Blend sugar and eggs. Whip the cream cheese until soft and creamy. Blend cream cheese in with egg and sugar mixture until smooth. Bake in 350° oven for 20 minutes. Cool slightly. Mix lemon juice and blueberry pie mix. Spread on top of cheese mixture. Serve topped with whipped cream.

Mrs. James B. Austin, III (Ann Franklin)

DADDY'S DESSERT

Serves 10-12

1 box (12 ounces) Vanilla Wafers
2 eggs
1 stick butter, melted
1 box (16 ounces) powdered sugar

1 teaspoon vanilla
1 can (1 pound 4 ounces) crushed pineapple, drained
½ pint cream, whipped and sweetened
1 cup chopped pecans

Crush Vanilla Wafers and spread in the bottom of a 9x13x2 inch pan. Beat eggs and add to the melted butter. Add powdered sugar and vanilla and spread over the vanilla wafers. Over this, spread the pineapple, then the whipped cream. Sprinkle nuts over the top. Refrigerate overnight to let flavors blend.

Mrs. William Comerford (Pat Nunley)

CHEESE PASTRY

Yields 3 Dozen

1 package (8 ounces) cream cheese
1 cup butter
2 cups flour

½ teaspoon salt
Grated lemon rind
1 egg, beaten
Sugar

Combine first five ingredients. Form into dough and roll out on board. Cut into circles. Brush with beaten egg and sprinkle with sugar. Bake in 350° oven.

A little preserves may be put in the middle of each pastry before baking. Press sides together before baking, and make bite sized.

Sally Bivins

PECAN COOL WHIP

Serves 12-18

½ cup margarine
1 cup flour
4 ounces pecans,
 finely chopped
1 cup powdered sugar
1 package (8 ounces)
 cream cheese, softened

1 container (13½ ounces)
 Cool Whip
2 small packages
 vanilla instant pudding
3 cups milk
2-3 bananas

In a 9x13 inch ungreased pan combine margarine, flour and ½ cup pecans. Bake in 350° oven 10-15 minutes. Do not overcook. Cool. Combine powdered sugar, cream cheese, 1 cup and 2 tablespoons Cool Whip. Spread this mixture over cooled crust. Prepare pudding using only 3 cups milk. Spread over the cheese mixture. Refrigerate until firm. Slice bananas and layer over pudding. Spread on a layer of Cool Whip. Top with pecans.

May be made with 1 small chocolate and 1 small vanilla pudding or lemon pudding omitting bananas. Freshly whipped cream with sugar and vanilla may also be used instead of Cool Whip.

Mrs. Prescott Haralson (Jo Anne Grimm)

GLAZED PEACH CRÉME

Serves 10

2 packages (3 ounces each)
 peach Jello
2 cups boiling water
¾ cup cold water

1 pint vanilla ice cream
1 can (8¾ ounces)
 sliced peaches

Dissolve one package Jello in one cup boiling water. Add cold water and chill until slightly thickened. While this is thickening, dissolve second package of Jello in remaining boiling water. Add ice cream and stir until melted and smooth. Pour into serving bowl and chill about 1 hour or until set but not firm. Arrange peaches on gelatin-ice cream mixture. Top with clear gelatin. Garnish with whipped cream if desired.

Mrs. William Comerford (Pat Nunley)

ORANGE SOUFFLÉ

Serves 12

¾ cup sugar
1 tablespoon unflavored gelatin
⅛ teaspoon salt
1½ cups cold water
4 egg yolks, slightly beaten

½ cup orange Tang
1 cup heavy cream, whipped and sweetened
4 egg whites
½ cup sugar

Combine ¾ cup sugar, gelatin and salt in saucepan. Stir in water and heat to just boiling. Stir a small amount of hot mixture into egg yolks, before adding yolks to pan. Cook and stir over low heat until mixture coats a metal spoon, 2-3 minutes. Remove from heat, stir in Tang, and chill until thick. Fold in whipped cream. Beat egg whites until foamy, not stiff. Add ½ cup sugar, 2 tablespoons at a time. Beat until stiff peaks form. Pour into 2 quart soufflé dish and chill until firm, at least 6 hours.

Mrs. James C. Ballard (Barbara Lloyd)

CARAMEL CORN

Yields 8 or 9 Quarts

8 or 9 quarts popped corn
2 cups brown sugar
1 teaspoon salt
1 tablespoon vanilla

1 cup butter
½ cup light Karo syrup
½ teaspoon soda

Place popped corn in large roasting pan. In saucepan mix sugar, salt, vanilla, butter and syrup. Boil 5 minutes, add soda, and stir vigorously. Pour over corn and toss. Bake in 225° oven for 1 hour stirring every 15 minutes. Cool. Store in airtight container.

Mrs. Wayne Smith (Julie Massey)

POPCORN BALLS

15 Medium Popcorn Balls

1 cup sugar
⅓ cup water
⅓ cup white corn syrup
1 teaspoon salt

⅓ stick (2⅔ tablespoons) butter
1 teaspoon vanilla
7 or 8 cups popped corn

Combine all ingredients except vanilla and popcorn, in a 2 quart saucepan. Cook over medium heat until syrup gets very thick (250°) and holds a drip from a spoon. Remove from heat and stir in vanilla. Pour over popcorn and let stand for 5 minutes. Wet hands and form balls the size desired. Cake coloring can be added to syrup, to give very festive popcorn balls.

Mrs. Charles Rittenberry (Cynthia Lindley)

PEACH ICE CREAM

Yields 1 Gallon

6 eggs
1 cup sugar
1 teaspoon vanilla
2 cans (29 ounces each)
shortcake peaches

⅔ cup sugar
½ pint whipping cream,
whipped, not too thick
Milk

Blend eggs and 1 cup sugar, add vanilla. Mix well. Add peaches and ⅔ cup sugar. Fold cream into egg and peach mixture. Pour into freezer container, add enough milk to fill it within 2 inches from the top. Freeze in ice cream freezer.

Mrs. Barnett Man (Velva Barnett)

SARA SORELLE'S COFFEE ICE CREAM

2½ cans sweetened
condensed milk
2 tablespoons powdered
coffee mixed with
½ cup water

1 quart half and half
1 teaspoon vanilla

Mix ingredients until well blended. Freeze in a 3 or 4 quart freezer.

INDEX

317

Vegetables

Amarillo Junior League Cookbook

The Junior League of Amarillo

1700 South Polk

Amarillo, Texas 79102-3151

Name

Street Address   Telephone

City   State   Zip

TITLE	QTY	PRICE	TOTAL
Amarillo Junior League Cookbook		$16.95	$
Beyond the Rim: A Taste of Amarillo*		$24.95	$
Texas residents add 8.25% sales tax			$
Shipping and handling**			$
TOTAL			$

*Available fall of 2003
**$4.00 for first book; $2.00
   for each additional book

Payment Method: [   ] MasterCard   [   ] VISA
                  [   ] Check payable to The Junior League of Amarillo

Account Number   Expiration Date

Signature

To call or fax an order:
Phone: 806-374-0802 / Fax: 806-374-8229

*All proceeds from the sale of this book will be used
for community projects and programs.*

Photocopies accepted.

Amarillo Junior League Cookbook

The Junior League of Amarillo

1700 South Polk

Amarillo, Texas 79102-3151

Name

Street Address   Telephone

City   State   Zip

TITLE	QTY	PRICE	TOTAL
Amarillo Junior League Cookbook		$16.95	$
*Beyond the Rim: A Taste of Amarillo**		$24.95	$
Texas residents add 8.25% sales tax			$
Shipping and handling**			$
TOTAL			$

*Available fall of 2003
**$4.00 for first book; $2.00
  for each additional book

Payment Method: [ ] MasterCard [ ] VISA
                 [ ] Check payable to The Junior League of Amarillo

Account Number   Expiration Date

Signature

To call or fax an order:
Phone: 806-374-0802 / Fax: 806-374-8229

*All proceeds from the sale of this book will be used
for community projects and programs.*

Photocopies accepted.